ROOTS

Published by Melbourne Books
Level 9, 100 Collins Street,
Melbourne, VIC 3000
Australia
www.melbournebooks.com.au
info@melbournebooks.com.au

Title: Roots: How Melbourne became the
live music capital of the world
Author: Craig Horne
ISBN: 9781925556957
Publisher: David Tenenbaum
Cover design: Marianna Berek-Lewis
Book layout: Ellen Yan Cheng

Back cover : Photo of Judy Jacques, courtesy Judy Jacques
Inside front cover: Poster courtesy Paul Neuendorf
Inside back cover: Poster design David Dickson

NATIONAL
LIBRARY
OF AUSTRALIA

A catalogue record for this
book is available from the
National Library of Australia

ROOTS

HOW MELBOURNE BECAME
THE LIVE MUSIC CAPITAL OF THE WORLD

CRAIG HORNE

M
MELBOURNE BOOKS

For my wife Karen,
who taught me to look for the role of women in everything.

And to my children,
Alex and Dylan who I love and admire.

FOREWORD

Victorians can't get enough live music. Particularly local acts, in intimate sticky venues, where the singer's sweat slaps you on the face like the salty foam of a Bell's Beach wave as you call out for more, more, more!

I often get asked about the secret to Melbourne music's success. What's in the water? Why do Victorians continue to attend live music in record numbers? How can we boast the most live music venues per capita in the world, when there's never been more competition for the entertainment dollar and live music audiences and venues are declining in major cities around the world?

In his fascinating and insightful book, Craig Horne provides some of the answers about how an isolated city on the other side of the world from the big bang of music became a globally recognised live music city.

In a rollicking ride that traverses the socio-political history of Melbourne from the early 20th Century, Horne analyses how the foundations were set for Melbourne Music City. Written with an insider's view — Horne has continually worked as a musician in Melbourne for almost fifty years — the book traces Melbourne's evolution as a live music capital from the early part of the 20th Century to the present day.

Along the way book reveals many secrets. Who knew for instance that the precursor to ASIO had fabricated lurid evidence against a visiting African American jazz band in the 1920's resulting in their expulsion from the country and the banning of African American bandleaders from White Australia until the 1940's. Who also knew the link between Melbourne's Modernist Art Movement and the Australian Communist Party who together were early promoters of trad. jazz in Melbourne. That it was the youth arm of the Communist Party and the Eureka League that sponsored Graeme Bell's Jazz Gang on a tour of Eastern Europe, Paris and London in 1947. And that the Communist Party had helped usher in the revival of Australian folk music in the 1950's and 1960's. It could only have happened in Melbourne.

I discovered local live music as a teenager in the 1980s, when bands with curiously Australian names like the Painters & Dockers, This is Serious Mum, the Meanies and Shower Scene from Psycho played all-ages shows at the Sidney Myer Music Bowl and all ages initiatives like Rockin' the Rails on trains. I was hooked on the energy, absurdity and community and joined up on the spot to be part of the cause — whether playing in bands, hosting club nights, DJ-ing, reviewing, reporting or lobbying.

When I lobbied for AC/DC to be honoured with a laneway name, I knew the band had tenuous links to Melbourne, but they moved here (and penned their ground breaking first two albums here) because of the live music opportunities.

The stats back it up.

When Music Victoria conducted the first census on live music in Melbourne in 2014, it revealed 465 regular live music venues that promoted performances at least twice a week. The follow up census in 2017 found this number to have dropped by two, but non-traditional venues in houses, at art institutions like Melbourne Museum and NGV were on the rise.

Now you can find live music at most sporting and cultural events, from Spring Fashion Week to the Australian Open. Victorians just expect it to be there.

Multi-national touring music behemoth Live Nation recently discovered that for the first time since they entered the Australian live music market, that ticket sales to their events in Victoria were higher than in New South Wales, despite the population disparity.

A recent report into recorded music listening habits commissioned by the Victorian Music Develop Office revealed that more than 60 per cent of Australians attend a live music event at least once a year, and in Victorian, 55 per cent preferred to see Australian music over international music — above the 49 per cent national average.

It can be easy to take for granted that we can see any style of music any night of the week, and discover the best new music through community radio stations such as Triple R, PBSFM and 3CR.

It's because the champions — whether musicians, volunteer broadcasters and advocates – that drive this ecosystem and community largely do it for love over money, which is at the heart of this book.

Horne, with the aide of some hilarious personal anecdotes and insights, pays tribute to the true heroes of the Melbourne music scene — the musicians, who continue to record and perform, rain hail or shine.

He also investigates 'the Melbourne Sound' and the 'Melbourne Method', where musicians benefitted from their isolation, and inventively incorporated many styles and elements into their own unique sounds.

This book has provided me with a newfound admiration for the trailblazers musicians of Melbourne, including Graeme Bell, Judy Jacques, Smoky Dawson, Margret RoadKnight, the Thunderbirds, Joe

Camilleri, Andy Baylor, Vika and Linda Bull, plus the journeymen who keep the whole show on the road, Jeff Burstin, Bruce Haymes, Stephen Hadley, Paul Williamson, Sam See, just to name a few.

And I will look differently on Melbourne streetscapes imagining the magic brewing inside the sacred venues of yesteryear: St Kilda's Jazz centre 44, Lorne's Arab Café, Little Reattas, the Thumpin' Tum, the Sarah Sands and the many Italian coffee houses that supported live music in the northern suburbs.

Like Horne, I have dedicated the best years of my life to live music. When I first saw those memorable bands as a teenager, I had no idea how they would help shape my life.

In 2014, after a 20 year hiatus, my band reformed. And the gift of live music, which had provided me with so much pleasure and brought me so many thrills, friends and memories — gave a bit more, when we were was offered the opportunity to perform alongside inspirations of mine like the Painters and Dockers, the Meanies and the Cosmic Psychos at legendary venues around Victoria. My live music adventure had come full circle. The gift that keeps giving.

Patrick Donovan
CEO Music Victoria

INTRODUCTION

THE LIVE MUSIC CAPITAL OF THE WORLD

News bulletins led with this headline when the Melbourne live music census was released early in 2018: more live music venues per capita than any other city in the world, that's what the census highlighted. Over five years between 2012 and 2017 there was a twenty percent increase in the number of gigs in the city and an increase in audiences to over 112,000 people every Saturday night. That's an AFL Grand Final's worth of people combing the city and looking for that 'hydrogen jukebox world,'[1] as Allen Ginsberg once called it; all those people looking for the speed and sound of music made in Melbourne.

So what specifically is it about Melbourne that, according to the Melbourne Live Music Census in 2017, allows it to support around 553 live music venues as compared to, according to a *Sydney Morning Herald* article[2] 453 in New York, 385 in Tokyo and 245 in London despite its population being a fraction of those major world cities? I mean, let's be honest, Melbourne's weather can be brutal at times, every road awash then, minutes later, sun so hot it drills holes in footpaths. You've all heard that cliché about four seasons in one day. But despite flaky weather, the footy, the movies, Netflix, YouTube, Melburnians are committed to going out in great numbers in rain, heat, hail, sleet to listen to live music and find those bands and singers they've heard on records or downloads or discovered on 3PBS or 3RRR or read about in the street press. Is this a new thing, a passing fad? No! Melbourne has been a live music capital for generations, arguably almost a century, and the story of how it became an internationally recognised live music capital is amazing.

It is remarkable that a little city, thousands and thousands of kilometres away from the musical motherland has been able to establish a culture that has been magnified by music where — according to the Music Victoria census — around 3500 musicians and tens of thousands of patrons on any given weekend night engage in a kind of magical exchange, which for generations, has sustained the crystal ju ju that is the music we love. All this in the face of hostile planning law, the dead hand of rotting corporatism, booze, sexism, drugs, the nihilism of changing fashion and technology. What has been the process that has allowed our musicians to create a sound so vital it gives you chills, a sound often overpowering, a sound so recognisably Melbourne? That's what I hope to answer in the pages of this book.

The story of live music in Melbourne is very much linked to the story of jazz. Jazz was played in the grand dance palaces, community spaces and town halls of the southern capital from the '20s up to the '50s. It was then that purveyors of roots music — which is defined as incorporating blues, country, folk, rhythm and blues, and rock influences — joined their jazz colleagues in the halls, clubs and coffee lounges, and later, bars and pubs of Melbourne. It's a big story. It's a story that has a political and social subplot, a story tied to the history and culture of Melbourne. Every story has heroes and ours has thousands of them — the musicians of Melbourne. Those men and women who were born in Melbourne or made the city their home, whose skill has allowed them to play across genres and styles, and who will, for a hundred bucks a gig, lump their basses, tenors, trumpets, trombones, keyboards, guitars, drum kits and amps through ice-chopping Melbourne winter days and nights to play like the confident masters they are. They go to root of things: a jazzy waltz, a full-on country jamboree. They never let the singer stand naked. With everyone sitting in with everyone else there is an inevitable cross-fertilisation: licks are incorporated, phrases are borrowed and a sound emerges, a Melbourne sound that is at once rakish and debonair.

Some might say the Melbourne sound goes to the very soul of the form that's being played. That's because Melbourne musicians are enthusiasts and not academics, which means they play from the heart and not the head. Some may find this approach a little eccentric at times, ragged even, but it's a sound that's unique. It's a sound I've heard up close from the barroom floor and from the ringside table of the stage, and I have seen first-hand how these Melbourne masters blow the fog away.

One thing this book isn't is a list. It is not a comprehensive, exhaustive examination of every jazz band or all the roots artists that have played and made a name for themselves both in Melbourne and beyond. What it will examine — and hopefully explain — is the altered consciousness, the reality or the 'invisible republic' (to paraphrase the music historian Greil Marcus in his book *Invisible Republic: Bob Dylan's Basement Tapes*)[3] of the Melbourne jazz and roots scenes.

CHAPTER 1

'CHANGE IS GONNA COME'

A warm north-easterly breeze sailed me down Collins Street in Melbourne on the eve of Australia's 1972 Federal Election. I was both nervous and excited; nervous that the Gough Whitlam-led Labor Opposition would fail in its attempt to win government and sweep away twenty-five years of conservative rule, and excited at the prospect that it would succeed. I wanted to take my mind off politics, so I was on my way to the Melbourne Town Hall to buy a ticket to The American Blues Concert, an event promoted by Kym Bonython and featuring Buddy Guy with Junior Wells, Arthur 'Big Boy' Crudup and Australia's Jeannie Lewis.

It had been an eventful two years since I had first sat on the Lord Mayor's seats at the Melbourne Town Hall back in May 1971. That night I had an epiphany when I saw Daddy Cool, a band I had only half heard of, play a show that's now etched in folklore, an event that turned an audience into a shrieking, bounding asylum of loonies. It resulted in DC signing a record deal and producing 'Eagle Rock', an unofficial Australian anthem that sent the band to the top of the charts and me to the rehearsal room. That Melbourne Town Hall show would see Daddy Cool go to America, and would set me on a musical path I'd follow for the rest of my life. But that was only half of it.

In 1971 I left school, enrolled in a business course, hated it, dropped out, learned 'Born to Be Wild', 'Jumpin' Jack Flash', 'Carol' and The Animals' version of 'House of the Rising Sun', played the odd gig, rehearsed some more and got a job with a trucking company. That lasted all of nine months before I ran screaming from the company's Footscray Road Freight Terminal pursued by a tattooed, six-foot-four predatory contractor who wanted me to be his boy!! I certainly didn't want him to be my man!!! I ran hard down Footscray Road and — panting and shaking — I fell into the musty, comforting and protective arms of the Victorian Public Service.

That was April 1972 and the monolith of Victorian politics — the arch conservative Henry Bolte — was Premier. He had been there forever, well since 1955 at least, but would not be for much longer: the electorate had turned on him. Henry was a rough-hewn autocrat: he smoked, he drank, he swore and he gambled, often all at once and often before lunch. Henry was a farmer, a bully and a builder. Bolte used debt — up to fifty-eight percent of the state's economy — to build things like the Tullamarine International Airport, the State Electricity Commission, the Gas and Fuel Corporation, Latrobe and Monash Universities, schools, hospitals, roads and the underground rail loop.

But by 1972 Bolte was a man out of his time and the public had had enough of him — especially young people, we hated him. We hated him because he'd pulled down half the inner city and built ugly high-rise towers on the denuded land. We hated him because he had no sympathy for environmental issues, and for his contempt for the cause célébre of the day, opposition to the Vietnam War. We hated him because he hanged Ronald Ryan in the '60s, civil libertarians were an anathema to him and he loathed trade unions — and trade unionists. We hated him worst of all because he was a buffoon; he had no time for artists, musicians, academics or the glories of Melbourne's Victorian architectural heritage, and he wanted to jail women who aborted their babies together with their abortionists. He had to go, the public and his party wanted him to retire, even Henry understood that his days were numbered, but he wouldn't go just yet, not until he was good and ready, and he was finally ready in August 1972.

In April of the same year I found myself walking through the heavy oak-hung doors the Public Works Department at Number 2 Treasury Place East Melbourne. The Public Works Department (PWD) was one of the original Victorian public sector departments and to my nineteen-year-old eye its public servants seemed to be of a similar vintage. Old, bald, badly-dressed men sat smoking and coughing behind heavy timber and leather-inlaid desks, banging stamps onto bits of paper then filing them into 'Out' trays where they were collected by pimple-faced, disaffected youths pushing shaky trolleys over worn linoleum-covered floors. The nicotine-stained walls peeled paint and mice squabbled in the wall cavities. In 1972 PWD was, to paraphrase LP Hartley, a foreign country; they did things differently there.

'Catholic, are you Catholic?' I was asked more than once, especially when I rubbed the ash streak off the forehead of a colleague …

'What the fuck are doin'?' asked the middle-aged man reeling from my touch.

'Sorry, you had this smudge.' I stuttered in reply.

'Of course I have a smudge you fuckwit, it's Ash Wednesday, aren't you Catholic?'

'Well, no … I'm nothing really … maybe notionally Church of England!'

'That explains a lot, what the fuck is a Protestant doin' in the Public Works Department, this is a Catholic Department, why aren't workin' in Education or Treasury?'

I suddenly realised why I was left alone most lunch times when half the office disappeared up the hill to sit on the pews of St Patrick's Cathedral and the other half walked across Spring Street to the

Cricketers Bar of the Windsor Hotel to suck back half a dozen darts and drink as many pots of beer as humanly possible in the allotted forty-five minute break. After lunch the office mood changed from one of grudging activity to one of raucous mayhem, defined by loud, teasing banter punctuated with the sound of transistor radios pumping out the droning call of the mid-week races, or in summer, the slow thwump of cricket commentary. Phones rang, bets were placed on TAB accounts, cigarettes were chain-smoked, and the clank of franking machines and the clatter and ding of typewriters became white noise underpinning the general muck-up of the office.

So what could a nineteen-year-old Protestant do? I couldn't find solace in female company; the only women who worked in the Victorian Public Sector in 1972 were typists and machinists who were generally my mother's age. Back then the public sector was a man's world; women were precluded from working in the hallowed administrative stream of the public service — something to do with women making way for returning World War Two servicemen. But the war had finished twenty-seven years before and no one had thought to change that particular recruitment policy, not the non-tertiary educated, male, job for life Departmental Secretaries and certainly not the rough as guts Premier. So what to do?

What I did was find Thomas' Music Store, then located in the Southern Cross Hotel on the corner of Bourke and Exhibition Streets. It was there I met my saviour and music educator, Alan Lee, a record salesman, vibraphone playing guitarist and pianist, and bandleader who developed deep associations with John Sangster and Jeannie Lewis. Alan Lee — an emotional and extraordinarily generous man.

I don't know why Alan took a shine to me, but he did. Maybe it was my obvious desperation to talk to a human being that wasn't an embittered, brain-damaged, middle-aged career alcoholic or an ex-serviceman suffering from what we would now understand as Post Traumatic Stress Disorder, the types of people who together made up the personnel within Accounts Records and Reports, my PWD workplace. I told Alan I was a singer in a rock-and-roll band and that I was desperate to expand my musical horizon. He asked me what I listened to and I reeled off the names: Daddy Cool, Elvis, Stones, Beatles, Kinks, Dylan, Cream, Neil Young, Doors, Janis, Joni, the usual early '70s fare. Alan smiled, nodded his head and said, 'I get it …' and then he proceeded to take me back to the musical origins of my favoured bands, back to Howlin' Wolf, Muddy Waters, Little Walter, Robert Johnson, Elmore James, Blind Willie McTell as well as the Jimmies, Read and Witherspoon. He played me Dave Van Ronk, Tom Paxton, Janis Ian, Odetta, The Band, Miles Davis and John Coltrane, Dizzy, Bird, you name it.

I sat most afternoons in a Thomas' sound booth, headphones on, my sandwiches by my side, discovering a whole new world of music revealed to me by Alan Lee, music that was not known to me — blues and roots (I found country and western swing a little later). In 1972 I spent half of my meagre salary on records and blew the rest on gigs like Creedence Clearwater Revival at Festival Hall, John Mayall, Led Zeppelin at Kooyong, and the shambolic Joe Cocker show, just to name a few.

On a particular lunchtime in late November 1972 Alan suggested I might like to come to The American Blues Festival gig at The Town Hall.

'You must hear Buddy Guy and Junior Wells and Arthur Crudup who of course wrote Elvis's "That's All Right Mama". Oh, and I'll be playing with Jeannie Lewis by the way.'

He explained that he played vibes and general percussion on a couple of tracks that would form the basis of the Sydney-based jazz vocalist's award-winning 1973 album *Free Fall Through Featherless Flight*.

'Sure, why not, I'd love to hear you perform!'

Arriving at the front of the Melbourne Town Hall I pushed through the crowd gathered at the entrance, walked through the foyer and took my place, third row and center stage of that great auditorium. I looked around the room: there was the magnificent organ dominating the back of the stage, the balconies, the ornate walls and ceilings. It was exactly as I remembered it from the Daddy Cool gig in May of the previous year. But there was a major difference … the audience. Sure, there were the freaky young men with beards and long hair, and the girls wearing cheesecloth, feathers and beads. But this was overall an older audience; there was the odd clean-shaven face, even one or two tailored jackets, and a smattering of the women wore more conservative couture compared to their younger sisters. I did notice, however, the ubiquitous joint being shared along rows of concertgoers from all age groups — apparently the desire to get stoned transcended age and class within the jazz and blues fraternity.

Finally the lights went down and an emcee, I think it was Kym Bonython, introduced Jeannie Lewis. Her band shuffled on stage and took their places behind their instruments; drums, bass, keys — and there was Alan with his vibraphone. Jeannie smiled, said hi, and launched into 'Motherless Child', her vocal soaring over the shimmer and swirl of the band. Hers was a transformative show made for dreamers and lovers. Was that the Dylan Thomas poem 'Do Not Go Gentle into that Goodnight'? Wonderful. Then 'Till Time Brings Change', followed by 'Feathers and Donna'; a stunning support by Jeannie, politely appreciated by the audience. Jeannie often quoted Phil Ochs: *Ah, but in such an ugly time, the true protest is beauty.* Well this was an ugly time; we were still fighting in Vietnam and, in attics in Melbourne's inner city, we were still hiding young men who refused to join that government-sanctioned Asian killing machine. What Jeannie did that night was pure protest, a howl against the rank, stultifying conservatism of the Australian government and its dribbling obsequiousness to America's Asian war. Luckily, in twenty-four short hours, that was all about to end.

Arthur Crudup followed and I couldn't have imagined a more contrasting experience to the ethereal Jeannie Lewis. He walked on stage wearing ill-fitting trousers with a box guitar slung around his neck. He looked frail, sick; those years living in a packing crate in Chicago singing blues in the freezing streets while working as a laborer and bootlegger had taken their toll. So too had the endless fight for recognition and royalties for his songs, including 'That's All Right Mama' and 'My Baby Left Me', both recorded by Elvis and a million other white boys. Standing on that Melbourne stage he seemed broke, humiliated and beaten. As he once said, 'I realised I was making everybody rich and here I was poor.'[1]

Crudup stood motionless in front of the microphone and looked stage left. A member of the road crew came out and put his arms around Crudup and tuned his guitar, then slunk back to the dark, leaving Arthur alone and exposed. But then, as Crudup started to play and sing, a miracle happened. 'That's Alright', 'Mean Ol' Frisco Blues', 'My Baby Left Me', 'Walking Cane'. This was deep, dark blues born in bondage, this was powerful and disruptive, this was the Devil's music. Suddenly it was 1935 and we were truckin' around irreligious Clarksdale in Mississippi lookin' for freedom and the road to glory. I smiled and clapped, exultant in the sound of Crudup's reedy-shouting vocal and boot-thumping rhythm. Crudup was the real thing and a primer for what was to follow.

Alan Lee had given me the lowdown on Louisiana-born guitarist Buddy Guy and Memphis-born harp player Junior Wells in the week before the show. He described Buddy as a killer sideman, a house guitar player at Chicago's Chess Records who had featured on classic recordings of Howlin' Wolf and Muddy Waters back in the mid-'60s. Junior Wells was also a Muddy Waters alumnus, a wild pioneer of amplified harp; he was also a singer songwriter who had released the classic 'Hoodoo Man Blues' with Buddy Guy on guitar in 1966. I bought the album on the recommendation of Alan and couldn't get enough of it: 'Snatch it Back and Hold It', 'Hoodoo Man Blues' — classic blues. I also bought the singles 'Messin' with the Kid' and 'Little By Little', both killer tracks and both sung and recorded by Wells. But I needed to see Buddy and Junior live; I needed to *see* them create that visceral, wild mercury sound — and suddenly, there they were, shuffling onto the stage at the Melbourne Town Hall. Guy was resplendent in a suit and carried a red ES 355 Gibson (not his trademark Stratocaster) and Wells wore a white shirt with checked trousers. The duo was complemented by a meaty bass player and a drummer, both of whom could have been straight out of the Chess Records house band and probably were. What a performance — Guy's spearing Gibson tone and zigzag attack, Wells's growling vocal and honking harp. 'Snatch it Back' got the Town Hall moving, followed by the bass-driven 'Honeydripper' (soon to be a staple of Jo Jo Zep and the Falcons' set list). 'Bad Bad Whiskey' was in there somewhere, as were 'The T-Bone Shuffle', 'Messin' With The Kid' and 'A Man of Many Words' with its New Orleans feel; and the band took it down with 'Ships on the Ocean'. The whole thing concluded with the meat cutter groove of 'Hoodoo Man Blues' and 'Little By Little'. The audience was on their feet, they'd been set free, and they called for more — but there was no more. That low-down, dirty, voodoo blues was over, for now. And so the audience politely filed out of the door and disappeared into the black Melbourne night.

As I left through the foyer I thought about what a contrast the night had been to the Daddy Cool gig eighteen months prior. There was no house wrecking, no dancing in the aisles, just mature appreciation of two stunning blues performers in their prime: a robust, magical encounter with history. It was also a glimpse into the direction Melbourne's emerging blues and roots scene would take, dominated initially by two bands — Chain, and Jo Jo Zep and the Falcons — and supported by Broderick Smith's duo of outfits, Adderley Smith Blues Band and Carson.

I often reflect how fortunate I was to be at the Melbourne Town Hall that night, a night that had a huge influence on the multitude of Melbourne performers and musicians who were in the audience. In my case, it planted a seed, I was too new to the art form to immediately run to a bar and start playing Robert Johnson's 'Crossroad Blues', but I knew something had moved. Like Sam Cooke said, 'Change is Gonna Come,' and I knew that it was gonna happen fast. A door had been unlocked, and I was about to explore what was on the other side. Meantime I'd work in the public service — not a bad option, given that Bolte had been replaced in August by the reformist Rupert Hamer, who was about to introduce wide-ranging reforms to the public sector that would greatly favour young people of potential. I'd also keep rehearsing and hope that one day I too would feel the visceral, stark emotion that was, and is, at the heart of this most spirited of musical forms, a form on full display that December night at the Melbourne Town Hall. Thanks Alan Lee.

CHAPTER 2

THE *ROOTS* OF *JAZZ*

American black music is self-evidently deeply political in the important sense of having clear and perceived connections with the oppressed position of black people in American society … to some extent the blues negotiate the tensions between opposition to the status quo, accommodation to it, and transcendence of it through the joy of sensual release …[1]

*B*lues and *roots* are words that have an elemental quality, words you can build something with, words that, for many, have a personal resonance that make nerves quiver like piano wires.

The Encyclopedia Britannica[2] says blues originated in America's South in the early twentieth century and developed from nineteenth century field hollers and funeral processions. From there it evolved into music played by itinerate singers, guitarists and piano players. It contains elements of jazz, ragtime and church music and, according to the BBC News Magazine,[3] was initially made broadly popular by W.C. Handy in 1912 when he published his song 'Memphis Blues'. Its roots go way back to Africa, the drums, the rhythm, the ju ju.

Essentially, though, blues is a lyrical vocal form and at its core is emotion: think Bessie Smith, Howlin' Wolf, Muddy, Etta. Sure there's slide guitars, bottles and paper bags full of twelve bar forms, but at its heart, at its elemental base, is a blues feeling, a dark weapon that can cut your heart in two.

Roots music incorporates elements of the blues; it also incorporates folk music, country, rhythm and rock. But on a deeper level there's the howl and whisper of working men and women heard in its ballads. Originally it was music made by white rural workers in the Deep South of America, but then it grew to incorporate the hopes and sorrows and convictions of everyday people's lives. It's sung and played on porches, in churches, in the fields, in bars and concert halls. It incorporates Cajun, zydeco, gospel. It's a form that can tell us about the history of a whole people in the face of changing social conditions. It's a music drawn from the lived experience of ordinary people, it's a music that gives dignity to identity and celebrates being alive.

All these forms of music are organic. After World War Two, rural black workers moved north to Chicago, Detroit and the West Coast in search of a better life, and the blues adapted to the social and economic conditions it found in each location. Suddenly urban themes bled into lyrics, electricity and amplification were added, the blues got loud, they were infused with groove, they became sophisticated. The West Coast blues were championed by T-Bone Walker; John Lee Hooker came from Motor City, but it was Chicago that produced the electric Muddy and Wolf and Elmore James, Little Walter, Koko Taylor. And so in America in the '40s, '50s and early '60s, blues became the language of the urban black industrial working class.

Roots music drifted to the city. Woody Guthrie, the Reverend Gary Davis, Peggy Seeger, Josh White, Joan Baez — they ended up at

The Gaslight and Cafe Wha? in Greenwich Village, New York City. As did this little frostbitten Jewish fella from Hibbing, Wyoming, a boy in search of destiny in the heart of Modern Gomorrah. John Hammond, the AR mastermind of Columbia Records, the man who discovered Billie Holiday, Charlie Christian, Cab Calloway, Benny Goodman and Count Basie said that when he first heard Bob Dylan he felt he incorporated the tradition of blues and jazz and folk.[4] So, if you want to know how roots music has adapted and changed over time, listen to Bob.

So to summarise, the blues isn't just one thing. Son House said that: 'The blues ain't nothin' but a low down achin' chill.'[5] Sure, that's one thing it is. But the blues can be a good time too, Junior Wells and Buddy Guy gave us a good time at the Melbourne Town Hall back in '72 but they also gave us that low down achin' chill. Roots can do that too; that's the thing about folk culture, it comes in many forms, from historic Irish ballads, to bluegrass, jazz to reggae, R&B, Cajun … Dylan. At their essence blues and roots music gives voice to the disenfranchised and repressed; it's the sound of the lived experience of people, and in Australia — and Melbourne in particular — we lapped up both genres.

Melbourne has always been a kind of magnet that has attracted all things American to our shores, be it Fords, fashion, language, movies, and of course music, be it jazz, country, folk and blues. Yeah, Melbourne loves American music, but we're not American. Our blues and our roots didn't come from 'walking behind a mule back in slavery time …' like it did for American blues singer Booker White[6] our blues was coloured by the songs first heard on convict ships.

What we did was take the form and feeling of blues and roots music and adapt them to our cultural, social and political circumstances, and in the process we created something uniquely our own.

Jazz Roots — Dixie Blows into Melbourne

Jazz too was a musical form that came straight out of the United States. Like country music, jazz was made popular in Australia via the introduction of a radio in the early twentieth century. What we heard on our radiograms we adapted to our lived experience here in Australia, especially in Melbourne, and there is no better illustration of this process than the career of Graeme Bell, a career we will examine in detail in the following chapter — but first, some historical context.

Nineteenth-century Marvellous Melbourne was booming like a thunderstorm; we were the Chicago of the south, that's what they said, a city that grew from nothing like Lodz or Odessa. It was gold that made Melbourne boom and bloom, gold that made it rich. Buildings rose from the grey clay, marvellous buildings like Parliament House, the State Library, the Exhibition Buildings, Treasury, the Courts, the Town Hall and Post Office. Melbourne was brash, boastful, and modern. Train lines snaked over empty fields, and newfangled cable trams ran down wide Victorian boulevards lined with Italianate terraces dripping with ornate, wrought-iron balconies. At that time many Melburnians were on the make; some were speculators, others gamblers, squatters, sportsmen. They searched for glory like that dumb copper Burke and the lost navigator Wills. Art, theatre, and culture were secondary to avarice in Melbourne in the nineteenth century, though of course there were those with pretensions.

As Andrea Baker points out, music entrepreneur George Coppin had arrived in Melbourne from Liverpool and gained control of the Theatre Royal. He staged operas, some of which, it is said, rivalled concerts staged at London's Covent Garden. 'Gold rush optimism sparked the golden age of Melbourne's classical music and opera scene. Between 1850 and 1890, thirteen music venues were built along the Hoddle grid in the CBD.'[7] Her Majesty's and the Princess Theatre are just two examples of theatres built during the Victorian era in the Renaissance Revival style.[8] But it was the Melbourne Town

Hall and the Athenaeum on Collins Street that would mainly host performances by Melbourne's first musical superstar, Dame Nellie Melba. Melba was Australia's first diva and she ruled the world stage, appearing everywhere from St Petersburg to Vienna, London to New Zealand and even America. Her career spanned from 1880 until her death in Sydney in 1931.

Melbourne may have been marvellous and its streets lined with gold, but in some ways they were also filled with empty pleasantries. The boom couldn't last. Land prices were out of control; rapacious land speculators had moved in, bought up vast tracts of dirt and sold them on at wildly inflated prices. London banks lent freely to buyers who were then hocked up to the eyeballs. It was a land boom and inevitably the bubble exploded, which led to debt, a financial crisis and a deep economic depression. Property values in central Melbourne plummeted and did not return to their 1880s levels until the late '50s.

But Melbourne in the 1890s wasn't just a time of economic crisis, there was a cultural shift going on, courtesy of a couple of touring outfits from faraway America. The companies brought with them African-American syncopated dancers, spiritual choirs and ragtime piano players. Suddenly amidst the economic gloom some excitement was injected into Melbourne's nightlife and its vaudevillian theatres filled with people eager to experience the exotica of those African-American entertainers. Ragtime music was a new kind of entertainment for Melbourne and seemed to complement the seedy side of life found in the barbershops, gin joints and opium dens hidden in laneways off Little Lonsdale Street.

The origins of this new music were mysterious. That it was of African-American origin was not in doubt: it came from the blues, from hunting songs and the chain-gangs. Some argue that way back in the first half of the nineteenth century this wild syncopated music was born when black slaves — some from Africa, some from the Caribbean, some from the interior of the American South — gathered on Sundays in New Orleans' Congo Square to play music and cross-pollinate their traditions. The music evolved overtime from its hard-luck, down-home origins, to become what we now know as jazz.

Christian Blauvett[9] argued that New Orleans Creoles were the principal founders of an emerging jazz genre. Creoles were the mixed-race descendants of black and white ancestors and typically identified more with European culture, rather than African culture. After the Jim Crow laws of 1890 classified the city's mixed-race Creoles as 'black', they were only allowed to play with other black musicians. This brought a greater musical fluency and technical skill to black music, as many Creoles were trained in classical music. This new Creole musical mix, soon to be known as jazz, incorporated the African tradition of rhythm and improvisation with a schooled European approach that emphasised harmony and different forms of instrumentation (saxophones, trumpets and pianos).[10]

Jazz was initially played in the sporting houses of Storyville by pioneers like Jelly Roll Morton who, its rumored, peeked in at those rockin' and rollin' couples doin' what they do and played in time to the rise and fall of those shakin' money-makers. In fact, the word 'jazz' may have come from the slang 'jass' which had an association with New Orleans bordellos, jasmine perfume being the favored scent of the city's prostitutes. Others argue that jass referred to a woman's rolling derriere,[11] which, since time immemorial, has got a lot of mojo workin'.

A few cool Melburnians in the '20s sure got their mojo working when jazz — labelled *dangerous* in '10s New York Times because of its brothel origins — came to town.

'As the '20s got underway, the new styles of jazz swept away the elegant dancing of the Edwardian ballroom; jazz was not only a new style, it was a new sound. Instruments that had been excluded from serious music, banjos, saxophones and drum kits reinforced the rhythmic drive of the music.'[12]

In respectable, suburban, '20s Melbourne, gardenesque housing estates spread along newly-electrified tram routes. Streets were filled with conservative, male-dominated households that looked to Empire for guidance, excluded liquor, and frowned on the modern, Americanised spectacles of the cinema, the dance hall, and commercial music. These vulgar entertainments had polluted middle class Melbourne via the recent availability of the gramophone, radio, and of course the movie theatre. It was through these mediums that jazz, and its symbol of lasciviousness and moral collapse, the flapper, appeared in the dance halls and supper clubs of Melbourne.

'The flapper was a girl who 'jazzed' her appearance, she bobbed her hair, painted butterflies on her knees, put on her Charleston dress, her 'art silk' stockings and her swinging beads and danced the night away.'[13] The flapper even swung those long beads in time to arguably Melbourne and possibly Australia's first all-girl jazz dance band, The Thelma Ready Orchestra.

The line-up for Thelma's orchestra was: Thelma on banjo, Kath McCall, piano, Lena Sturrock, violin, Alice Organ, saxophone, clarinet and cornet and Lillian Stender, vocals and drums. And they played everywhere. They held down long residencies at the Mayfair Café in St Kilda, the smart and very modern Venetian Room at the Hotel Australia, not to mention the Menzies and Oriental Hotels. They also played two or three nights a week at society weddings and feature events at Melbourne's premier reception venue; Nine Darling Street, South Yarra. If that wasn't enough, the orchestra had a regular gig at radio 3DB as well as two mornings a week at the King's Theatre on behalf of the *Herald* newspaper.

Jazz, or a form of it, seemed to have infected every female musician in Melbourne. Suddenly all-female dance bands, like those led by Eve Rees, Marion and Dora Lightfoot, Val Summerhayes, Agnes Smyth, Alic Dolphi, Grace Funston and the aforementioned Thelma Ready, were playing regularly at dance halls, balls, receptions and on the vaudeville stage.

Thelma Ready understood that her all-ladies band was something of a novelty: 'a drawcard with the gentlemen', as she put it. Their drummer Lillian Stender was a particular attraction, with her 'natural voice and lovely personality'.

'She had IT. All the men fell for her. I had a job to control her. A few fights went on. Although Lillian had learned the drums, she was never a good drummer. Lily got by on her personality, her looks and her voice…'[14]

By the '30s Melbourne was jumping, and all-female jazz/dance bands were a huge attraction. Eve Rees and her Merrymakers, with its piano, saxophone, trumpet and drums line-up, played every night of the week. Eve told Kay Dreyfus, 'What a tremendous amount of work we got! … Mayoral balls, CWA dances, cafés lodges, clubs, weddings, parties…receptions of all kinds …'[15]

Jazz was changing Melbourne. Some opinion leaders at the time said it was destroying the minds and morals of the young, that it was a dangerous and demoralising fad at counterpoint to the morally-correct, white Anglo Saxon, suburban sensibility of middle-class Melbourne. But jazz had resonated with the young ramblers and gamblers of the inner-city; it had infected the city like the Spanish flu. St Kilda and Fitzroy, for example, were wide open to all things American: jazz, flappers, Hollywood movies, cool-cat language and gangsters like Squizzy Taylor. Emulating his hero, Chicago's Al Capone, Taylor filled the streets of Carlton, Collingwood, Fitzroy and Richmond with bullet-holed bodies, debris and sadness.

If you believed the newspapers, inner Melbourne was awash with jazz, crime and sex. *The Truth* newspaper was full of articles about sly grog sloshing out the back of lolly shops, cafés, hairdressers and grocers, mostly in Fitzroy, Collingwood and Port Melbourne, and mainly sold by destitute women trying to turn a quid. When the law cracked down on the trade, many sly groggers turned their attention to the sale of the then legal-cocaine. You could buy a packet of snow on Little Lonsdale Street for two bob, making coke the drug of choice for many denisens of the inner city. Others had more creative uses for the wonder drug: a trainer and stablehand were arrested by police when their horse, Valdoid, won the 1923 Moonee Valley Yaroke Handicap by half the straight and at long odds; turns out the horse was doped up to its bridle with coke!

Inner Melbourne sure was roaring in the '20s, but then things went a little too bit too far for our god-fearing, racially pure authorities. In 1928, when African-American Sonny Clay and his band came to town, all hell broke loose. As Jeff Sparrow explained in *A Short History of Communist Jazz*:

'When Sonny Clay toured with his band The Colored Idea, the Commonwealth Investigative Branch — the forerunners to ASIO — devoted themselves to monitoring the musicians, determined to prevent them "consorting with white women".[16] Eventually, the uniformed police raided an after-concert party. The *Truth* explained what they found: "Empty glasses, half-dressed girls, and an atmosphere poisonous with cigarette smoke and fumes from liquor — and, lounging about the flat, six negroes".'[17]

In their inimitable journalistic style, the *Truth* newspaper's headline screamed:

'Blackout for Sonny Clay's Noisome Niggers ... Australia wants not another coon ...'

Following a sustained media campaign from *Truth*, which respectable papers like *The Age* joined; a parliamentarian raised the matter in the House of Representatives in Canberra.

'After reading out headlines like "Nude girls in Melbourne flat orgy" and "Raid discloses wild scene of abandon; flappers, wine, cocaine and revels", he asked, "Does the Minister not think that in the interests of a White Australia and moral decency, permits to such persons should be refused?"'

The Minister agreed — and six band members were deported. It would not be until 1954 that another band led by an African-American musician would be permitted to tour our sunburnt shores, a huge cultural and musical lost opportunity, for the whole country, but especially for Melbourne.[18]

Melbourne's reception towards African-American jazz musicians contrasted to that offered by European cities such as Paris, where jazz was introduced to the French by segregated black soldiers stationed in France during World War One. African-American soldiers — led by Lt James Reese, a well-respected New York bandleader — marched their music through two thousand miles of tiny farm villages and concert halls across France. Everywhere Reese led his 369th Harlem Infantry Regiment band, they created an exciting musical revolution. The French went crazy for jazz and the African-American musicians who played it.

After the war, many African-American musicians, dancers and entertainers returned to France. Many settled in, and delighted cabarets and club audiences of Paris' Lower Montmartre, which became known as Black Montmartre. Club owners and club-goers from all over the world couldn't get enough of the syncopated rhythms. In the early '30s Louis Armstrong, Duke Ellington and Coleman Hawkins — and later Ella Fitzgerald — were treated like royalty by Parisians and so these musicians toured often, up to and after World War II.

Not in sunny white Australia however where politicians and the conservative press had dismissed jazz music and musicians as decadent, degenerate and a direct threat to our racial purity. Such disapproval from community elders, however, spurred many young people to explore the hidden pleasures of this new and exciting music.

Initially jazz was hidden in the popular songs of America's Tin Pan Alley inspiring Melbourne's more curious and adventurous musicians to delve further. This study led to jazz appreciation societies emerging across town, and saw both amateur and professional musicians emulate what they heard on records from Chicago and New York. Suddenly jazz bands were the cat's pyjamas and jazz musicians were cool — especially hot stylists like Melbourne's own multi-instrumentalist Benny Featherstone and the trombonist-bandleader Frank Coughlan. These bands played a mixture of jazz and popular swing for eager dancers to do the Lindy Hop and Charleston. They played to packed crowds at venues like the Palais in St Kilda or the exotic Green Mill with its state-of-the-art rubber sprung floor, atmospheric lighting, and convenient location across the river from the Flinders Street Railway

Station. Frank Coughlan also played informal group sessions at venues like the Fawkner Park Kiosk, as well as gigs at The Melbourne Town Hall.

You can still hear what those 'cool cats were puttin' down' through the wonders of wire recording. In 1925 American band leader Ray Tellier had an eighty-two week run at the Palais with his outfit the San Francisco Orchestra, during which time the band recorded 'Yes Sir That's My Baby'. This song, along with Bert Ralton's Havana Band's 'I Want to be Happy' were the first Victorian jazz age recordings.

Then the roaring twenties gave way to the depressive thirties. Suddenly the capitalist world was being blown apart and chaos was driving its fist into the faces of the poor. The '30s saw a third of the working population unemployed; the poorer suburbs were hardest hit, as were those aged 20-29 and over forty. Even those who managed to keep their jobs had their wages cut and their taxes increased. Homelessness was rife, children starved, families were torn apart. Those of the working class were reduced to rubble, but the affluent middle class mainly survived. But what's that I hear? A new sound had crept into the financial ruins of Melbourne, and that new sound was Dixieland jazz — but only those living in a working household, those with food in the icebox, cream-coloured drapes and an HMV radiogram, took any notice.

CHAPTER 3

MODERNISM, COMMUNISM, HOT JAZZ & GRAEME BELL

Jazz is a tree. It has many branches that reach out in many directions, it goes out into the far east and picks up an exotic blossoms ... everywhere it goes east, west, north, south, it produces many different coloured flowers and picks up many influences ... but as you go down into the earth, you'll find blue-blooded-black roots deep in the soil of black Africa which is the foundation of everything, because it is [the African beat], the most listened to beat in the world ...[1] (Duke Ellington)

Dixieland jazz originated in New Orleans at the turn of the twentieth century and was played mostly by its African and Creole American originators: Sidney Bechet, Louis Armstrong, King Oliver, Kid Ory. Dixie bands typically featured piano, saxophone, trumpet, bass and drums and some may have also included trombone, tuba, clarinet, banjo, guitar and washboard. This wild mercury music caused a sensation in African-American communities across the United States, with its shards of attacking horn, its disorientating rhythm, and its stab first and ask questions later attitude. However, perhaps unsurprisingly, the first commercial recording of jazz music was not made by its intense and passionate originators but by five white crackers cashing in on this new sound: the Original Jazz Band. In 1917 this inauspicious bunch climbed the stairs of the Victor Talking Machine Company on 38th Street in New York City and recorded a stinking pile of 12 bar crap known as the 'Livery Stable Blues'. Highlights of this musical mess included a clarinet making the sound of a rooster, a cornet whinnying like a horse and a trombone mooing like a cow; Pat Boone and Vanilla Ice would be proud.

By the '30s it wouldn't be this piece of cultural appropriation that would be played by Melbourne musicians, but one of more traditional jazz, played by a couple of serious students of the genre with unorthodox chemistry — the Bell Brothers. Although not the first to play Dixieland jazz in Melbourne, they would be its principal exponents.

Graeme Bell was a classically trained piano player and his brother Roger blew horn. The two Scotch College boys fell in with some jazz dudes from their school, like 'Lazy' Ade Monsbourgh, and started playing clubs, coffee houses, pubs and specialist jazz venues like The Embers as well as jazz appreciation societies. It was the Bells that got things swinging.

In the '40s, jazz appealed to the young almost as much as it horrified the establishment. During the war, many local musicians came into contact with Americans who updated them on developments in the scene. Melbourne became the centre of a local enthusiasm for 'hot', or traditional '20s New Orleans style jazz,[2] with its emphasis on improvisation and authenticity and which paralleled new directions in the visual arts and literature. In 1941 for example, Graeme Bell's[3] Jazz Gang formed a Victorian Jazz Lover's Society and staged regular gigs at The Stage Door on Flinders Street. The Gang co-produced a program of boogie-woogie piano, blues and traditional jazz, with supports from such people as a young pianist Don Banks and blues singer Vivian Roberts along with guitarists Joe Washington and Spade Davis. Bell writes that, 'To date, this was probably the most adventurous staging of jazz music in Melbourne.'

But the Victorian Jazz Lovers Society shows were important for another reason: they were co-produced by Harry Stein, sometime drummer but fulltime leader of the Communist Party-aligned Eureka Youth League. Harry would have a significant role to play in both the evolution of jazz music in Melbourne and in bringing Graeme Bell and his take on the traditional jazz form to the attention of the wider world.

Picture this: it's among the darkest days of World War II. German U-Boats have blasted the British fleet to bits in the Atlantic and the Nazi Army has marched into Greece. Auschwitz has expanded to increase the production rate of bodies and up to 34000 Jews are slaughtered in ditches by anti-tank guns over a two-day period during Operation Odessa, while almost simultaneously, Liverpool is reduced to rubble by the Luftwaffe. Meantime, Rommel roars across the African desert, Moscow is under siege and Japanese Zeros sink most of the US fleet anchored at Pearl Harbour. With the world on the brink, Graeme Bell and his Jazz Gang formed a partnership with the Communist Party of Australia to bring their two-beat hokum to the jazzbos of Melbourne.

Bell's band poured out their polyphonic blues improvisations every Saturday night at The Stage Door. Roger Bell's cornet played the melody on songs like 'Shimmy Like Your Sister Kate', while Ade Monsbourgh on clarinet or valve trombone and Pixie Roberts on clarinet improvised around Roger's wailing voice. Jack Varney on banjo or guitar chorded away as Lou Silbereisen on bass or tuba kept the oom-pah rhythm driving through the song, propelled by the great Russ Murphy on drums, as soldiers about to fight in the burning sands of Africa or the rugged mountains of Greece danced with their sweethearts like there was no tomorrow. In a boiling whirl of organic sound, they lost themselves for a few stolen moments in multi-dimensional, unembellished madness, a madness hotter than a Vickers machine gun.

Aside from Harry Stein and his comrades at the Eureka Youth League, the Bell boys were also hanging out with Melbourne's modernist, artistic avant-garde, led by John and Sunday Reed at their Heide farm in Heidelberg. It was at Heide that the aristocratic Reeds and their painting protégés (such as Sidney Nolan, John Sinclair, Joy Hester, Daniel Vassilief, Adrian Lawler and Albert Tucker) read and dissected modernist authors like Dostoyevsky, Aldous Huxley, T.S. Eliot, D.H. Lawrence and Virginia Woolf. The assembled patrons with their artists, writers and musicians in tow, pored over art books that reproduced the European modernism of Braque, Matisse, Cézanne, Gauguin and Picasso. At the same time the modernist painters were also creating their own Antipodean artistic revolution: think Nolan's Ned Kelly series and Tucker's *Images of Modern Evil* exhibition, not to mention John Perceval's *Survival*, to name a few. They drank wine, ate Sunday's roasts and listened to recitations of works by Rimbaud and Eliot by modernist writers like Max Harris and Michael Keon. All the while, Nolan, Tucker, Counihan and others painted and fought and fucked and created an always unique, often disturbing artistic Australian voice. It was a voice that was underpinned by Bell's jam sessions, a voice that still resonates today.

My uncle Alf Roberts and aunt Jean lived on a dairy farm next door to the Reeds in the '30s; in fact it was Alf who sold them eleven acres for 1314 pounds in 1934 allowing John and Sunday access to the Yarra River. I'm not sure if my farmer uncle's family were fully prepared for their neighbours' exuberant bohemianism, the visual and sexual experimentation of John, Sunday, Sidney Nolan and their various modernist acolytes. Nor would they have fully grasped the shock and spark of the blazing art and literature exploding under the roof of the Victorian farmhouse next door just off Bulleen Road. My cousin John however fully understood the lascivious behaviour he observed his neighbours engaging in all those years ago:

> *There were wild parties, jazz bands, with drinks running freely … and in summer there were always nude men and women swimming in the river or luxuriating under the shade a red gum. I was a teenager and wanted to see more of what went on under those trees.' But Uncle Alf knew what was going on in the shade of those arching red gums, 'He nailed hessian bags to the fence separating our farm from the Reeds, hoping to block out the view. But us kids just went swimming in the river and all was revealed!*

Graeme and Roger Bell were in the eye of the intellectual storm surrounding Heide. The Bell boys' band played at swing parties hosted by John Sinclair in a converted garage owned by the Reeds and over the road from their Victorian farmhouse. As well as the Reeds, communist intellectuals and fellow travellers, modernist artists, writers and their satellites explored the universe and the inner substance of things, got off on cheap booze and each other while the Bell band supplied the musical backdrop. To quote Lesley Harding and Kendrah Morgan 'Roger Bell's soaring trumpet was heard across the empty farmlands …'[4] up and down the Yarra Valley.

The Bells also played 'hot jazz' at the Reed-supported Contemporary Art Society's exhibitions, where the living art of Nolan, Tucker, Noel Counihan, Adrian Lawler and Joy Hester was first displayed, much to the horror of Melbourne's conservative right wing art establishment. Bell, in his autobiography Australian Jazzman quotes Melbourne's *Truth*, describing, in modernist terms, the scene at the October 1941 CAS exhibition, held at the Hotel Australia on Collins Street and featuring the Bells' band, Graeme Bell's Jazz Gang:

'Long-haired intellectuals, swing friends, hot mommas and truckin' jazz boys rubbed shoulders on friendly terms. While swingers hollered 'Go to town!' and jitterbugged in the aisles, the intelligentsia learnedly discussed differences between the rhythms of hot jazz and the pigment of Picasso.'

The close association between jazz musicians and artists was seen as decadent by Melbourne's conservative art establishment. J.S. McDonald, then-Director of the National Gallery is quoted by Bell describing Melbourne's Modernist Art movement as the:

'Product of a generation revelling in jazz, jitterbugging and the elevation of the dress model to stardom ... [they are]committed to ungainly attitudes ... the exalting of the discordant and ugly!'

Bell himself described his association with the Contemporary Arts Society as 'a most important event' that not only led to further gigs, but also cemented close political and personal relationships for a new generation of artists and musicians. As Bell wrote:

'We jazz musicians and the contemporary artists discovered that we were in the same camp. To be modern or anti-conservative during the prevailing climate was to be anti-fascists and therefore left wing. If anything was anti-conservative in the early '40s it was jazz. It was a matter of record that the conservative forces in the arts were linked to right-wing politics ... leading writers like Max Harris saw jazz as part of the total art phenomenon ...'

The connection between these artists and left-wing politics (via Graeme Bells' association with Harry Stein and the Eureka Youth League) was cemented when the two men co-produced shows at The Stage Door in Flinders Street under the heading 'Young Jazz Lovers'. The partnership between modernist artists, writers, jazz musicians and progressive politics was unique within Australia. As Bell wrote: 'Other [Australian] cities, however, particularly Sydney, had nowhere near the rebellious vitality in art, jazz or literature that there was in Melbourne.'

The artistic rebelliousness of the '40s could be at least partially explained by the psychology of 'the outsider'. Melbourne's young, bohemian subculture ran in counterpoint to the suburban cultural establishment. This establishment was led, at the time, by the likes of media giant and father of Rupert, Sir Keith Murdoch, J.S. McDonald and Murdoch's artistic acolyte, the soon to be National Gallery of Victoria Director, Sir Daryl Lindsay. At this time these cultural troglodytes were busy digging a hole to nowhere in their conservative suburban graveyards, while trying desperately to dismiss the politically progressive, polyrhythmic dynamism of Nolan, the Reeds, James Gleeson, Max Harris, Michael Keon and jazz musicians like Graeme Bell and his Gang. Lindsay refused to buy any modernist paintings for the NGV, and Murdoch dismissed the whole movement as debauched.[5]

The real action was not at Lindsay's Toorak mansion, or Murdoch's bucolic spread on the Mornington Peninsular, but out in Heidelberg at the Reed's joint, where guests found release letting the Bells' music dump them like a wild wave. That barn sure rocked; not only was it the scene of wild modernist mayhem, but also the venue where Graeme Bell and his newly acquired young wife, Margo Byass, held their wedding party. Bell writes:

'The rort …was held in John Reed's barn … all the artists, writers and jazz musicians of note were there … for the all-night jam session … it was a mad and restless night.'

Another modernist clique descended on the Bell's new South Yarra apartment, where artists, musicians, racing drivers, sportsmen, writers and African-American servicemen would participate in Saturday afternoon drinking and jazz jam sessions. It was all about trying to escape the general gloom of the war years …

As the war progressed Graeme Bell's Jazz Gang continued to wail away in subterranean university college jam sessions, and four nights a week at their residency at the Swing Inn coffee house on Flinders Street, above the Young and Jackson's Hotel. At weekends the gang played the Pacific Hotel in Lorne as well as other regular jazz gigs all around town. The band at this time featured Graeme on keys, Roger on trumpet and Ade Monsbourgh on trombone. It was a line-up that, although still somewhat fluid given the demands of the war effort, remained largely intact until the end of hostilities.

Jazz, parties, dances, art shows; '40s Melbourne would have been, compared to the rest of world, a surrealist daydream largely untouched by the horrors of the past six years. When the war ended in September 1945, Europe and much of Asia lay in ruins. Great cities such as Warsaw, Kiev, Tokyo and Berlin were piles of rubble and ash. In the Soviet Union, 17000 towns and 70000 villages had been wiped off the face of the earth, and by the end of 1945 the largest population movement in European history was underway.

It's estimated that between eleven and twenty million people had been displaced by the war, leaving some 850,000 people starving in displaced persons camps across Europe by conflict's end.

Britain, too, was bankrupt, leaving bombed-out cities such as Manchester, Liverpool and London with little money to rebuild. Things were made even more uncertain when Prime Minister Churchill proclaimed that 'From Stettin in the Baltic to Trieste in the Adriatic, an iron curtain has descended across the continent...' which ushered the entire Western World into a Cold War with their former ally, the Soviet Union.

Even though Australia had lost over 27000 servicemen and women in the struggle with the Axis powers, in comparison to Europe we had emerged relatively unscathed. Some would say we prospered from it; the war had accelerated the development of Australia's manufacturing industry which led to a significant fall in unemployment. Australia also emerged from its isolation from the rest of the world when then-Prime Minister Ben Chifley announced a mass migration program at the war's end. Between 1946 and 1960 the program pushed an annual increase in Australia's population of 2.7percent per year and contributed to the development of a cosmopolitan society and a more outward-looking nation.[6] With a rising population and an emerging manufacturing industry, we were well-placed to prosper from the post-war boom.

Culturally, the surge in economic prosperity mixed with a collective feeling of relief, following the privations of both the war and the Great Depression in the previous decade meant that people were looking to relax and celebrate. The people wanted a goodtime, they deserved it, and the Melbourne jazz scene was primed and ready to deliver. Throughout the war and especially in the lead up to peace, there had been an explosion of jazz gigs across town, many attracting both American and Australian servicemen and women stationed in the southern capital. And the Bell boys were in the thick of it.

From the early '40s Graeme Bell and his Jazz Gang played regularly at the Palais Royale, the Trocadero (previously the Green Mill), and the Exhibition Buildings, as well as at many of the town hall dances staged throughout Melbourne, according to Bell's autobiography. In addition, the band played a regular Sunday session at Admiralty House on Exhibition Street, plus the odd special event — like a dance for three thousand people held in a huge factory in Morwell. There were also the lucrative, wild private parties where booze flowed and Albert Tucker's 'Victory Girls' ran hot. Graeme also played piano with various bands at places like the Geelong Palais and the Heidelberg Town Hall. Then there were gigs at the Power House on Albert Park Lake, Manchester Café opposite the Melbourne Town Hall and, later, the Green Knoll Café, which soon morphed into the Horst Liepolt's Café and Jazz Centre 44, located on the corner of Acland Street and the Esplanade right opposite Luna Park (more on this venue later). Maybe it was in the war years during which foundations were laid for Melbourne to become the nation's live music capital.

Like a lot of contemporary Melbourne musicians, Graeme and Roger were also filling their diaries with guest spots in other people's bands, sitting in when key personnel were shipped off for military duties. Graeme worked with Russell Jones' band every Saturday night at The Power House, and even spent a few months playing with Claude

Carnell's band in Mackay, Queensland, performing for US soldiers as part of an American Red Cross show band. Graeme's absence left the way open for Roger to join clarinettist Pixie McFarlane and regularly sit in with Benny Featherstone's Dixielanders. This gig led to a residency at The Rainbow Room, with Don Banks, Lyn Callen and Laurie Howells. When Featherstone joined the Merchant Navy, Roger and his band, the newly-named Roger Bell's Dixieland Jazz Band, took up their Saturday spot at the Heidelberg Town Hall. Roger's six-piece band played alternate sets with Hal Lloyd's Strict Tempo Dance Orchestra, a radical move at the time. It the brainchild of promoter Bill Glennon, and the idea took off like a rocket; suddenly there was a circuit of Glennon-sponsored events around town. This led to regular gigs for Roger and the band.

In the war years, Melbourne's music scene was fluid, with side musicians running from gig to gig subbing in for unavailable players. With half of Melbourne's jazz musicians enlisted in the armed forces, people like Graeme Bell who was exempt from war service due to medical grounds (he suffered from an inflamed vertebra) and Roger (who was working as an engineer in a protected industry and therefore also exempt) were in high demand. They adapted different styles of music for a variety of audiences; a jazz club, a swing band, a wedding, a private event (what we would call a corporate event today). There was also an occasional recording session.

Graeme and Roger could both read music charts, an advantage over their self-taught colleagues. As well as being outstanding musicians, they were also blokes who were easy to work with, an important prerequisite for a sideman and almost as important as musical ability. Most importantly, the more they were out there gigging, the more they were on band-leaders' radar, and more gigs came their way. This is a practice that continues in Melbourne to this very day.

——//——

Right up to the '70s the format of alternating a contemporary band with a full orchestra persisted at the Heidelberg Town Hall. By then the venue was a little daggy and Melbourne was alive with groovy discotheques that had sprung up all over the city: Berties, Sebastians, The Thumpin' Tum — Q Club was even hip in comparison. But, for me anyway, the Heidelberg had two great attractions. The first was the Heidelberg Town Hall Big Band. What a thrill it was to hear that twenty-piece orchestra, with its full brass and reed section, keys, guitar, bass, percussion and drums in full roar. The second was The Charlie Gauld Trio (oh, and the gorgeously sophisticated office girls that seductively shimmied around the town hall all night long, but I was 15, they were unattainable, we move on).

My friends and I, along with a couple thousand others, would make our way to the Town Hall on Upper Heidelberg Road on a Wednesday or Saturday night. We would go to see Jill Glenn, Colin Cook, and Olivia Newton-John; I remember seeing her sing solo and with her old Go Show/Bandstand partner Pat Carroll. These artists, among others, would sing the hits of the day, backed by that mighty twenty-plus-piece band. When Jill Glenn did her 'Little Egypt' routine or swung her hips and did the hoochie-koo while singing 'Big Spender' from Sweet Charity, man I nearly popped my cork. Colin Cook also did a pretty good Joe Cocker impersonation when he performed the Mad Dogs and Englishmen version of 'The Letter' with the band. After an hour or so, the singers and band would take a break, everyone shuffling outside to smoke a gasper or talk bullshit or try to chat up one of the office girls or whatever.

After a half-hour or so, we were back inside and ready for — in my case — the main event. For me, the real highlight of the night was when the Charlie Gauld Trio took the stage to play the progressive rock hits of the time. Charlie was arguably one of the greatest guitar players in the country and a legend of the local music scene, having come out of Melbourne's '50s go-to house band the Thunderbirds, which had also included Harold Frith on drums and Peter Robinson on bass, who went on to co-form with Laurie Arthur the Strangers. The Thunderbirds had backed Betty McQuaid on her hit recording of the John D Loudermilk song 'Midnight Bus' as well as Johnny Chester on his version of the Johnny Kidd and the Pirates hit 'Shakin' All Over'. Listen to Johnny's version of the song on YouTube; that's Charlie Gauld wangin' that surf guitar, and what a cold blast of icy reverb that sound is!

Charlie could play anything; funk, flamboyance or invention. The first time I heard Jimi Hendrix's 'Purple Haze' and 'Foxy Lady', as well as Cream's 'Sunshine of Your Love' they were being played by Charlie at The Heidelberg. He stood expressionless and resolute behind his aviator sunglasses and extracted, it seemed to me, the same fire and fluidity from his Burns guitar that Hendrix and Clapton had managed to pull out of their Stratocasters. It was psychedelic, it was funk, it was blues, it was rock — Charlie Gauld played them all.

Many years later, Jeff Burstin and myself were playing a little acoustic gig on a Sunday afternoon at the Palace Hotel on Burke Road in Camberwell. Suddenly, a little old man wearing enormous sunglasses shuffled into the room, pulling with him a shopping trolley full of old newspapers. He sat down at a table and ordered a beer, pulling out a handful of yellowed newsprint and flicking through them, stopping occasionally to drink from his glass. He intermittently looked up and smiled at us, or swivelled around the room as though looking for someone. He'd drain his beer, read his newspaper, order another pot and repeat. I'd recognised who he was at once.

'I reckon that's Charlie Gauld there,' I said to Jeff between songs. 'I'd know him anywhere.'

When we took a break I approached Charlie and asked if he was who I thought he was. Of course I was right. I told him what an inspiration he was to me, that he was, in my young teenage eyes, the greatest guitar player I had ever seen. I told him he was a legend, I said it was an honour to meet him, and then I saw, through his dark glasses, his eyes moisten, so I shut the fuck up.

'Thanks …' was all he whispered. I bought him a beer and asked if he would like to sit in with Jeff and me.

'Please play my guitar, it would be such a thrill if you did …' I gushed.

'No, no, I don't play anymore, sorry. I was hoping Wayne [Duncan, our then bass player and an old friend of Charlie's] would be here today?'

'No sorry Charlie, it's just the little duo today.'

'Oh right! I was hoping to see Wayne, maybe next time … you were great by the way, I just wanted to see Wayne.'

With that he repacked his trolley, drank his beer and shuffled out the pub's front door. Charlie Gauld died soon after and with him went a little piece of Melbourne's rock'n'roll soul.

The Eureka Youth League, Communism and all that Jazz

Throughout the '40s and '50s, and into the '60s decade of rebellion, the Communist Party of Australia (CPA) developed significant relationships with cultural and artistic movements. The youth wing of the CPA, The Eureka Youth League (EYL), played a particularly important role in the attempt to forge an alliance between musicians and communism. First through jazz, and then through two folk music revivals, the EYL sought to use music to recruit members and to foster its ideological and political struggles. In the end, the EYL's and CPA's relationship with both jazz and folk was tenuous. Yet along the way, the music itself flourished. This, then, is a story of tensions between and paradoxes surrounding the Party and musicians sympathetic to it. Yet it is also a story about how the cultural life of Australia was greatly enriched by the EYL's attempt to use music as a political tool …[7]

Back in 1942, newlywed Graeme Bell was hangin' with the Reed push, playing hot jazz and pissing-on at the Fawkner Hotel in Toorak Road, or spending time at his flat in South Yarra. Drinkin' at the flat was *de rigueur* with the hip bohemian crowd and everyone who was anyone was there — jazz musicians, music critics, Michael Keon. It was at the Bells' Adams Street flat that Sid Nolan turned out monochromes of nudes painted on blotting paper with the aide of a dipped finger in a jar of red pigment. Groovy baby.

But then the planets aligned, and Graeme and Roger Bell's life would change forever when Harry Stein of the Eureka Youth League, the youth arm of the Communist Party of Australia invited the Bells to play at Stein's Eureka Hot Jazz Society at 104 Queensberry Street North Melbourne. What was going on here? Why would a card-carrying communist support and promote a bunch of avant-garde jazz heads like Bell and their modernist artist mates?

Maybe Stein and fellow members were true Bolsheviks, in the pre-Stalinist sense. Like Harry's Eureka Youth League, the pre-Stalinist Russian Bolsheviks encouraged a national cultural pluralism, a kind of democratisation of art where progressive artistic movements would become a dynamic force in society, hopefully resulting in modernity becoming accessible to everyone. In the immediate aftermath of the 1917 revolution, Lenin's Commissar of Education Anatoly Lunacharsky turned over the Russian art schools to modernist artists such as Marc Chagall, whose staff included Malevich and El Lissitzky. According to Robert Hughes in *The Shock of the New*:

'Lunacharky, who was determined to see the birth of "an art of 5 kopecks" — cheap available and modern — created the Higher State Art Training Centre in Moscow … which turned into the Bauhaus of Russia, the most advanced art college anywhere in the world, and the ideological centre of Russian Collectivism … where the modernity of rivets, celluloid, aeroplane wings replaced primitivism and mysticism.'[8]

Maybe Harry Stein viewed things similarly to his Bolshevik comrades. Maybe he too wanted to establish Melbourne's very own democratically available modernist jazz centre right there in Queensberry Street, a place where everyone, not just the denisens of the Trocadero or Palais de Danse, could access this dynamic music. He certainly wanted to establish a space where jazz musicians could play, swap ideas and be supported by both a sympathetic promoter and a receptive audience. If this fitted into a broader communist vision for Stein at the EYL Hall in North Melbourne then perhaps it was successful.

The war was clearly approaching its end. Together with the Soviet Union, the Allies had invaded Germany and were pushing the Nazi Army back to Berlin. Hitler suicided, the Germans unconditionally surrendered in May and now there were just the Japanese to deal with in the Pacific. For Melburnians it was time to emerge from the depression, fear and monotony of war and embrace the warm miracle of peace. That's what happened, though not overnight, at the EYL Hall in 1945.

Down the road apiece was Camp Pell, an American Army Camp set up in Royal Park. It was there that thousands of cashed-up, unbound, jazz-loving US soldiers were in search of a good time. Ironically they would find it at Commie Central, EYL Hall. Jazzbos and their girls dug the band, danced the Lindy Hop and disappeared together into the anonymity of the blackout. It was, to paraphrase T.S. Eliot, a still point in a turning world. It was a time of anticipation. There was a sense of existing in a kind of dream, where — to quote Eliot again — the past and future had gathered. There was nothing to do but dance and wait.

Then the bomb annihilated Hiroshima and Nagasaki, turning men, women and children into shadowy outlines on walls. Japan surrendered in September and war was over, for now. Camp Pell was dismantled but the EYL jazz scene lived on — in fact, it thrived. Pretty soon the Queensberry Street hall became a musical magnet for every jazz cat in Melbourne, especially when Graeme Bell's Jazz Gang rented the space from Harry and the EYL to run a regular hot town cabaret every Saturday night. The cold, cavernous Victorian Hall was transformed into an atmosphere of a Parisian *café-chantant* by visual artists like Tony Underhill who painted neoclassical figures on huge pieces of paper and hung them on the walls. Artist/set designer Warwick Armstrong also painted a semi-abstract design of Salome dancing before Herod for the stage backdrop. Graeme Bell himself designed a modernist depiction of a clarinet player for the band's music stands. A piano was rolled out of Graeme's mother's house and into the club, front of house staff were recruited from the ranks of girlfriends and wives, and suddenly, to immediate success, the Uptown Club was born.[9]

Bell had experience hosting dances, and had learnt a thing or two about building a crowd. As he wrote,

'When you've got something to market and a ready-made outlet doesn't present itself, you create your own.'[10]

Years before, Bell had hired places like Leonard Cabaret at the St. Kilda Baths for a regular Sunday night dance. The whole enterprise was a kind of cottage industry; he printed tickets himself and made each patron a club member. This had the bonus of creating a mailing list of jazz enthusiasts that could be added to as he expanded his entrepreneurial empire. For the opening of the Uptown Club, Bell broke out the franking machine and hit the post office, and designed posters and notices.

When the Uptown Club finally opened it was a full house from day one. Couples danced to blues shouters, boogie-woogie piano, and of course the red-hot sounds of Graeme Bell and his Jazz Gang. It was a venue straight out of a Scott Fitzgerald novel, a place where ladies could rouge their knees and roll their stockings down.

'Put your lovin arms around me, like the circle round the sun,

I want you to love me momma like my easy rider done ...'[11]

Soon 104 Queensberry Street North Melbourne was the place to be for every respectable jazz-cat in town. This was true no matter how young they were, like John Sangster, the teenage, cornet-playing schoolboy from Vermont. In his autobiography, *Seeing the Rafters,* Sangster describes how every Sunday he would kiss his Presbyterian Church Choir singer father goodbye and catch the train to North Melbourne to see Graeme Bell's jazz band go gangbusters. Sangster was drawn to Roger Bell's cornet technique, writing that he 'played it clear and strong.' He was also inspired by Lazy Ade Monsbourgh: 'He was a revelation, I marvelled as he played his rich valve trombone like he was straight out of Bourbon Street in New Orleans.'

Occasionally, tuba, banjo and washboard replaced drums and bass in the band. When this occurred, a new smooth, light rhythm could be heard purring behind Graeme's front-line players on songs like Bell's 'Blue Tongue Blues'. Upon hearing this, Sangster was hooked, and he went on to become a powerhouse in Australian jazz, touring with Bell and his band from 1950 to 1955 and playing various instruments including drums, cornet and vibraphone.

Sangster went on to play with Don Burrows and even joined the progressive rock group Tully in 1970. He toured with the rock musical *Hair* and wrote scores for television, documentaries, films and radio. In 1973, Sangster released a series of popular *Lord of the Rings*-inspired albums that started with the *Hobbit Suite.*

By 1946 the Uptown Club was in full roar. Every Saturday night it was packed with, a young crowd of university students, artists, musicians, dancers, plain jazz enthusiasts, and even the Chilean Consul's daughter, Alma Hubner, one of the Bell's band most ardent supporters. As Bell wrote:

'Admission was 3s3d and we played from 8.15 to 11.45pm. At the time it was an offence to drink alcohol where people were dancing or within 100 meters of premises where there was dancing. You couldn't even go out to your car parked around the corner the corner to take a swig without being booked.'[12]

As alcohol was not allowed, soft drinks were sold in the foyer, along with cups of coffee and tea — although there was grog smuggled in via medicine bottles and the odd Dexedrine tablet to speed things up a bit. Graeme Bell and the Uptown Club weren't going to challenge the *Le Lido* on the Champs-Elysees for sophistication, nor was it, for fear of being closed down by authorities, able to challenge Melbourne's overarching cultural conventions.

The First Australian Jazz Convention

In December 1946, Bell, Ade Monsbourgh and Harry Stein helped unite Australia's jazz fraternity by organising the first Australian Jazz Convention, held in the EYL's Hall in Queensberry Street.

As Jeff Sparrow observed,[13] Australia's musical isolation at this time was so intense that jazz-heads habitually accosted American sailors on the docks to ask them if they had any records. This isolation was, at least in part, the result of two events: the Australian Government's banning of imported recordings in '40, and the paucity of overseas musicians visiting our white-Australian shores. After the Sonny Clay episode, it was not until 1954 that another band led by a black musician was permitted to tour.

Australia was a Federation in name only in the '40s; more accurately, perhaps, we were a loose collection of self-contained states and territories, separated physically and culturally by distance and inferior communications. Jazz enthusiasts lived in islands of polyrhythmic isolation in our capital cities or worse (in terms of access to jazz), remote rural locations. Jazz lovers and musicians alike were in desperate need of an opportunity to meet, discuss current musical trends and ideas, and simply just play and have a good time. The Australian Jazz Convention provided that opportunity.

As Bell wrote, for five days in 1946, jazz musicians and music lovers from all over Australia descended on the EYL Hall for a series of lectures, concerts, jam sessions, workshops, record programs and discussions. Graeme Bell gave a talk on the music of Louis Armstrong, Dink Johnson, and Jelly Roll Morton. Bill Miller presented material under the heading 'Origins of Jazz', featuring field recordings of Alan Lomax and including blues, 'Negro' lullabies and chain gang work songs. Concerts sold out, jam sessions went long into the night, ideas were swapped, and a lot of hot Australian jazz was played. Bell later recalled, 'We were all walking on air. Here were these musicians from Sydney Hobart and Adelaide — few of us had previously met — who had been searching out this music that we had. Their aims were the same and they talked the same language. The rapport was almost unbelievable.'[14]

The lecture papers given at the conference were later published in the John Reed/Max Harris literary and artistic avant-garde journal *Angry Penguins,* which again reflected the association hot jazz had with the modernist movement at the time.

The convention did however highlight certain characteristics associated with the Melbourne 'traditional' or 'hot' jazz scene that were not shared by other mainland cities. There was, for example a notable absence of Sydney bands from the first jazz convention. This was largely because Sydney didn't support a lot of traditional jazz music, it being a Melbourne-based phenomenon at the time. In his book *Black Roots White Flowers*, Andrew Bisset speculated that Sydney bands were more mainstream. He writes:

'In Sydney there were more commercial ballrooms and more money for entertainment, especially during the war. If a musician reached a professional standard on his instrument then he had a good chance of making a living by it in Sydney, provided he played the music that was popular. Because of this, Dixieland was despised as something you rose above. But in Melbourne, [where]... many good musicians remained amateur, they were free to pursue their own interests, [consequently] Dixieland musicians researched their subject thoroughly, they knew more tunes than their Sydney counterparts, they sharpened their talents, their bands stayed together longer because there was nowhere to go, so they developed their own style and eventually created their own jobs.'[15]

jazz notes

presents

graeme bell and his dixieland band

in

riverboat jazz

Saturday, 2nd December, 1944

Tickets - 5/- each

Paddle Steamer "Mississippi" leaves Princes Bridge at 2 p.m. sharp

This ticket must be presented at the wharf or admission will be refused

Graeme Bell, Pianist, and Leader of Australia's Leading
Dixieland Band.

THE MANCHESTER CAFE

has much pleasure in announcing
the special engagement of

GRAEME BELL & HIS FAMOUS DIXIELANDERS

Commencing Mon. 24th Feb. week nights from 9-11 30 p.m.

Light Refreshments and Supper served
continuously

Minimum Charge — 1/6

Manchester Unity Building
C/r Collins and Swanston Sts.

YOUNG JAZZ LOVERS

In Co-operation with Jazz Lovers' Society.

Present

THE HISTORY :: OF JAZZ ::

at the

STAGE DOOR

276 FLINDERS STREET, CITY
SATURDAY, AUG. 9th
at 8 p.m.

Programme Features:

GRAEME BELL and his Jazz Gang

BOOGIE - WOOGIE PIANISTS

GEORGE FONG, University Special

DON BANKS, 17-year-old Wonder

BLUES SINGERS
VIVIAN BESSIE
ROBERTS
ROGER BELL and
GEORGE TACH

Record Session of Rare Recordings by Gordon Ford, Jazz Critic

ADMISSION 2/2.   THIS PROGRAMME ADMITS YOU.

Renwick Pride

Wear Your Maddest Hat   ★
to the All League . . . .

Mad Hatters' Ball

on

SATURDAY, NOVEMBER 18TH, 1944

at

162 CHAPEL STREET, PRAHRAN

Dance to Graeme Bell's Hot Band

8-11.30 p.m.   Admission 2/7

The madder the hat the bigger the prize.   R. Brilliant, Hon. Sec.

GRAEME BELL

AND HIS

DIXIELAND BAND

❖ ───────── ❖

INVITE YOU TO DANCE TO THEIR MUSIC

AT THE

PRAHRAN TOWN HALL

ANY FRIDAY NIGHT IN THE MONTH OF

This Ticket is Complimentary and will Admit   *Persons*

Art work by Graeme Bell

THE
PALAIS ROYAL
Presents the First Provincial Appearance of the All-Conquering

GRAEME BELL

Tues.
Oct.
26

Tues.
Oct.
26

And His Australian Jazz Band
(By Courtesy of the Australian Broadcasting Commission)

☞ See, Hear & Dance to this Sensational Jazz Group
who Astounded the Critics on their Recent World Tour

NOTE: In Addition to Feature Numbers Graeme Bell's Band will play Alternate
Dance Numbers with Frank Phelan's Harmonists, whose Programme will
be on a 50—50 Basis.

8—12   SUBSCRIPTION 2/11 (incl. tax)

S. A. Joy & Sons, Printers.

THE
TROCADERO
BRINGS YOU

Continuous Modern Dancing

TO AUSTRALIA'S INTERNATIONALLY FAMOUS
BAND LEADERS

Frank Coughlan & Graeme Bell

Every Thursday and Saturday

GALA OPENING:
DERBY NIGHT, SATURDAY OCT. 31st

★

PROGRAMME:

MONDAY — MODERN — CUP EVE GALA.
                                    CARNIVAL NIGHT.
TUESDAY — MODERN
WEDNESDAY — CONTINUOUS 50-50, 2 Bands.
THURSDAY — CONTINUOUS MODERN, 2 Bands.
FRIDAY — MODERN.
SATURDAY — CONTINUOUS MODERN, 2 Bands.

★

For Better Dancing
Trocadero Ballroom
(JUST OVER PRINCES BRIDGE)

NORM CHAPPLE, Manager.

MELBOURNE'S FINEST BALLROOM

LEGGETTS

AUSTRALIA'S LARGEST DANCE FLOOR

Presents

Graeme Bell
and his Dixieland Band
(OF STAGE, RADIO AND RECORD FAME)

On Wednesday Next, September 1st
Admission as Usual 2/6 inc. Tax and Cloakroom

Don't Miss this Night with...

GRAEME BELL
and his
DIXIELAND BAND

Just arrived from Overseas where they were acclaimed as THE WORLD'S BEST.

See them in a half hour's
STAGE SHOW
then swing into action and
Dance until 11.30

With Graeme Bell plus Lin. Challen
(Continuous Dancing)

Owing to all the floor space being needed, there will be
NO BEGINNERS' CLASS on this night.

Leggetts for Dancing
EVERY EVENING RIGHT AT PRAHRAN STATION

Graeme Bell and Charlie Blott
present

JAZZ PARADE

(A Portrayal of the Best in all forms of Jazz)

at the COLLINGWOOD TOWN HALL,
(10 minutes from city)
NOVEMBER 30, 1948 at 7.45 p.m.

✶ FREDDIE THOMAS AND HIS 18 PIECE ORCHESTRA
(featuring the Music of Stan Kenton plus original arrangements)

✶ DON BANKS AND HIS BOPTET
(the only authentic be-bop group in Melbourne)

AND

✶ GRAEME BELL AND HIS AUSTRALIAN JAZZ BAND
(first Concert appearance since their phenomenal ABC tour of Australia)

LAZY ADE'S QUARTET - - PIXIE ROBERTS TRIO
THE ONE AND ONLY WILLIE McINTYRE (pianist and singer)

Your Compere — **Bob Horsfall** *Kind permission 3KZ*

Admission 2'-, 3'-, 5'- plus tax
Booking at Allans 6 days in advance

IMPORTANT — BE EARLY

einer der letzten authentischen
Blues Sänger

Deutsche Jazz-Federation   präsentiert

GRAEME
BELL

and his australian Jazzband

It's a tribute to the vision of early pioneers of the Australian Jazz Convention that it continues to this very day. The Convention, in its 73rd year at the time of writing, is now permanently held in Ballarat annually and is the longest continuously running jazz convention in the world.

Then it was 1946; Bell was playing hot jazz at the Uptown Club, and the Eureka Youth League was booming. At Heide, Sid Nolan was spreading his tins of Ripolin and bottles of oil on the scrubbed long table in the dining room; on the walls were charcoal drawings of bearded heads.

Brisbane poet Barrett Reid said of that moment:

'I saw real paintings, free authentic, for the first time. I had arrived [at Heide] just as the Kellys were nearing completion; the large hardwood panels, the cardboard studies, the many drawings and water-colours, captured and controlled my eyes.'[16]

What Reid saw that day was an example of modernism engaging with popular imagination, through the vehicle of the Ned Kelly story. Nolan's genius was to take the motif of Kelly, the black square letterbox, and, as Harding and Morgan wrote in *Modern Love*, mix local folklore with a lyrical bush setting in which Kelly appears as a kind of Australian Everyman. With the help of Nolan's work, over time, the outlaw came to personify what many Australians thought about themselves: a race of anti-authoritarian men (no sheilas here mate, and *no shirt lifters!*), rebellious and alone, riding a stallion heroically through the great green grey of the Australian bush towards a blue horizon, beyond which lay immortality. Through Nolan's Kelly series modernism came into the mainstream.

A similar phenomenon in the hot jazz scene would take place in February of the following year when, according to Bell's autobiography, Harry Stein phoned him to ask if he and the band wanted to go to Prague.

Stein went on to explain that the World Youth and Students Convention, a leftist youth festival, would be held in the

Czechoslovakian capital between July and August of '47, and youth organisations from all over the world had been invited to send delegates. Sporting bodies, gymnasts, dance troupes, choirs, and so on were going, why not a jazz band? The Eureka Youth League would sponsor the event and Harry Stein would accompany the band as tour manager. Fares would be raised in a collaboration between the EYL, the trade union movement and the band.

It's interesting to note that modernist artist and CAS mainstay, Noel Counihan was also sponsored by the left to travel to Czechoslovakia in the '40s as part of an Australian delegation to the first World Peace Conference held in Paris. Counihan worked in Prague, Hungry, Poland and finally England for over three years, also establishing an international reputation.

Bell's association with the Contemporary Art Society and the modernist art movement in general had helped mould the band's philosophical outlook and gave it cachet with a progressive, sophisticated audience in the first half of the decade. But it would be Bell's association with the Eureka Youth League and the left wing political movement in the second half of the decade that would, as Bell himself wrote, 'Launch us as almost a household name and [give] us international exposure.'[17]

The media had got hold of Bell's imminent European tour. The Bell band would be the first Australian jazz group to tour overseas, a rarity for anyone from the performing arts, or really from any walk of life at this time. This gave the band huge publicity; it meant photos in the papers and radio and newsreel coverage. This generated a buzz which, in turn, led to massively increased audiences at places like the Uptown Club, as well as a five-night-per-week residency at the Manchester Café.

The tour may have also indirectly led to another huge leap in the career of the band: their first recording contract with Columbia Records, a subsidiary of EMI. In those times a recording contract opened many doors; airtime on city and country radio was guaranteed because of the small number of records released in Australia straight after the war. As Bell wrote, 'Coupled with the overseas tour, this [recording contract] was a double that was hard to beat. It was like pressing two magic buttons simultaneously ... and in the right place ...'[18]

To say Graeme Bell and his Dixieland Jazz Band (as it was now known) was a hit in Prague would be an understatement. Crowds of six thousand people or more at their concerts were normal. Bell observed that 'The audience reaction ... was something none of us will ever forget ... they threw their hats in the air, whistled and cheered as we went into our programme ...'[19]

The band's performances were filmed for newsreels and the footage was shown in movie theatres all over the world. Articles about the band appeared in Czech, French, English and Russian newspapers, with one paper declaring, 'Usually we think of Australia only as the land of the kangaroo, emu or good sheep wool ... none of us would have thought that Australia produced true, pure jazz ...'[20]

Following the Prague convention the band stayed on to play a month-long, nine-show-per-week residency at the prestigious Fenix Club in Prague. This led to an invitation to cut six sides in the Rokoska Studios for the Czech label Supraphon; the tracks from these sessions were exported all over the world in later years. Bell was always proud of the results; he wrote that 'Forty years later these records stand the test of time for balance and clarity and yet I think only two microphones were used, one for the front line and the other for the rhythm section ...'[21]

The tour continued in Bohemia and Moravia, with a brief return to Prague for a one-night stand at the historic Smetana Hall. Featured on the bill was famed Czech poet Egon Kisch, well known in Australia for the dictation test imposed on him by the Australian government when he tried to visit before the war. Kisch had been asked to write out a passage in Gaelic, which of course he couldn't manage; he was subsequently deported back to Czechoslovakia.

From Czechoslovakia it was on to Paris, where the band was a huge success. During this stint the band played an enthusiastically-received gig at the Hot Club of France and conducted a recording session for the French Pacific label; the tracks would be subsequently released on a Swaggie album some years later. Then there was a series of frenetic gigs and residencies all over London and Great Britain, including at the prestigious Leicester Square Jazz Club. As a result of this nearly six-month European tour, and later European visits, Graeme Bell and his Dixieland Jazz Band were credited by the American music journal Downbeat magazine as starting the European traditional or trad jazz revival, and being ... 'unquestionably the greatest jazz band outside America.'[22]

Trouble in Paradise

However, all was not well with the modernist movement at home. The Bells' overseas absence had coincided with Australia descending into a cultural miasma of fear, conservatism and bigotry; the source of this crisis, in part, could be placed at the feet of the Cold War.

Australia had just emerged from World War II after experiencing the horrors of the Great Depression. Its people were exhausted, and looking to live out their life in a quiet, safe suburb. The desire for security replaced curiosity; pursuit of a career (for the male of the household), accumulation of assets, raising of children, and the keeping of an English-style garden were the matters of importance for most Australian families. There was, however, trouble in paradise.

The Atomic Age had arrived, bringing with it not only the promise of cheap power, fuelling a new industrial revolution, but also the possibility of annihilation. The Soviets had the bomb, so did America: it was a fight that could potentially kill us all.

Conservative state and federal governments and the right-wing press spread panic, fear and Cold War hysteria. The Minister for

External Affairs Richard Casey fuelled anti-communist Cold War paranoia by bringing to the nation's attention a 'Nest of traitors in the public service.'[23] Reds were everywhere, apparently: in trade unions, the teaching profession and universities. Nowhere was safe.

Additionally, as wool price plummeted and inflation rose, the economy slid into a recession. A horror deflationary federal budget followed, leading to a surge in unemployment, with wages stagnating and black smoke rising over the Bonegilla migrant camp near Albury as inmates rioted.

It's all the fault of those wogs, we collectively screamed, and the Government agreed. Menzies responded to the economic crisis by severely cutting Australia's migration program from Britain and Europe, much to the relief of many Australians, including members of Her Majesty's Opposition. In the nation's capital, the Honorable Queensland Labor Senator Archie Benn compared immigrants to cane toads, complaining they never should have been introduced in the first place.

This economic and political uncertainty resulted in many Australians turning on the Government. For a while it seemed the Menzies regime would come to an end — but they still had a trick, in the form of a communist threat, up their sleeve. Then on the eve of the 1954 election, they were handed a gift from the security-intelligence gods in the form of the Petrov Affair.

Vladimir Petrov was a minor Soviet diplomat who had been courted by ASIO for many years; they managed to convince Petrov to defect in the caretaker period before the election (fancy that?). When Petrov's wife was being flown back to Moscow by Soviet officials it stopped in Darwin for refuelling giving an opportunity for our brave boys in blue to swoop; she was spectacularly escorted off her plane in the full view of the waiting Australian media (I wonder how they found out about it? Separation of powers; No?) by a couple of burly Federal Police officers and reunited with her husband in Sydney. The nation cheered and in the days leading up to the election, citizens devoured related stories of Soviet espionage on our shores — and then, wouldn't you believe it, the Menzies Government was returned, with a thumping majority!

Anti-communist hysteria also led to a split within the Labor movement. It was led by arch-Catholic Bob Santamaria, the leader of a grouping of conservative, ALP affiliated trade unions known as the Grouper faction. Santamaria justified splitting from the ALP on the grounds that communists had infiltrated many of the trade unions associated with the party, and consequently wielded too much power. The split resulted in the formation of the ultra-conservative Catholic-dominated Democratic Labour Party that subsequently formed a close political alliance with Menzies' Liberals, an alliance that kept the ALP out of government both federally and in Victoria for well over two decades.

These were indeed desperate times, and Melbourne's progressive artistic scene was not unaffected. Albert Tucker was just one of the many artists to flee Australia at this time, stating:

'The realisation that art has its own forms, structures and principles; and for me a far greater validity than politics ... the artist his own specialised form of energy which will assert its self regardless of any opposition.'[24]

Sidney Nolan and Arthur Boyd followed Tucker's lead. The aim of these artists was not to walk a collective path to modernism, but rather undertake their own solitary artistic journey, one that moved them away from our shores and resulted in their becoming what Albert Tucker described as 'refugees from Australian culture'.[25] John Reed reported that the postwar years had seen 'some organic change ... in the community, a lessening of sensitive awareness, or perhaps a mere dissipation of energies into numerous channels, irrelevant to creative talent.'[26]

This 'dissipation of energies' led directly to the collapse of what had been one of Reed's greatest achievements: the dynamic Contemporary Art Society.

This new social and artistic conservatism was felt most keenly in Melbourne; as Richard Haese wrote, 'the Melbourne scene had been the liveliest, and the change of cultural climate was felt most intensely there.'[27] And with Melbourne's cultural landscape fast resembling a pile of indurated clay, what was the impact felt within the jazz scene?

It firstly had the effect of breaking the nexus between the modernist art movement and jazz: they no longer could be described as a cohesive whole. With the collapse of CAS, and with many of its key practitioners living in exile overseas, there was no-one left on the visual arts scene to fight the good (left-wing, artistic) fight. This probably had a real impact on Bell, and on the jazz scene in general.

Let's go back a little to the time when the Graeme Bell Australian Jazz Band — they had been renamed again — returned home from their triumphant European tour in August 1948. By then, the band's international career had been launched and the Bell boys were household names throughout the country. Bell explained, 'By the time we reached Melbourne, the publicity was quite overwhelming and we wondered what we had started. All capital dailies were running stories with photos … we were also filmed by Cinesound Newsreel …'[28]

Even the conservative Australian Broadcasting Commission wanted a piece of the action and dangled a lucrative contract in front of the band. But there was a catch; in order to sign the ABC contract the band had to satisfy 'Aunty'. Bell had to agree that 'I [Bell] was not going to place a bomb in the middle of Collins Street or paint a hammer and sickle over the door of St Paul's Cathedral or do anything a communist was supposed to do …'[29]

Bell managed to do this by agreeing that he and the band would sever all connection with communist fronts like Eureka Youth League, including the Australian tour organised by the EYL to 'pay back' their sponsorship of the band to Prague.

The band was broke on their return from Europe and as Bell explained in his autobiography; being on the road is expensive, and despite six months of packed houses there was little to show for it.

The ABC contract would not only wipe out any outstanding debts, it would secure the band's immediate future. It was no contest; the EYL lost their poster boys for recruitment to the cause.

The decision meant that things got decidedly hostile between the band and their former comrades. Audrey Blake from the EYL shot both barrels in an article published in the EYL's Youth Voice:

'When Graeme Bell's Band left Australia all were members of the Eureka Youth League. We gladly accept their resignation. People with such lack of principle have no place in our ranks ... Without the League, the Bell Band's European tour would have been impossible. The Bell Band, who are now interested only in money, have placed themselves beyond the pale of all progressive elements in the Australian labour and democratic movement ...'[30]

This proved to be a turning point in the relationship between left wing politics and the Melbourne jazz scene. Up to this point, people like Harry Stein believed that jazz music should be championed by the Communist Party, and that, in turn, it would play a significant role in recruiting musicians and young people to the left. But by the end of the '40s, fascism had been defeated, the Cold War was in full swing, a new social conservatism was on the rise and there was no longer the same commitment by artists to left wing causes. A new era of artistic individualism had arrived.

Visual artists such as Tucker and Nolan, and Graeme Bell and his band were artists first, not politicians or political organisers. They had sympathies for left wing causes, but were no longer part of a united, modernist 'art movement'. The EYL and the Communist Party of Australia had undoubtedly helped facilitate the emergence of a vibrant live music scene for hot jazz in Melbourne. But ultimately musicians are, as 'autonomous agents,'[31] a cultural reality seen as treacherous by an increasingly Stalinist-dominated Communist Party of Australia.

The flirtation between jazz and the EYL, and its unhappy outcome, reinforced the view of puritanical CPA hardliners like Paul Mortier: that jazz was not a progressive force in society but rather a decadent pollutant that would turn sons and daughters of good Marxist families away from the working-class cause. Mortimer is quoted by Ashbolt and Mitchell:

'To the extent that we fail, their minds will continue to be gripped musically by the inanities of Tin Pan Alley, or the eroticism of Bessie Smith ...'[32] Mortimer was instead advocating young people turn to folk music which, during the '50s became the natural home for radical youth. But that's another story; it will be explored shortly.

Mortier had much in common with Methodists at this time; both socially conservative and both infused with a joyless commitment to the one true cause. But he had much more in common with Stalin and his war against Russian culture, where modernist filmmakers like Sergei Eisenstein and artists like Chagall were forced to flee Soviet shores in pursuit of artistic freedom overseas. If artists didn't emigrate, they fell under the Soviet boot for fear of the death camps. Musicians like Shostakovich conformed to Stalin's sterile socialist realism because failure to do so would risk his being tried as an enemy of the people during the purges. The Stalinist era eliminated an entire generation of the Russian internationalist avant-garde, replacing it with conformist mediocrity pumping out propaganda.

Meanwhile, Bell and his band had reached a pinnacle of their creative power. Their ABC concerts were a huge success both critically and financially, with the Melbourne *Herald*'s music critic John Sinclair stating that the Bell band played 'vital jazz in its purest form ...'[33] The band played town halls up and down the east coast and recorded thirteen radio programs for broadcast on ABC stations right around the country. Graeme Bell remembered the tour fondly:

'After the scruffy accommodation and travelling conditions we [endured] in England, the ABC's first class and very efficient arrangements were not hard to take ... grand pianos tuned on the day of the concert, taxis to and from hotels, press receptions, supper after the shows ... [we were well] looked after ...'[34]

After the ABC tour ended the band was back on the road, this time with ex-Duke Ellington trumpet player Rex Stewart. Together they played sixty country towns in all, from Port Augusta in South Australia to Sale in Victoria and up to Yass in New South Wales. The tour was the most comprehensive of its type ever undertaken in Australia, giving many country people their first chance of seeing a live jazz show.

Following the Rex Stewart tour, the newly named 'Graeme Bell and His Australian Jazz Band' travelled back overseas, beginning with England, Scotland, Ireland and Wales. This tour included a Royal Command performance for Princess Elizabeth in 1951, and a tour of war-ravaged Germany with the Delta blues singer Big Bill Broonzy. There the band was met with reception that Bell described as 'over-whelming'; jazz had had been banned during the Nazi regime and was now a living symbol of freedom for the German people.

A touring jazz band, for German girls, also presented a chance to exercise these freedoms; as Bell explained in 2006, 'German girls would hide in the band bus behind the seats, and when the band would take off, in the middle of the snow, on these long journeys, they'd reveal themselves, some of them would wear wedding rings so that they could get into the hotels with the members of the band and pose as their wives, and they'd purposely speak bad German.'[35]

The tour included fifty-eight concerts in two months in the European snow through January and February and although very well organised, the cracks were beginning to show. By the end of the European run, the band ran out of steam.

The end of an era

By the early '50s, Graeme Bell and his Australian Jazz Band had fallen apart. According to Bell after the European tour things began to get a little strained domestically, wives and families were fed up waiting for their men to come home. After five years of constant touring, the band had lost its joie de vivre and most of its members wanted out. 'Lou and Pixie were all for going on, but the rest of us wanted to quit for a while, so we cancelled the whole thing …'[36]

It was, perhaps, a case of too much of a good thing: too much touring, too much music, too much booze and too much partaking of the pleasures of the road. Bell's jazz career subsequently took a backseat; instead, he played piano as an arranger-for-hire in other people's bands while concentrating most of his energy on his emerging business interests.

Bell had co-founded the Swaggie record label in 1949, alongside his brother Roger, Ade Monsbourgh, Pixie Roberts, Lou Silbereisen and Mel Langdon. Swaggie was the first Australian-owned record company dedicated to recording Australian jazz music. The label was a cooperative and continued as such until it was sold by the partners to Nevill L. Sherburn some four years later.

Bell also hosted *The Platter Parade,* a radio program which broadcast once a week on 3UZ. He tried his hand at jazz promotion as well, touring a number of American jazz musicians around Australia. Ever the businessman, Bell made a point of recording with the touring international artists on his Swaggie record label, including English trumpet legend Humphrey Lyttleton, providing a bank of material for later release.

Bell continued to play live, but what he presented was, in his own words, 'a musical smorgasbord … with programs cluttered with novelty and hokum … playing ragtime and boogie pieces [which] appealed to the general public.'[37] Bell got through all this by hitting the bottle, apparently the booze blurred out the reality of playing music for the money and not for the art.

Then in 1954 Bell received an offer to tour Korea with the dynamic young singer, Yolande Wolffe (Bavan). The offer was too good to refuse, and so Bell put a band together. It included John Sangster (his old fan from the Uptown Club) on trumpet, Jack Baines on clarinet, John Costello on trombone and Jack Banston on drums. The tour lasted three months and even took a swing through Japan.

However, Bell was moving further and further away from the hot jazz that had made his name. He played dinner music in Tokyo for the English military, and cabaret in Kyoto. Back in Australia he played piano in the orchestra pit for an ice-skating show at the Theatre Royal in Adelaide, then moved to Brisbane to take up a six nights-a-week residency playing jazz standards at the Bennelong with John Sangster. This was a wild period for Bell, he drank too much, played bad music, was broke and became depressed.

Then, luckily, an offer came from food and wine expert Len Evans. He wanted to put together a traditional jazz band to play the prestigious Oasis Room at the Chevron Hotel in Sydney; other band members included Bob Barnard on trumpet, Norm Wyatt on trombone and Laurie Gooding on clarinet. The Chevron Hotel in Kings Cross was Sydney's poshest and swingingest night-spot of the era, and Bell, upon joining the band, was now back playing what he was famous for: energetic, direct, uncomplicated hot jazz, an approach forged in the dance halls and clubs of Melbourne.

CHAPTER 4

THE
JAZZ EXPLOSION

THE MELBOURNE'S CASUAL DANCE SCENE
AND JUDY JACQUES

B ell's absence from Melbourne's live scene in the late forties and early fifties was filled by a new generation of musicians and bands. This included Tony Newstead and his Southside Gang, with sometime Bell drummer Don Reid and the indefatigable Abe Monsbourgh on trombone. Other bands were led by the likes of Frank Johnson, Jack Allen, Len and Bob Barnard, and pianists Lee Anderson and Don Banks. All may have incorporated into their line-ups Pixie Roberts on reeds, or Frank Traynor on trombone, Lou Silbereisen bass, Dick Tattam, trumpet, Max Walley drums — it was simply a matter of finding out who was available and grabbing them for the night. This fluidity of band membership became a feature of the Melbourne fifties jazz scene; the emergence of the casual jazz dance scene had left bandleaders struggling to keep pace with the demand.

From about 1954 onward, every spare community space in Melbourne was swinging to the sounds of Frank Johnson's Fabulous Dixielanders, Len Barnard's Famous Jazz Band, The Yarra Yarra Band,

The George Watson Big Band, and The Kenn Jones Band, just to name a few.

Club 431 in St Kilda Road staged a Sunday night gig hosted by Frank Johnson's Fabulous Dixielanders, who also played The Cambridge Club in South Yarra and the Atherton Club in Oakleigh. Len Barnard's band played Ormond Hall and the Powerhouse Rowing Club as well as the Maison de Luxe in Elwood. All of these bands played places like the 14-foot Sailing Club in St Kilda, The Bullfight at the Elwood Lifesaving Club, The Point Ormond Kiosk, Black and Blue, The Memphis Club, The Glen Iris RSL, Basin Street, The Middle Park Life Saving Club, The Driftwood Number 1 and U Clubs, The Embers, The Keyboard Club, Katarina's Cabaret, Birdlands, not to mention and the host of holiday gigs in Dromana, Sorrento Hotel, Portsea Hotel, The Arab and Beach Hall Palace in Lorne, Isle of Wight in Cowes, the list is endless. Musicians ran from one venue to another, swapping gear and music charts, grabbing a beer and a fag in the car park, running up the steps and onto the stage.

Musician Jeff Hawes wrote that Melbourne's casual dance scene was unique in Australia: 'I had relocated to Sydney (at this time) and the casual dance craze had not occurred in the harbour city, no doubt due to the club culture and their poker machines. In Sydney jazz was performed in pubs and wine bars.'[1]

Sydneysiders had Bondi and Manly beaches as well as semi-tropical weather and the pleasures of the flesh that were on full display down Darlinghurst Road in the Cross. Jazz dances held in Melbourne, where soft drinks and cups of tea were served by a women's auxiliary, would have seemed rather quaint to our Sin City neighbours. But casual jazz dances helped Melbourne build a new life for itself.

Judith Durham in her biography *The Judith Durham Story: Colours of My Life,* described the scene at the time:

'Musicians were first to organise these events [casual jazz dances] and when they caught on with the jazz crowd, promoters were quick to jump in. Jazz was incredibly popular [at this time], there was a real

Plus these famous topline Radio and Bandstand Stars:—

★ **VICTOR JOHNSON & HIS 12 MAN ORCHESTRA**
  ROGER BELL & HIS DIXIE LAND JAZZ BAND
★ **TED LEVISON,** Ace Vocalist and Everybody's Favorite.
  ALLURING MADELAINE WALSHE SONG STAR
★ **JOY BURNS,** Dugout Song Star.
  BRUCE GEORGE
  AMAZING BOOGGIE WOOGGIE RHYTHM PLAYER

GEORGE WATSON
and his
"DUGOUT DANDIES."

PLAY ALL YOUR FAVOURITES INCLUDING
RAGTIME COWBOY JOE
GOLDEN WEDDING
OLD MILL STREAM
PIANO MAN
PARRADIDDLE

with GEORGE himself on the drums
Plus   **A DIXIE LAND** Speciallity

"THE MARCH OF THE BOB CATS"

2-7   —   A D M I S S I O N   —   2-7

cult movement in those days ... town halls were packed to the rafters every week end with teenagers ... it had a character all of its own.'[2]

The casual jazz dance scene generated its own Melbourne 'look' as well, skin-tight corduroys worn with sloppy joes, desert boots and all topped off with a duffle coat. A perfect outfit for young women to dance the stomp and cake-walk all night long.

Not only did the jazz scene provide work for musicians, it also encouraged their versatility; an ability to play different styles and approaches and in a range of combinations, from small groups right up to big bands. As the pace of work increased so did the fluidity of line-ups, which in turn helped create a recognisable Melbourne approach to playing jazz that could be described as energetic, direct and uncomplicated.

The Barnard Brothers

Len and Bob Barnard were crucial to igniting the Melbourne jazz explosion of the '50s. Drummer and piano player Leonard (Len) Barnard and his cornet-playing brother Bob first came to prominence in 1949, when they played the Jazz Convention in Melbourne. Around 1954, they formed the Len Barnard's Dixieland Jazz Band. The band variously included Doc Willis, Frank Traynor on trombone and the ubiquitous Abe Monsbourgh on tenor sax. They played a host of Melbourne venues including the Palais Royal, and had a long residency at the Mentone Lifesaving Club.

'They were terrific days, roaring days ... although none of the bands [in Melbourne] sounded the same, they all had an Australian sound, it was the rhythm section that did it ... most had banjo and tuba ...'[3]

It was the Len Barnard band that recorded the first Australian long-play album with Parlophone, a recording that included his whizz-kid brother Bob on cornet. With a taste for Louis Armstrong and Bix Beiderbecke, Bob was a precocious talent. By 1952, at the age of nineteen, Bob had unseated Roger Bell as Australia's most popular and best cornet player, a title he carried while he and his brother toured Australia in 1954. Bad weather and bad management meant Len and Bob lost their shirts, leaving Len to work in Brisbane for a while before coming back to Melbourne to play a regular gig at the Palais de Danse and sitting in with a host of Melbourne bands.

Bob in the meantime toured up and down the east coast, trying the scratch a living as a trumpeter for hire. But then fate would intervene in the form of — you guessed it — Graeme Bell. Bell threw him a lifeline by booking him in for a gig in Sydney, and Bob dropped everything to be there — but at the last minute, the gig fell through. With tickets booked for Sydney and gigless in Melbourne, Barnard went anyway, and it proved to be a fruitful decision. Bell put together his revered 'All Stars' jazz outfit with Bob on trumpet, Harry Harmon on bass and Alan Geddes drums. The group would stay together throughout most of the '60s. Bob went on to form his own band in Sydney, recording with Graeme Bell's great Swaggie label and appearing regularly on television up to the '80s.

The Barnard Brothers played with Australian jazz royalty, including Don Burrows, John Sangster, Judy Bailey, Doc Willis, Graeme Lyall, and Tony Gould. Bob was described 'world leading ... If recorded evidence and the firsthand knowledge of witnesses who have toured the United States can be accepted, [Bob Barnard] is at least equal [to] any trumpeter playing in the traditional style anywhere in the world ... there is a majesty about his music which is balanced by a glorious lyricism.'[4]

And Len too was in constant demand as jazz music's consummate timekeeper. Like all great drummers, Len played the music rather than the drums, and he could play anything: from Dixieland trad to the cool modern jazz of Charlie Parker, Thelonious Monk, Miles Davis, Dizzy Gillespie, Miles Davis and others.

As the '60s emerged, Melbourne jazz musicians explored

new musical ideas. The Dixielanders nurtured a number of future Melbourne jazz legends, including trombonist and entrepreneur Frank Traynor who went on to form Frank Traynor's Jazz Preachers, Australia's longest continuously running jazz band. Traynor also made a huge contribution to Melbourne's live music scene as an entrepreneur. He founded the Melbourne Jazz Club in 1958 and Frank Traynor's Folk and Jazz Club in 1963, which played a pivotal role as an after-midnight jazz venue and a centre for the revival of Australian folk music. The club hosted folk musicians up to seven nights a week, and featured performers including Martyn Wyndham-Read, Danny Spooner, Brian Mooney, David Lumsden, Trevor Lucas and Margret RoadKnight.

Judy Jacques

Judy Jacques is a quintessential Melbourne musician, a woman who goes deep into the music, a seeker of the truth of whatever she performs. Jacques plays music that she feels is right for her rather than what is expected or popular. But the system works in a cynical way, especially if you're a woman. There are always expectations of how she should look, what she should sing and where she should perform. These expectations, imposed by men, are depressing and oppressive. It takes real courage to know what's right for you, and have the faith and ability to reach for it, often in the face of a lot of real resistance. Judy Jacques has had that courage right from the start.

Jacques was a teenage singing sensation in Melbourne. Born in 1944, she grew up in the marshy swamps of pre-bituminised Bentleigh and Moorabbin. When she looked out of her childhood window, she would have seen newly-built clinker brick houses lining the shoe-sucking muddy streets that were fast covering the flatlands surrounding Port Philip Bay.

Her dad was a baritone and her uncle a dancer; collectively, they lit a fire in her young mind. She first heard of a world beyond the primitive greyness of post-war Moorabbin on the radio. The radio showed her that nothing in her world was exactly right; it also inspired her to sing a version of 'Smoke Gets in Your Eyes' at the Pakenham pub at the age of eight.

The audience loved the young girl's performance, and Judy loved the experience; she felt the power of an appreciative crowd and she wanted more. She sang anywhere she could, at talent quests and sing-a-longs — she wanted to perform for anybody. Then she landed a regular gig on Melbourne radio station 3AW at eleven years old. As Judy explained: 'It was a way of getting out of Moorabbin and at the same time helped me deal with constant fear and shyness.'

She hooked up with her guitar-playing sister Yvonne and formed a duo the Two Jays, playing country music that included yodeling, said Judy 'I still love a good yodel', as well as hits by Elvis and the Everly Brothers. Then her uncle, Len Mooney, gave her some 78 recordings of Louis Armstrong and Ella Fitzgerald. That was it for Judy — she had found the real deal and she couldn't ignore it.

'Hearing traditional jazz at the age of fourteen via the freedom and ease of Ella's sweet melodic tones and Louis's lyrical trumpet set me on a path, I felt definite about what I wanted to sing. Jazz and traditional folk music existed side by side in the '60s and I soaked up everything … folk music told me that songs could be entire stories, verse by verse, just as African-American gospel music told me stories from the Bible.'[5]

At this age Judy left Bentleigh High School. She didn't want to waste time in the classroom; education didn't seem important. Within months, she was working at the Department of Civil Aviation and singing every Saturday night at the Moorabbin Scout Hall with a pop-rock band — fun, but not her thing. Then a friend from work took her to Dante's Inferno at the Glen Iris RSL to see the traditional jazz outfit the Melbourne New Orleans Band fronted by vocalist Paul Marks. Judy wrote to me in a long email about the experience of attending her first jazz club:

It was packed, not with slick-backed, greasy-haired, leather-jacketed rockers and their swinging skirt dancing girl-friends, but girls and boys in pressed shirts, duffle coats, cooks' daks and pointy toed shoes, they danced to music with a long history, music that asked to be respected. This was the music I wanted to be involved with. I boldly walked up to clarinetist [Nick Polites] and said, 'I can sing, and I want to sing this music, I want to know, can I come to rehearsal?' I was fourteen, the musicians in the MNOJB would have been of another generation or more, older. But Nick told me about a new young band that had just formed that were more my age, the Yarra Yarra New Orleans Jazz Band. He thought I would be more suited in age to sing with them. However, I did go to a MNOJB rehearsal; I was picked up from my parents' home in Moorabbin by Nick and drove to somewhere around Glen Iris; I sang one song. After the rehearsal, I was then driven home by a member of the band, but the [journey] became a nightmare. He kept touching me, stopping and reaching for me, pulling me towards him. I eventually shouted, 'Stop the car now!' and I got out and walked home. In my mind it was a long walk home, my first experience with forceful and dangerous men. Maybe I should've punched the bugger, just like my father taught me to do. Dad showed me how to throw a punch so I could get out of scrapes just like that one; he never wanted me to be a victim.

Over the years, I'd see that same man at parties or gigs and thinking about it now, I still feel anger. I'd avoid him, but sometimes he'd sidle up and make some sort of derogatory snide remarks and laugh, classic bullying behaviour.

Judy was a pioneer, belaboring the barriers that prevented women participating in the male-dominated jazz world of '50s Melbourne. It was a big ask for someone so young, but Judy had steely resolve:

Coincidentally and amazingly, … [at a time when] jazz was just being noticed [in Melbourne] John Wratten — who ran the Scout dance at the Moorabbin Scout Hall where I played with the rock band — decided to change the style of the dance from a rock to jazz, and had offered the gig to the Yarra Yarra New Orleans Jazz Band but on the proviso that I stayed on and sang with them.

They agreed, but reluctantly; there was resistance within the band. Don Hall (the band's drummer) and Bob Brown didn't want a sheila in the band, and tried to discourage her by calling her a good pop singer. As Judy wrote in our email exchange:

I felt pretty lonely in that first year singing with the Yarras; the band didn't necessarily want me around, nor did their girlfriends. I remember turning up to one of our first rehearsals in Camberwell. I stood at the front door knocking for twenty minutes before anyone would let me in!

But Judy was made of stern stuff; she went back every night until the band gave in and she became a permanent member.

After the band's initial tactics to get rid of me didn't work, the fellas and I became close friends, they were my mates, sharing with me songs and singers I should listen to. Rehearsals and listening sessions were something to look forward to. The boys were very clear about the style of jazz the band would play, so I was excited to be developing an understanding of style differences through their passions. Talk was nothing but jazz, jazz and more jazz. We'd listen to music that grew from a style closer to the early music of New Orleans and gospel, music closer to the roots of African-American Music, closer to the history and the politics of race.

The band was very selective and together we became an earnest mob of musicians always looking for the centre of the music. Any thoughts I'd had as a child of making a record for the top forty and being famous disappeared; an ego based

*career flashed like lightening and disappeared over the horizon
as all I wanted to do was sing music that mattered, to be part of
this band, part of this small enclave of musicians and friends,
and to show them that I could do it.*

Ironically, as the years rolled on with the Yarras, Judy did become
famous, or at least gained a cult following '… so much so that … every
girl in Melbourne seemed to be wearing her hair in Judy's style — long
with a fringe.'6

Largely as a result of Judy's popularity, the Yarra Yarra New Orleans
Jazz Band became a leading player in Melbourne's hot jazz boom of
the late '50s and early '60s. The band held down a weekly residency
at the Gas Works dance in Kew Town Hall, which regularly attracted
an audience of 1500 people or more. There was also Friday nights at
Boston in South Yarra and Sunday nights at St Kilda's notorious Jazz
Centre 44, which Judy described as:

*A bohemian hangout; it was packed with jazz aficionados,
poets, writers, painters, all were our regular audiences. I was
very young, the Yarra Yarras would start early and play,
sometimes all night. I'd take a break and folk singers would
drop by to take a set with the band; we did this most Sunday
nights for two years or so.*

And Judy kept listening and exploring this new and exciting world …

*I listened to everyone I could, George Lewis, Ma Rainey, Bessie
Smith, early blues singers, Josh White, Big Bill Broonzy and
Billie Holiday, Ella of course and Louis, then I heard the Gospel
Singers, Mahalia Jackson, Sister Rosetta Tharpe, the Patterson
Singers, Clara Ward and many more. I began regularly visiting
Thomas' Records asking for gospel imports, buying everything I
could from my meagre wage. I particularly admired Mahalia,
she used her entire range when she sang, she could climb high
and sweet, sailing up into her soprano range or drop down to*

*a bottomless depth with no breaks between that range, that's
what I heard, good singing and that's what I aimed to emulate.*

*The full extent of my vocal range [C below middle C to
high E-flat] was something I developed over years, through
experience and through classical vocal training — which I
needed when I sang Brian Brown's incredibly challenging music
some years later.*

In the meantime, she played the 1960 Australian Jazz Convention in
Kew, Melbourne, followed by the hugely successful Convention in
Adelaide in 1961. Judy was a sensation:

*I felt as if I was at the forefront of a new movement of music,
one that was for young kids in Melbourne, it was like the band
and the audience shared a special secret between them.*

By 1963 Judy was releasing records with the Yarras, playing regularly
at the Melbourne Town Hall's Downbeat, singing at Jazz at City Hall
concerts and appearing on television. There followed a sell-out *Jazz as
You Like It* Moomba concert hosted by Mike Walsh at the Melbourne
Town Hall. Judy recalled that 'The Hall was packed to the rafters as
5000 kids clapped, stamped and cheered.'[7]

Judy was always listening to new material: folk singers like Pete
Seeger, the Weavers, and of course Joan Baez; according to Ryan, Baez
was the first performer Judy heard singing folk songs in a language
other than English. It was also an important time for Judy for
another reason:

*Much of the folk music in the fifties and '60s had strong political
messages and the early '60s were somewhat of a political
awakening for me. I began to look and listen and ask questions,
especially about racial issues.*

Judy's eclectic musical tastes fit the Melbourne jazz/folk scene at the
time where jazz and folk clubs flourished cheek by jowl. When Judy
performed with the Yarras in coffee bars, she would sit in with folk

singers afterwards and sometimes contribute gospel songs, sharing the stage with Glen Tomasetti, Trevor Lucas, Paul Marks and Brian Mooney, who all sang English, Irish and Scottish songs as well as their own songs. She shared her love of folk, blues and gospel with Margret RoadKnight, which was the start of a life long friendship.[8]

Then at nineteen, Judy formed Judy Jacques and Her Gospel Four, the first popular gospel group in Australia. Judy recorded two highly successful EPs with the band, and is credited 'with de-marginalising black gospel singing in Australia resulting in ... hundreds of people packed into churches to hear her sing.[9]

Judy was now so successful that she could buy a little farm, Wild Dog Hill, in the St Andrews foothills north-east of Melbourne. There she regularly entertained touring folk and jazz artists, such as Peter Paul and Mary. Judy remembers very well that day when the trio sang and ate together: 'Mary Travers rode my horse Big Boy Pete. They talked about this amazing young singer-song writer Bob Dylan and I suspect their concerts introduced him to Australia.'

Judy also entertained the cast of the African-American US musical *Black Nativity* (renamed *Go Tell it on a Mountain* in Australia): 'They just gathered around my piano and away we went! Their magnificent voices are still with me.' Maybe what is still with the Black Nativity cast (Alex Bradford, Princess Stewart, Esther Rolle, Barbara White and the Patterson Singers) was the sight of her outside dunny and the smell of the pan awash with the results of the good time they were having eating and drinking at the Wild Dog!

But then, the demands of mainstream television could no longer be ignored. Says Judy:

> I could see for the sake of my career in a small country ... that the time had come to expand my repertoire and image. So when ABV2 approached me in 1966 to join the cast of ... Bobby & Laurie's Dig We Must with a fresh image, it was perfect timing.

Judy then went on to co-host *Start Living,* another teenage music show for ABC TV. Judy would sing the soul-infused material favoured by Dionne Warwick; it was, according to Ryan, 'a little challenging for producers.'

Around this time, Judy had a confronting encounter with legendary figure in Australian popular music, Johnny O'Keefe. It was an encounter that left her questioning the value of performing in Australia's music and entertainment mainstream:

In the late '60s I shared a show with John O'Keefe at Pentridge Prison in Melbourne. We became friends, he'd ring me at all hours of the night from exotic places, always had something to say, 'like what are you doing? Get out of bed, you should be up here singing' ... he came up to Wild Dog Hill a couple of times.

Eventually, he organised a few gigs in Sydney. I flew up and he picked me up at the airport in a Chevy convertible with the top down showing off all the cream upholstery. He took me to meet his parents and then he drove us around the streets of Kings Cross stopping many times to talk to people, everyone recognised him. He was spreading the word for the shows we were doing at an RSL over a couple of nights. 'Comin' to the show tonight Bill? Judy's singing too,' and on we drove. He was famous, he loved Sydney and Sydney loved him. John's hustle worked, the show that night went over extremely well.

But there was a problem, I was a little uneasy with my allotted role as John's pretty, blonde singing sidekick. Luckily I had a secret weapon in the form of a mate in Sydney, Kevin. He did my hair and makeup, poured the wine, organised the parties and generally kept me safe from harm. As well as the champagne, Kevin also kept a bottle of black hair dye handy and understood my ambition to be a bloody good singer and serious musician and not just a blonde, pretty poppet. So Kevin got to work with the black dye. Pretty soon my long bleached blonde hair, including my false hair-piece were transformed into a thick black mass that would have looked handsome on a horse.

I got to the gig and walked in for a quick run through with the band. My mate John was there and we'd planned to perform a duet for the show that night. He turned and looked at me … a dark cloud swept across his face. He stomped towards me and thrust his face close to mine and spat … 'I hired a blonde!!!' They were the last words spoken to me by Johnny O'Keefe.'

Judy, aside from dodging angry Australian rock legends, was at the toppermost of Australia's entertainment heap; but something wasn't quite right:

I was becoming disillusioned with 'entertaining', it was disappointing both creatively and musically, so in 1974 I chose to have a break from all appearances and re-evaluate my priorities. I took a year off, travelled overseas, wrote poems and songs, some of which incorporated the lyrics and poems of Eric Beach.

By 1975 I was back at Wild Dog Hill and slowly fell into what some may label as a 'delayed adolescence'. I rebelled against the show biz mainstream by rejecting the label of pop diva/entertainer that had been attached to me; I'd grown to hate that label so I ripped it off. Suddenly I was free to explore a more avant-garde, experimental direction in music, specifically free improvisation. Artistically it was the best thing I ever did, I was able to expand my vocal technique to incorporate a wordless language that enabled me to express what I had to say at the time.

This new musical direction led Judy to the Clifton Hill Community Music Centre, and Carlton's La Mama Theatre, where she collaborated with poets, dancers, writers, visual artists and actors. It was at this time that 'she had the freedom to invent and explore musical forms without feeling a need to gratify an audience.'[10]

This experimental phase resulted in a collaboration with poet Eric Beacher. The two jointly developed a show for The Pram Factory called *Lyrics and Blues, before taking it* on a rather disastrous tour through country Victoria. According to Ryan, the show incorporated Judy's more challenging atonal improvisations resulted in a Christmas Hills crowd rushing the stage shouting obscenities and throwing cans.

In her career, Jacques demonstrated a willingness to experiment with innovative musical forms and vocal techniques. They may have challenged some audiences, but they kept her creative juices flowing and kept her relevant, a point made by Bruce Johnson writing in *The Oxford Companion to Australian Jazz*: 'Jacques …[was] one of the very few [artists] to emerge from the jazz/folk boom of the early '60s and define a new phase in her career.'

Judy was artistically invigorated in the '80s. She rejoined the Yarra Yarras for weekly gigs and explored her interest in free improvisation; energy was coming from a million different places. By the late '80s Judy was the fifth member of the Brian Brown Quintet, with whom she played concerts, toured, and recorded for nearly twenty years. She also fronted Bob Sedergreen's Blues on the Boil for many years and participated in a reunion with the Yarra Yarra New Orleans Jazz Band to celebrate their 25th anniversary.

As the years progressed, Judy went on to teach improvisation at the Victorian College of the Arts and run classes at a number schools and colleges. She formed her own outfit, the Wild Dog Ensemble, with her husband, trumpeter Sandro Donati. It was with another of her bands, Lighthouse, that Jacques toured the UK in the late '90s, performing at the Edinburgh Fringe Festival.

In 2002, after five years of work, Judy released her album *Making Wings*. The twelve-track song suite was inspired by Flinders Island in Bass Strait, where her lighthouse-tending ancestors lived and where she now resides, following the destruction of her Wild Dog Hill property in the Black Saturday bushfires. The album didn't take any precautions: the band which featured Doug de Vries on guitar, Sandro Donati, trumpet Nicola Eveleigh, flute, Howard Cairns, bass Michael Jordan, drums and Denise Close, percussion sounded relaxed on the album, on top of their game. It's little wonder that *Making Wings* won the Bell Award for Australian Jazz Vocal Album of the Year .

Judy continued to perform jazz, gospel and folk music all through the 2000s. She has curated special concerts on her new Flinders Island home; she also paints, writes and reflects on her career, a career that was always based on her strong self-belief as an artist.

Modern Jazz

In many ways, the career of Judy Jacques reflected the evolution of Melbourne's jazz scene, from the hot jazz craze popularised by The Bell Brothers and others in the '40s to the more subliminal influence of cool, modern jazz.

Modern jazz (and bebop for that matter) took its time entering the musical consciousness of Melbourne-based trad jazz players. It took a younger generation of musicians, like Don Banks, Brian Brown, Splinter Reeves, Charlie Blott, Teddy Preston and Keith Houslow, to introduce the new, darker sound to Melbourne. Modern jazz is an intense musical form that evolved in America during wartime, courtesy of such luminaries as Miles Davis, Charlie Parker, Dizzy Gillespie, and Thelonious Monk. Its counter-melodies, complex harmonies and disruptive off-beats made it a difficult form for audiences more familiar with the danceable rhythms of traditional, hot jazz.

Modern jazz, which ultimately became synonymous with bebop, was largely hidden from Melbourne jazz-heads for many years. A US Musicians Union recording ban from 1942-44 meant this radical form went unheard here in Australia until the late '40s. But as the '50s progressed, a Miles started recording with Prestige and Blue Note, Parkers' Dial, Savoy and Mercury cuts became more available and suddenly jazz was not just about a goodtime and clichéd chord changes, it was about a deep personal expression through music. Charlie Parker explained the new jazz form:

'I realised by using the high notes of the chords as a melodic line, and by the right harmonic progression, I could play what I heard inside me. That's when I was born. Music is your own experience, your own thoughts, your wisdom. If you don't live it, it won't come out of your horn. They teach you there's a boundary line to music. But, man, there's no boundary line to art.'[11]

Brian Brown was considered the leader of the modern jazz movement in Melbourne around this time. Brown, along with his longtime musical partner Bob Sedergreen, brought the post-bop world of Miles Davis, Sonny Rollins, Coleman Hawkins and Stan Getz to the local jazz scene. They played a style of jazz that was always developing, a style the reflected the constant and often turbulent changes occuring in society.

When Brown slid this new creative, passionate jazz style under Melbourne's front door, it gained an enthusiastic following among the new generation of sophisticated jazz fans, who were attracted to its fluency, speed and shapely melodic invention-on-the-fly. In echoes of the Bell era of the '40s, Brown's music also resonated with artists and Melbourne's bohemian intelligentsia; for example the band was booked for a recording session at Bill Armstrong's studios and were greeted by a very hip crowd that included: Germaine Greer, the artist Clem Meadmore and a number of Melbourne's leading musicians including Chris Karan.

Jazz Centre 44

It was the Germaine Greers of the world, together with a menagerie of funky jazz freaks, who came to hear Brown and other post-bop musicians at Jazz Centre 44 in St Kilda.

According to the St Kilda Jazz Heritage tour Web site, a jazz club had been housed in the semicircular Federation building on the corner of Acland Street and The Esplanade opposite Luna Park since

1947. Operating under several different names including, Katarina Café, Catharina Cabaret and Catherina Club, most people remember the crazy, mixed-up bohemian hangout, where patrons danced the cakewalk, poets mixed with musicians, prostitutes came in from the street and Blue Note jazz was first heard in Melbourne, as Caterina's Cabaret. The club was managed right up to the '60s by the equally bohemian, chain-smokin', Ford Falcon-drivin' Irene Fredrikson (nee Tenenbaum); even though the building was owned by Horst Liepolt from 1957 and had been renamed Jazz Centre 44.

Six years after immigrating to Australia from Berlin, Horst Liepolt had started Jazz Centre 44 in the '50s, naming it after the year he'd first heard a Louis Armstrong record. Jazz Centre 44 quickly became *the* hipster place to hang out and hear progressive jazz. Regular trad jazz bands played the club, mostly on a Sunday night; bands like Bob and Len Barnard's outfit, the Melbourne New Orleans Jazz Band and the Yarra Yarra New Orleans Jazz Band featuring Judy Jacques. Judy described playing the Sunday night slot at the club, a slot she and the band filled for about two or three years:

> *You'd start playing at the regular time, then in the breaks when the boys were drinking a refreshment or two, a folk singer, or poet like Adrian Rawlins would come on stage and perform. We'd continue to interchange band with folk singers all through the night, then stumble down stairs when the sun came up. It was wild place and I was so young.*

Jazz Centre 44 was the only venue in Melbourne where existentialist writers, painters and thinkers came to hear modern jazz, as opposed to the mainstream stuff you heard in the community and RSL halls throughout Melbourne. The club was dark and chaotic, but you could see Luna Park's big dipper rise and fall and shake and rattle outside the window as tourists walked up and down the boulevard.

Ken White, a local acoustic blues vocalist and guitarist, was regularly booked to play his dark delta blues alongside mainstream jazz vocalists and Dixieland and Bebop ensembles at the club. He described the place as a 'less than sedate venue, booze could be got from under the counter, brawls were frequent and the jazz was furious.'[12]

White and his musical partner, Graeme Squance, were a nascent acoustic blues duo in Melbournein the early '60s. They were the first musicians in the country to play and sing real Mississippi Delta blues, early Muddy, Sonny Terry/Brownie McGhee, Sleepy John Estes, stuff like that.

But then Leopolt sold the Jazz Centre 44 and moved to America, the club became a waxworks and the jazz party moved on to the Green Man, the Colonial Inn, Outpost Inn, Little Reata, joints like that, places where jazz and folk, folk and blues, protest and traditional formed a mixed up crazy symbiotic bohemian milieu, a milieu that came to define the Melbourne music scene in the early '60s.

Sunrise, sunset, that's what happens in Melbourne, when one venue closes more open and the whole circus tumbles in and takes up residency. The jugglers and clowns then pick up their instruments and play as though nothing had changed.

LET'S *ROCK*

As the fifties slid by, the suburbs sprawled, the Cold War got chillier and Menzies sucked harder at the British teat. In Melbourne, rapid change was underway, at least in some corners of the city. The 1956 Olympic Games had provided an opportunity for those recent European immigrants to showcase the cuisine (and liquor) from their home countries to thousands of eager international visitors. Post Olympics, European eateries started popping up all over places like Carlton, Fitzroy and St Kilda, the migrant areas of Melbourne, where European-style nightclubs like Jazz Centre 44 also emerged.

But the suburbs remained largely Anglo-Saxon; migrants were yet to find the pleasures of the quarter-acre block, the septic tank, the silence of empty mud-sucking streets. Housewives made small talk over their back fences while their husbands worked in factories or offices, to the earn the money to fill the clinker-brick houses with soft furnishings, refrigerators and Pye televisions. Menzies ruled the country and made sure school children recited the national pledge every day before class … 'I love God and my country, I will honor the flag and serve the Queen and cheerfully obey my parents, teachers and the laws …' Like a conservative economic missionary, he preached the importance of free enterprise, hard work, home ownership, family values, materialism, belief in God and the Queen (not necessarily in that order) and the value of the occasional outing to the Dandenongs for a Devonshire tea. It was these Australian values, he assured us, that would be a shield against the threat of Marxist ideology, which would lay waste to our Australian way of life.

Some argue the '50s marked the end of the Enlightenment, when Melbourne's progressive artists and writers jumped on ships and headed for Europe. But for a sizable chunk of Melbournian teenagers the '50s were revolutionary. Finally young people had a music and a cultural attitude that spoke to them and separated them from the silent scream of their suburban life. Rock'n'roll had arrived and blown the old joint apart.

I was a preteen in the mid-'50s, sharing a room with my brother, older by seven years. We lived in the inner-north industrial suburb of Northcote, with its mixture of grand and not-so-grand Victorian homes standing alongside postwar utilitarian housing. Peter slept with an Astor radio by his bed, a radio from which, one night, I heard something that filled me with such intense emotion I didn't know what to do. Stan Rofe was spinning platters and producing music propelled by wildly kinetic rhythm; like most young Melbournians, my brother and I had never heard anything like it. I asked Peter what we were listening to and he said they called it rock'n'roll. Pretty soon it became an obsession: Elvis, Buddy Holly, Chuck Berry, Fats Domino, Little Richard, Brenda Lee, Jerry Lee Lewis and our own Johnny O'Keefe had produced a sonic cataclysm that shook our teenage lives to the foundations.

Robert Palmer wrote for *Rolling Stone* in 1990[1] that, when they asked Fats Domino what the origins of this new music were, he said 'Rock'n'roll aint nothin' but rhythm and blues and we've been playin' it for years down in New Orleans ...' Palmer explained; 'As far as Fats Domino was concerned, rock'n'roll was simply a new marketing strategy for the style of music he had been recording since 1949.' But that was only half of it. There was no clear precedent in R&B for an artist like Chuck Berry, who combined hillbilly, blues and swing-jazz in equal measure and wrote songs about teenage life that black and white teens alike found appealing. Elvis too had aspects of R&B, country and gospel in his sound, but as Palmer wrote:

'Popular music had never seen a performer whose vocal delivery, stage moves and seamless integration of influences as diverse as down-home blues, white Pentecostalism and hit-parade crooning remotely resembled Elvis Presley's.'

And where, outside the wildest, most Dionysian black storefront churches had anyone heard or seen anything like Little Richard?

Palmer notes that rock'n'roll was the only form of popular music that specifically addressed teenagers — there had been adult records, like jazz or adult pop, and kiddie records, but nothing for that burgeoning bulge of the baby-boom population caught between childhood and adulthood. Rock'n'roll enabled 'marginal' American teenagers the opportunity to express themselves not as purveyors of jazz or country, whose audiences were limited, but as a dominant force in the popular marketplace.

Initially, the impact of rock'n'roll was muted in Melbourne. It was perceived as a novel attraction, or, as the *Milesago* music site describes, 'an exotic import, something strange and dangerously alluring to the young musos and fans who saw and heard the American originals.'[2]

Most of the first wave of Australian rock stars came out of Sydney, and leading the charge in the late fifties was Aussie rock'n'roll pioneer Johnny O'Keefe. Alongside the 'Wild One' were other local rockers like Lonnie Lee & The Leemen, Digby Richards & The R'Jays, Col Joye & The Joy Boys, Alan Dale & The Houserockers, Ray Hoff & The Offbeats, Digger Revell & The Denvermen and New Zealand's Johnny Devlin & The Devils.

In 1956, however, *Rock Around The Clock*, featuring Bill Haley and the Comets, was released. In Melbourne, almost overnight, jazz and popular dance halls like Leggett's Ballroom in Prahran and Earl's Court in St Kilda switched to rock'n'roll, and town halls — perhaps most famously of all, The Preston Town Hall — became antipodean havens for rock sensibility.

Rock'n'roll spawned the bodgie and widgie scene of leather jackets, motorcycles, greasy hair, noisy Holdens and American dreams. And rock'n'roll was fun, played at a regular 4/4 beat and a decibel range only made possible by amplification. It was music made for dancing, not for intellectualising. Suddenly for teenage Melbourne, jazz and swing seemed lame, stuffy, gutless and flabby; they were dullsville, man. Rock'n'roll was wild, weird and hip. As David Nichols wrote in *Dig, Australian Rock and Pop Music 1960-1980*, 'The early rock'n'roll musicians did not spring fully formed into this performance mode: they had started out as jazz or country players, working in what we would now understand as a swing style.'[3]

One of Melbourne's premier instrumental rock bands, The Thunderbirds, grew out of the local bebop and modern jazz scene. They quickly moved on from playing Melbourne's Jazz Centre 44 to backing Johnny Chester, Malcolm Arthur, Margie Mills, Judy Cannon and Frankie Davidson at the Preston Town Hall and Thornbury's Arcadia Ballroom. Suddenly town halls and converted movie theatres from Preston to Frankston to Dandenong to Sunshine were packed with jiving teenagers. There was no person under the age of twenty unaffected.

In downhome Northcote, the rock'n'roll bug continued to infect my brother; his black hair was cut into an Elvis pompadour, he wore Hawaiian shirts, and later, he would drive an FJ. Rock'n'roll had become both seductive and exciting, like forbidden fruit. The trick was to find a way to taste it. We were too young to go to the Preston Town Hall and we had no pocket money to access the dark vinyl pleasures of Elvis or Johnny O'Keefe or Jerry Lee, or a device to play records, for that matter. Then one day we were asked by our dad to pick up a hat he had bought in Fairfield, one of those porkpie Stetsons, which he wore every day of his working life. I can see him now in the early morning fog, hat low, overalls clean, his lunch and *The Age* bouncing in his kitbag as he marched off to the bus in Darebin Road. He returned at night, the sky scarlet as lipstick. It was always around five that I'd see him walking slowly down Swift Street, the hat pushed back on head, his overalls smeared with work, the kitbag empty and his footfall slow and enduring. But I digress; the Stetson was to be picked up from a Fairfield hatter in Station Street, near the Coles Variety Store — it's a discount chemist now. It was sleek and grey with a feather in the band, and somehow even then I understood that hat was like a eulogy for another time. It was becoming old hat to wear one.

After collection, we ducked into Coles to check out the latest record releases, and there amongst the Patti Page, Burl Ives and Connie Francis was Elvis's latest LP release *King Creole*. The record was the sound track to the movie of the same name and arguably Elvis's best movie. Set in New Orleans, Presley plays 19-year-old Danny Fisher (a role originally intended for James Dean), who is struggling to graduate from high school when he accidentally stumbles into a singing career. The songs on the film's album — largely written by the great song writing team of team Jerry Lieber and Mike Stoller — were a mixture of Dixieland jazz and slinky blues, songs like 'King Creole', 'Hard Headed Woman', 'Trouble' and 'New Orleans', plus a smattering of schlocky crooning pop: 'Lover Doll', 'Young Dreams', 'Steadfast Loyal and True'.

My brother and I picked up the album. Walking north up Station Street I noticed that, along with the album, Johnny O'Keefe's single 'Shout', written and previously recorded by the Isley Brothers, had found their way into the paper bag holding my fathers hat. How did that happen? We elbowed and bumped our way up Station Street; rebels with a cause, headed for our neighbour's house. Our sidekick Lance Puche had a record player and we wanted to play the shit out of our vinyl booty.

Most Saturdays for the next few years we would huddle in Lance's bedroom listening to Elvis, JOK, Roy Orbison. Roy had a voice like an opera singer, as Bob Dylan had once said:

'With Roy, you didn't know if you were listening to mariachi or [Wagner] He kept you on your toes … he sounded like he was singing from an Olympian mountaintop and he meant business … he was singing with three or four octaves.'[4]

Then one summer, when Northcote's black volcanic soil, so sticky and adhesive in winter, cracked and shattered like a road in an earth quake — we got *The Summertime Blues*. In February 1959 Buddy Holly, Richie Valens and the Big Bopper went down in a plane crash in an Iowa field. Then Elvis disappeared into the army and Chuck Berry was in jail, convicted under The Mann Act of transporting a minor across borders. Little Richard found God and quit showbiz and Jerry Lee married his barely pubescent cousin and was blackballed by record producers and rock promoters alike. Then to compound the whole mess, in April 1960 Eddie Cochran was a passenger in a car driving back late at night from a gig in Bristol England. When the car reached Chippenham about midnight it spun out of control, hit a poll and threw the man described as … 'James Dean with a guitar', onto the verge. Eddie, the writer and performer of such classic songs as 'Twenty Flight Rock', 'Summertime Blues', 'C'mon Everybody' and 'Somethin' Else', died later that night in hospital, he was twenty-one years old. Almost overnight the rebel yell of rock'n'roll had been silenced. Then capitalism and the demands of the market economy conspired to turn our remaining rockers into adult entertainers.

By the late '50s-early '60s, corporate recording giants such as RCA, CBS, EMI and Australia's Festival entered the rock'n'roll market and turned its high-octane energy into pure milk and sugar. As David Nichols observed:

'Col Joye, Johnny O'Keefe and Dig Richards … had by now become established entertainers, compelled by professional requirements to broaden their palette.'[5]

In other words, corporate interests turned rock'n'roll outlaws into pliable pussycats. Johnny O' Keefe put out boringly safe singles like 'I'm Counting on You' and 'Just a Closer Walk with Thee'. Who was he kidding? In addition, flaccid *Bandstand* dominated our television screens, where Judy Stone, once a guitar-playing country star, was told in no uncertain terms that if she wanted a regular spot on the show she should 'drop the guitar', and 'just…sing and look pretty'.[6]

Suddenly no matter how hard I flicked that radio dial on the Astor by my brother's bed, I couldn't find anything worth listening to. We even stopped going to Lance's joint on Saturday's for our weekly record round up; the footy was far more preferable than listening to Elvis sing 'Wooden Heart' from *GI Blues*.

Then one night, as I listened to 3AR (the precursor to the ABC's Radio National), I heard a voice that drew me in like a magnet, a voice that was rich, dark, and lustrous, with an upper register that broke my heart. A soprano full of sadness, a miracle of a voice that could have come from a mountaintop; I had never heard anything like Joan Baez. She sang songs so dark the lyrics could have been ripped out of the Old Testament, songs like 'Silver Dagger' and 'House of the Rising Sun'. I was hearing stories about profit and sin, death, outlaws, and with 'All My Trials', the release from suffering that death can bring. I was hearing was folk music.

CHAPTER 6

WHAT THE *FOLK?*

'**P**ete Seeger suggested that the desire to listen to or perform folksongs was related to a growing interest in tracing one's cultural roots and national heritage as well as an upsurge of enthusiasm for do-it-yourself activities in an increasingly mechanised post-war world'.[1]

When the partnership between the Eureka Youth League and Graeme Bell fell apart in 1947, the Communist Party of Australia turned to folk music to attempt to further its political agenda. And folk became, in the '50s, a more natural home for radical youth. Richard Haese noted that:

'One of the central leitmotifs of radical left-wing thinking from 1944 onwards, then, was the recognition that the Australian labour movement, with its cultural cry of temper democratic, bias Australian, must provide the basis for contemporary political and cultural values. This chimed well with the first Australian folk revival, beginning in the '50s, which was decidedly nationalist in values'.[2]

The CPA sought to promote folk music as being about the Messianic worker, the shearer, mechanic, miner, meat worker, plasterer, steamfitter, ironworker — maybe the textile worker, nurse and secretary would be included under a different 'women's work' category, who knows? This music spoke of the underclass, the poorly paid and mistreated. But the danger was that the folk music the left wanted to promote would be one-dimensional, preachy, and subsumed by polemics.

The CPA excursion into folk music started with the 1953 premiere of the production *Reedy River*, a musical that captured the leftist principle of cultural nationalism. It was staged in Melbourne by the CPA-aligned New Theatre and was, to use the words of its director John Gray, 'our first Australian musical.'[3] It was a musical set during the Shearers' Strike of 1891, and featured singers, dancers and, in the case of the Sydney production, a bush band with a button accordion and harmonica. The Shearers' Strike was a key moment in the Australian Labor movement and led directly to the formation of the Australian Labor Party. This was a perfect subject for Communist Party bush song collectors like John Meredith, John Manifold and Russell Ward and presented radical nationalist sensibilities in an entertaining fashion. This was true, perhaps, for the *blokes* in the audience; not sure women would have necessarily related to the eulogised bush spirit, the rural stoicism, the ruggedness that underpinned the musical.

Championing the industrial, political, and human rights of women through the politically bleak '50s was a second order priority for the CPA. They were dealing with Cold War hysteria, the Petrov Affair, and the crimes of Stalin, as revealed by Khrushchev in 1956. All these factors sparked a stampede for the exit; as author and lapsed CPA member Dorothy Hewett bemusedly noted:

'A surprising number of ex-communists are joining the Scientologists. There must be something about their rigid methodology and thought-police processes that makes them feel at home.'[4]

But despite this crisis of confidence within the party, Melbourne's cultural nationalists pressed on with their mission. Wendy Lowenstein, the author Alan Marshall, and Edgar Walters collected and preserved Australian folk songs and folklore, which came from such seminal sources as performer Simon McDonald's traditional songs 'The Wild Colonial Boy' and 'Bill Brink'. Simon worked in rural Victoria, and performed his songs and poems in pubs and sheds and town halls for decades. Another source was Sally Sloane, a gifted singer and button accordion player from New South Wales. The emphasis in this period, as Warren Fahey has observed, 'was on scholarship and preservation rather than popular performance', with many events and concerts sponsored by folklore societies and even the Adult Education Association.

In the early '60s, a pioneering Folk Festival was organised by the Victorian Folklore Society and the Bush Music Club in Melbourne. The event, held over seven days, included concerts of traditional Australian folk songs and ballads, as well as lunchtime lectures by people such as Lowenstein and Marshall. There was also folk-dance demonstrations and sing-alongs in the Lower Melbourne Town Hall.

Many of the songs and traditional dances were collected by enthusiasts on impromptu Australian folk song collecting trips, where they would load up their cars with musical instruments, camping gear and sound recording equipment and head for the hills. Malcolm J. Turnbull highlights one particular trip in the very early '60s organised by Pat O'Connor, the Melbourne Folklore Society's Treasurer, according to Pat:

'We camped at Nariel Creek and discovered an old-time country dance was being held in town that night. The music was being played by several men who learnt it from their fathers and grandfathers … Shirley Andrews (President of the Bush Music Club an old-time dance collector) collected two local dances — the Berlin polka and Princess Club.'[5]

Shirley Andrews was not only a folklore enthusiast, she was a biochemist, Aboriginal rights activist, member of the Eureka Youth

League and later a member of the Communist Party of Australia.

The CPA's commitment to an Australian cultural nationalism via traditional folk music continued well into the '60s. The party had turned its back on anything resembling a progressive, modern approach to music at this stage, in favour of a people's culture based on the historical Australian bush tradition. It's no surprise that this hardline approach led to, as Turnbull described:

'Authenticity becoming a god within the traditionalist camp. Elderly bush balladeers like Duke Tritton, Simon McDonald and Sally Sloane, were venerated as "the real thing", simple people unsullied by city ways, passing on an unspoiled tradition which they had lived.'

Performers of such material were respected for their knowledge of the origins of the songs they performed, whether collected from sheet music, record, or oral sources, as well as the associated folklore from which the songs were drawn. According to Turnbull, performer credibility depended on the working-class affiliations, and songs could not be personalised or tampered with in any way; even harmonising was perceived by some traditionalists as sacrilege. A singer's accent was crucial for traditionalists where, as Turnbull recounted:

'Hillbilly or Irish rebel accents ... [and] operatically trained vocals, sounded out-of-place when applied (say) to Australian bush songs. Virtuosity could be suspect, with audiences and fellow-performers wary of singers or instrumentalists who seemed "too good". Honesty was at issue here — and the implication that commercialism automatically entailed a lack of honesty.'[6]

For many performers, it must have been confusing confronting to play in front of such a critical audience. Turnbull stated that:

'As a newcomer to the mid-'60s Melbourne folk scene, Fiona Laurence drew on Scottish songs she had learned in childhood from her Gaelic-speaking grandmother. She was nonplussed when she found herself criticised for not singing "orthodox" Scots songs — by which the folk establishment seems to have meant Ewan MacColl's repertoire.'[7]

But the orthodoxy of the bush ballad was not the only folk music available in Melbourne in the early '60s. The second strand had arrived in Melbourne via the coffee houses and dive clubs of New York's Greenwich Village, where the Gaslight, Café Wha? and the Kettle of Fish Tavern were preeminent. Bob Dylan described the atmosphere in those venues at that time:

'It was always packed [at The Gaslight] from start to finish — some people sitting at tables, some standing and crowding along the walls — bare brick walls, low level lighting and pipes exposed ... I played twenty minute sets ... it was hot in there and too claustrophobic, I didn't hang out ... but there was always, Van Ronk, Stookey, Romney, Hal Waters, Paul Clayton, Luke Faust, Len Chandler playing poker (upstairs) all through the night.[8]

These were places that, as Dylan describes, had a 'frantic atmosphere — all kinds of characters talking fast, moving fast, some debonair, some rakish.'[9]

The folk music boom had arrived in America via such performers as The Kingston Trio, Pete Seeger, Woody Guthrie, Joan Baez, Judy Collins, Odetta, Nina Simone, Tom Paxton, Phil Ochs, David Van Ronk, Peter, Paul and Mary and of course Bob Dylan. These artists played a more contemporary, politically-focussed repertoire.

Pete Seeger's 1963 tour of Australia was particularly influential on the local scene, not only for introducing folk audiences to the political songs of Seeger and his seminal band, the Weavers, but also because he presented the songs of contemporary writers like Dylan, Paxton, Ochs, Van Ronk. These were songs written by artists that were from the folk tradition but wrote material that was current. Seeger's tour inspired many from the Melbourne folk scene to follow the US example, because, to state the bleeding obvious, there was a lot to protest in Melbourne in the '60s.

Bob Menzies had introduced conscription into the army for twenty-year-old Australian men following his commitment of troops to fight and die beside their American allies in Vietnam. Australian troops would join US soldiers to defend the corrupt regime of South Vietnam against the nationalist, communist-supported militia of the North Vietnamese People's Army.

Culturally, Australia was a backwater. Novels like James Joyce's *Ulysses*, D.H. Lawrence's *Lady Chatterley's Lover* and Nobokov's *Lolita* were banned, as were films such as *La Dolce Vita*, Fellinis' *Satyricon*, *Blow-Up* and *Zabriskie Point*. In addition, Australians were still encouraged to genuflect towards Her Majesty, who Menzies 'but saw pass by and loved 'til the day he died.'

In Victoria, Premier Bolte was busily deconstructing inner-city Melbourne by pulling down Victorian-era housing and replacing it with high-rise concrete towers. He also engaged in the judicial murder of Ronald Ryan, and fought anyone that looked vaguely like a unionist or a teacher.

An old work colleague of mine, Elizabeth Rennick, was a Herald journalist in the '60s. She relayed the proceedings of one of Bolte's press conferences at the time:

> *Every Monday at ten o'clock; five or six hack reporters were ushered into a room by Syd Kellaway, the one-man media unit for the Victorian Premier — for the first of the week's daily press briefings. A middle-aged woman would follow the press contingent balancing a tray with a silver tea pot, china cups and a plate of cream biscuits. When the little fat man from the Minister's office arrived, smoking a corked tipped cigarette, everyone immediately fell silent.*

Henry Bolte was at his desk and he immediately began to banter with journalists; they nattered about football, the weekend races at Flemington and the quality of the call on 3UZ, It was as though he was standing at his back fence gossiping to a neighbour. But the convivial suburban scene was soon shattered when a journalist plucked up the courage to ask the Premier what he was going to do about striking teachers.

Bolte crinkled his face and those bulging eyes that delighted a generation of cartoonists stared back at the questioner for a few moments until he replied, 'They can strike until they're black in the face. It won't make any difference.'

'But they have threatened to sit on your door step in protest until they get what they want,' the journalist responded.

Bolte smiled, took a drag from his cigarette and quipped …

'I don't have a door step low enough …'

The room erupted in laughter; journalists loved Henry's earthiness, his bushman's wit, but most of all they loved his very quotable quotes.

Another of his quotable quotes came when a journalist asked about rumors of Bolte's pending retirement:

Bolte: Nah, not true. What paper did you say you were from, son?

Journalist: The [anti-government] Sunday Observer.

Bolte: Well, you got the story wrong. I'm joining the board of your paper.

Journalist: In that case I'm going to quit.

Bolte: You better, son. Because you're the first c*** I'm going to sack when I get there. Cue more laughter …

While Henry held court in Treasury Place, there was something else going on in Melbourne. It was happening in places that served coffee after dark and stuff they called pasta. For some, these places were decadent, filled with outlaw artists playing guitars and preaching revolution. But the coffee houses of Melbourne were simply places where young people could gather to hear deep and penetrating music, songs about unionists and immigrants and women left destitute by their men — songs like *Barbara Allen* with maybe twenty verses. In

Melbourne's coffee houses, no-one played the two-minute, thirty-second pap sung by Pat Boone or Frankie Avalon heard in high rotation on the radio.

The coffee house, where jazz and folk meet

Music critic Robert Shelton maintains that the folk boom grew out of a generalised malaise which afflicted urban youth in the '50s. Children born in to the American (and Australian) middle class in the 1941–50 period confronted:

'A society in which the automobile, the television, the research laboratory, the transcontinental market, and the retail franchise … would begin to displace the railroad, the radio, the factory, the regional market, and the local business'.[10]

In the late '50s and early '60s, coffee houses were where people went to listen to folk music. They were a clear confirmation of the extent to which local developments reflected the state-of-play in America. Maybe it was a reflection of young people's changing cultural elegances away from Britain, where folk music emanated primarily from pubs, to the U.S., where the coffee house was the places to go to find the inner-heat of folk.

For Melburnians, the folk seed was planted in the surf-coast village of Lorne in 1956 when The Arab Café opened its doors. The bluestone and canvas café was the brainchild of three young brothers: Graham, Alistair and Robin Smith. Their vision of sun, sand and surf, enhanced by cappuccinos served by tanned, tall, blonde-haired girls, was designed to take advantage of an influx of overseas visitors to the 1956 Olympics. The joint took off like a rocket. From the time The Arab opened its doors between Christmas and Easter, it served, according to Malcolm Turnbull two thousand patrons a week, and pretty soon this little piece of bohemia was a must-see destination for MG driving thrill seekers. An article published in *The National Times* in 1981 reflected on the cultural contribution The Arab had in the early '60s:

'It was the days before big jets, when anything other than Fletcher Jones trousers, Smoky Dawson and meat pies was considered exotic. Here was a place that offered a smattering of styles, Italian café society mixed with the American beat scene as well as a novel bit of Australiana — perving on near naked and unattainable beachgirls.

As Turnbull writes:

'Soon after opening the café, the Smith brothers expanded their operations to take in a dance-hall 200 yards away. Fitted out "with Australiana and Beach chic" and reopened as the Wild Colonial, it played host to the cream of Melbourne's trad jazz bands from 1958 until 1964, including Frank Traynor.

'As well as playing at the Wild Colonial's enormously successful jazz dances most evenings, artists would be called on to entertain patrons at the Arab.'[11]

These artists included beat poet Adrian Rawlins and folksingers Paul Marks, Brian Mooney, Peter Laycock, Martyn Wyndham-Read and the luminous Glen Tomasetti. The practice of interspersing folksingers as a change of pace at the Wild Colonial jazz dances, and jazz players interspersed with folk singers at The Arab, soon caught on. It would lay the foundation for a whole range of jazz/folk venues all over Melbourne, including the famous Frank Traynor's Folk and Jazz Club.

Places like the Melbourne Jazz Cellar, Gassworks, Café Ad Lib in South Yarra, The Jolly Roger in St Kilda Road, Hernando's, and the Treble Clef were early adapters. According to Malcolm Turnbull writing on Warren Fahey's Folk Lore blog, music wasn't the only thing that got people through the doors of the Ad Lib; it also offered great Italian cooking and dark corners where the gay community could discreetly hook up. Music was an aural condiment to all the other stuff going on; patrons either paid attention or, more often, didn't. Turnbull observed of the crowd:

'Audiences were primarily student-based and, by extension, middle class. Well-educated young adults, white … and generally city-bred, immersed themselves (or dabbled, at least) in treasure-troves of rural music, the blues, labour anthems and topical song. In Britain, by contrast (according to a '60s survey), nearly 70% of folk club members described themselves as manual workers, and only about 5% as students.'[12]

Tom Lazar opened The Reata on High Street in Malvern in 1960, with decorations that were Greenwich Village chic; fishing nets hanging from the ceiling, candles in VAT 69 bottles, red-and-white gingham tablecloths. Tommy filled the café with pasta and folk singers, hoping to attract the non-conformist, intellectual crowd. There was Paul Marks — credited to be the first performer in Melbourne to crossover from jazz to folk — young blues pioneer Trevor Lucas, Martyn Wyndham-Read David Lumsden, Brian Mooney, Tina Date, Glen Tomascetti, and Gary Shearston.

On Sundays, popular afternoon concerts were staged at the café, amalgams of jazz and folk performances and poetry readings. Often people were packed so tight inside that it was hard to breathe. Patrons spilled out into High Street, queueing round the block. But Lazar was a businessman, and reconciling business and artistic sensibilities was, as Turnbull observed, a dilemma confronting most folk/coffee lounge proprietors:

'Singers who attracted cult followings were an anathema to businessmen who wanted quick and steady turnover of paying customers, not devoted observers, or penniless friends of artists who sat on one or two coffees a night.'[13]

Lazar got sick of his café filling up with people staring at the singer on the stage, their imaginations working overtime, but with their wallets and purses firmly shut. He was also tired of his money-spending diners complaining about the singer onstage, because all they wanted to do was eat their dinner and talk about azaleas with their friends. Turnbull writes of one particular incident at Lazar's when the banjo-playing Garry Kinnane was tossed a pound note with a curt request to 'take your banjo up the other end of the restaurant.'[14]

Lazar was not a huge folk fan — but he was a fan of paying customers. So he acted on their complaints and shook those long-haired laggards and deadbeat folkies out of his Malvern-money-maker and moved them to his new city venture, Little Reata. But soon he encountered similar problems there as well, finally abandoning the staging of folk music at both cafés at the end of 1964.

This left the field open for an uptown club that took folk music seriously, a place where artist, audience and patron were moving in the same direction. Frank Traynor opened that club in 1963.

To some extent, Melbourne's early '60s music scene reflected the changes seeping through the city at the time. Melbourne was politically progressive, hosting the Australian Council of Trade Unions as well as Australia's anti-Vietnam war movement, and the first of the nation's Moratorium Rallies at the end of the decade. But Melbourne was still, in many ways, at a cultural crossroads. There was the Melbourne of the suburbs, with their televisions and Holdens and where, mainly men, would work in factories or offices as their 3.5 kids scuffled off to hastily-built schools in places like Thornbury or Sunshine or Macleod. This Melbourne was optimistically conservative. But there was another more exotic Melbourne emerging in the early '60s.

After the war, as previously mentioned, migrant ships brought Europeans and the Olympics bought tourists. More Italian and Greek restaurants opened in Melbourne; Pellegrini's, Drossou's Greek restaurant, Campri, Florentino, Lorne's Arab. Wine was drunk, often in brown paper bags, and espresso was brewed. The university students that frequented these places discussed Camus, ate bolognese and drank Fergusson's red. They browsed the pamphlets stacked on the counters, which canvassed everything from women's rights to union causes and anti-war rallies.

These places attracted teenagers like 15-year-old Ross Wilson, the future singer and songwriter of Daddy Cool and Mondo Rock.

Wilson and his mate Keith Glass would start at the jazz clubs, such as The Onion Patch in Oakleigh, or the Beaumaris Community Centre. But when the dances closed, they jumped on the train and headed to the jazz and folk coffee houses of Melbourne. One of the bands they encountered were the Red Onion Jazz Band; as Wilson told me when I was researching my book, *Daddy Who?*, 'As a teenager the first regular gigs I went to … were jazz dances. I used to follow the Red Onions with Gerry Humphrys on vocals and clarinet.'[15]

The Red Onions sprang out of Beaumaris, a bunch of school friends who taught themselves to play and scoured for authentic material like Louis Armstrong, Clarence Williams, King Oliver and Bix Beiderbecke. Brett Iggulden (trumpet) Bill Howard (trombone) and Alan Browne (drums), plus Gerry on clarinet and vocals, were not copyists, much to the disgust of the authentic jazz brigade. The Red Onions were about the feel of the music, and their performances were always a balance of authenticity and spontaneity.

The Red Onions were enormously popular, with a devoted following that included young Wilson and Glass. Glass described the Onions packing out the church and community halls of Melbourne's bayside suburbs in those pre-Beatles days, with Gerry singing a Satchmo/Cab Calloway style on such favourites as 'Ice Cream (You Scream)' and 'The Girls Go Crazy'. When the girls had stopped going crazy and the night was over, young Wilson and Glass would head for the midnight train, trying to avoid the trouble in the streets because, at that time in the early '60s, the Melbourne teenage scene was split between the cool, often middle class jazz lovers with their duffle coats and corduroy trousers and the more working-class rockers resplendent in leather jackets, greasy hair and stove pipe trousers. Glass described the scene at the time:

'The Jazzers had to run the gauntlet of antagonistic Rockers from the nearby town hall dances who wanted to cause the long- haired poofters some bodily harm — we were heading to Traynor's in the city.'[16]

Frank Traynor

As a reminder, Frank Traynor was a New Orleans, tailgate-style trombonist as played in the King Oliver, Louis Armstrong and Jelly Roll Morton bands. He initially played with Len Barnard's band before cutting out on his own and forming the Jazz Preachers, a band that he led for almost thirty years. Frank was larger than life; he was a complex man, contradictory, not given to compromise, he was quick to anger. After one concert, he rushed a politician who had picked up his trombone, grasping him by the throat and shouting, 'Put that down!'

Frank was always on the lookout for something new and mostly — according to multiple sources — that something new wore a skirt. When Traynor's opened its doors in October 1963 the jazz/folk marriage was formally consummated and the marriage became a distinctive feature of the Melbourne scene at the time.

Traynor had come across folk music while playing a long residency at the Wild Colonial Inn in Lorne whose sister venue, as we recall, was The Arab Café. It was at the Arab that Frank came across folk music and the darkly mysterious Glen (Glenys) Tomasetti. Tomasetti, the guitar-playing contralto was, according to Turnbull, the queen of the local scene in the early '60s. Politically committed, she was blessed with a soaring voice and an ability to get inside a song by emphasising the song over the singer. In the chops and three veg world of Melbourne in the late '50s early '60s both Tomasetti and The Arab were something else.

It was also at the Arab that Traynor saw a natural affinity with folk music and traditional jazz, as he later recalled:

'They had mutual respect for one another, particularly because they were both taking their music from folk roots, they were both a bit underground, they were both totally sincere in what they were trying to do with their music and had a great personal belief in it; there being a message of truth in the music.'[17]

Traynor was in many ways reflecting a worldwide trend where folk and jazz musicians were finding a natural affinity between the two genres. Bob Dylan for example wrote in his autobiography that as a young man living in New York:

'I [was] listening to a lot of jazz and bebop records, records by George Russell, or Johnny Cole, Red Garland, Roland Kirk, Gil Evans — Evans had a recorded rendition of Ella Speed the Leadbelly song... there were a lot of similarities between some kinds of jazz music and folk. 'Tattoo Bride', 'A Drum is a Woman', 'Tourist Point of view' and 'Jump for Joy' — all by Duke Ellington — they sounded like sophisticated folk music.'[18]

In Australia, Frank had an idea. What if a serious music venue could present folk and jazz under one roof? Traynor was sick of playing dance tunes and crowd favourites at jazz dances and society parties, and the folkies were tired of being drowned out by the noise and chatter and coffee cups at cafés. So he hooked up with Tomasetti and they became business partners and lovers.

Initially Tomasetti curated the series of Sunday afternoon folk concerts at the Emerald Hill Theatre in South Melbourne and Frank helped out. The cream of Melbourne's folk singers at the time, Martin Wyndham-Read, Paul Marks, and Brian Mooney, as well as Tomasseti herself, descended on the place. The Sunday sessions also had poets like Adrian Rawlins and jazz musicians like Gerry Humphrys on the bill. It was a scene inspired by the coffee houses of New York, where Dave Van Ronk would play a set followed by Tiny Tim, followed by Beat poet Allen Ginsberg, followed by a set by Lenny Bruce. So cool, so bohemian, and so far removed from the complicated psychological bargains being made in suburban Melbourne at the time. Jazz, folk, politics and poetry coalesced easily on Melbourne stages in the early '60s.

The success of those Sunday sessions were a light bulb moment for Traynor. He saw that folk music could pull a big crowd, while jazz attracted the black beards and eclectic girls, the non-homemaker types, just the type Frank loved.

Frank Traynor's Folk and Jazz Club

And then, in late '63, Frank found the space he was looking for to put together a venue of this own — a dingy building at 237 Exhibition Street on the corner of Little Lonsdale. Finally, Frank Traynor's Folk & Jazz Club — commonly referred to as Traynor's — opened its doors. A letter signed by Frank, and co-signed by Brian Mooney, Martin Wyndam-Reed, Margret Smith, Ade Monsbourgh and Jim Beal, was sent to anyone who was interested. It announced that Traynor's would initially open Friday and Saturday nights with folk music from 8pm to midnight, then jazz 'of the rent party nature' from midnight 'til 2am. 'Light refreshments will be available and there will be a small admittance charge'.

One of Traynor's most successful early events was Glen Tomasetti's 'Folksingers and Minstrels Club', moved over from the Emerald Hill Theatre. Tomasetti followed her South Melbourne blueprint, mixing jazz and folk music with a bit of Adrian Rawlins thrown in, and Melbourne's bohemian push loved it. It was Traynor's business acumen that led to Melbourne being acknowledged as the country's centre of commercially successful jazz and folk, and his influence that led many Melbourne-based jazz performers to embrace folk music.

Paul Marks had started life as a blues player in the '50s, singing with the Melbourne New Orleans Jazz Band and playing traditional folk songs at Traynor's and Reata through the week:

'I had emigrated to Australia in 1956 and soon met Frank Traynor, Bob Barnard and the rest of that talented lot, and started singing with Frank and Bob down at Mentone life-saving club.'[19]

He then moved on to folk forming The Paul Marks Folksinging Group. Their initial performance was met with hostility, according to jazz musician Nick Polites:

'The audience threw pennies when Marks first tried out his folksinging group at the Esquire in Glen Iris; within a couple of weeks, however, the young patrons were "eating out of his hand" and "it became the talk around town".'[20]

Trevor Lucas, who would relocate to London at the end of the '60s to join Fairport Convention, marry Sandy Denny, then embark on a successful career as a record producer for Australian bands like Redgum and Goanna, was another to move between jazz and folk. He told music paper *Go-Set* that he started singing in a traditional jazz band in Melbourne before moving on to folk, playing regularly at Traynor's and recording an album. 'Australia (and Melbourne particularly) was,' he said, 'a particularly stimulating place to work.'

Danny Spooner also got his start in music at Traynor's. He'd arrived in Australia from Britain in 1962 and realised there was an audience ready to appreciate his traditional English folk repertoire. At Traynor's, Spooner heard Martyn Wyndham-Read, who many have dubbed one of Australia's greatest performers of traditional English folk, as well as Brian Mooney, David Lumsden, Trevor Lucas and Margaret RoadKnight. Danny had a prodigious memory and a determination to learn — he quickly incorporated Australian bush songs, Canadian-French whaling songs and American material into his repertoire.

Traynor's was unique, and there was nowhere else quite like it, though there were examples of similar crossover venues like the Primitif in Brisbane, the Shiralee in Perth and maybe the Troubadour in Sydney. But Traynor's had something special:

'From the outset, and throughout its lifetime, Traynor's provided patrons with a mix of both jazz and folk music. The jazz formally started after midnight (Fridays and Saturdays) although jazz-buffs would start to wander in around 10.30; accordingly, management was careful to ensure (where possible) that blues singers were scheduled for the last few folk sets of the evening. There was generally a big exodus (three quarters of the audience) just before midnight, then the diehard jazz musicians would start to roll in from their gigs elsewhere around town.'[21]

But it was its bohemian quality that proved as much a magnet to audiences as the music, as described by *Herald* newspaper arts critic Leonard Radic:

'There are no neons outside the centre. Not much light inside, either. Two candles on the wall, a few low-watt shaded lamps hanging from the ceiling. Hessian draped across the window of this one-time espresso café shuts out the outside world … You go in by the side door. At first you cannot see. The atmosphere is dim, but not smoky. Reminds you of a similar dive in Soho. What was its name? Le Caveau? Anyway, the name fits pretty well. The cashier's desk is a low table, neatly stacked with shillings and two-shilling pieces. In the background the patron stands flicking through a roll of notes. "Two? That'll be 10 bob. You'll find a seat inside". If you're lucky. Seats, when eventually you spot a pair, are low canvas affairs with inclined wooden seats. Very good for ceiling watching. Kegs take the place of tables.'[22]

Radic described the patrons as young, earnest, a mix of schoolgirls and university students, uniformly dressed in black where coffee was served in mugs, one shilling each. It was serve yourself in the annexe, where your cup might leak but, 'this isn't the Menzies (at Monash University), so you don't complain.'[23]

Traynor's was a non-booze coffee lounge. Food was limited, cheese and biscuits, but you wouldn't wanna eat it anyway. There was one spotlight over a small raised platform where folk singers performed sitting on a barrel, the crowd sitting enraptured in complete silence. The coffee was brewed in a large stockpot and served black or white. Then then was this weird cocktail they called Black Death, a mixture of cola and claret…yum. But you could get a drink:

'The post-midnight jazz meets were always liberally oiled with wine provided by King & Godfrey in Carlton and served with prepackaged cheese and biscuits or pastries provided by a local Jewish baker, the coffee itself came from Grinders in Carlton.'[24]

Then, inevitably, the Glen Tomasetti/Frank Traynor relationship ended in tears. Ken White, that proto-blues performer and a Traynor's resident, remembers Tomasetti throwing Frank's records down onto Exhibition Street one night after she discovered that Frank was doin' that tail dragger thing all over town. Traynor was, after all, the quintessential *backdoor man/what the men don't know the little girl they understand.* Tomasetti sure understood.[25]

But wait, there was more! Young nascent blues and roots musicians like Ross Wilson, Keith Glass, Broderick Smith, Tom Cowburn of the Spinning Wheels and Chris Stockley were just some of those suburban teenagers drawn to the Traynor's dark door, not only to check out the folk singers and the gorgeous women, but also to visit a very important piece of Melbourne's musical infrastructure at the time: Tony Standish's record store, or to give it its formal name, The Frank Traynor Folk Club and Heritage Record Shop.

Tony Standish — The Heritage Record Shop

Tony Standish was a journalist, adventurer, and traveller, and a blues, jazz and folk freak. He'd been on the road for nine years before making it back to Melbourne in 1963; he described his adventures:

'I'd made it to New Orleans, spent time in Canada, drove a '49 Dodge all over the USA and Mexico, and travelled from Louisiana to Liverpool on an old Liberty ship, the S.S. Sue Lykes. The last five years of my six-year sojourn in London had been spent as an assistant editor on the British jazz magazine, Jazz Journal.

'It had been an idyllic job for a young jazz aficionado. The pay was meagre, but this was more than offset by the opportunities to meet, photograph and interview famous players, to go backstage at concerts, to gain free entrance to clubs and events otherwise closed to the average fan. Sinclair Traill, the magazine owner/editor and my boss, also allowed me time to run my own small record company, Heritage Records, which issued limited edition blues and jazz LPs and EPs.'[26]

Back in Melbourne, Standish spent a few months working in a bookstore before the call of jazz and record retailing became too much for him. Then fate intervened.

One day he was standing at the corner of Exhibition Street and Little Lonsdale Street looking through a dusty window of a vacant shop. Suddenly, there was another face alongside his own and peering equally intently. It was Frank Traynor who was checking out the very same shop.

And that was how the Frank Traynor Folk Club and Heritage Record Shop came to be — the Folk Club downstairs and Standish's upstairs in a tiny room with a window overlooking a leafy kindergarten on the opposite corner.

In no short time Standish's store became the hangout for jazz and blues freaks of Melbourne. It was Tony that introduced many Melbourne musicians, like Ross Wilson and Broderick Smith to the likes of Howlin' Wolf, Muddy Waters, Sleepy John Estes and John Lee Hooker. Standish's store must have looked vaguely extra-terrestrial:

'We papered the walls with spare covers of an LP I'd issued in London by Papa Charlie Jackson and Blind Blake. I contacted a feller named Norman Pierce in California who ran Jack's Record Cellar and Pete Russell in Bristol, UK, who also ran a specialist jazz record business. Both agreed to supply LPs at a small discount. We were in business!'[27]

Standish's though was not open all hours, he wasn't silly enough to think he could make a living out of flogging jazz and blues (and folk) records in a big country with a tiny population. He was open Thursday and Friday evenings and from 10am to 2pm on Saturday. Bring your own cans.

The shop proved to be a magnet for folkies, blues nuts and music lovers in general as Tony explained:

'The folkies from downstairs — Brian Mooney, Martyn Wyndham-Read, Danny Spooner, Margaret Howells, Graham Squance, Kenny White — were always popping up for a chat or a social sip; a hard core of jazz and blues musicians and collectors streamed across the threshold, most clutching a six-pack; and the young people of jazz, blues, folk, such as Barry Wratten and the members of the pioneering

Adderley Smith Blues Band, including Kerryn Tolhurst often came visiting. It was all happening and this at a time when a twelve-inch LP sold for fifty-two and sixpence a throw.'[28]

Ken White, a regular customer of Standish thought that he had reach nirvana when he walked through Standish's front door:

> I grew up in Clayton in the '50s and was introduced to jazz and folk by haunting local YCW dances and the rock scene. I was an apprentice furniture maker, but loved guitar. I was taught to play by a local woman she was a little wild, but great. She introduced me to a lot of stuff and recommended I go down to Frank Traynor's and check out that scene. Best thing I ever did.[29]

Ken ended up living at Traynor's while playing his blues in the little coffee lounges around town like the Cats Whiskers in Frankston, Black Magic, van Gogh's as well as the real deals like Little Reata and Reata's, the Colonial Inn, Outpost Inn and Dan O'Connell's in Carlton, all thanks to the education he was receiving from Tony Standish.

> It was when I was staying at Traynor's and became aware of Tony Standish that I really got educated in the blues, Doc Watson, Robert Johnson, Reverend Gary Davis, Muddy Waters, Howlin' Wolf, Little Walter, stuff from Louisiana and the Delta, I heard it all first at Standish's. His shop was like the university of the blues and we were all graduates.[30]

Traynor's provided a centre for Melbourne's folk and jazz scene through its seven-nights-a-week folk and late-night jazz jam sessions. It was also an important source of musical education and inspiration for a generation of Melbourne musicians and music lovers, encompassing much of what was, and is, the Melbourne approach to music. Traynor's embodied a certain bohemian larrikinism of that time; its musical format tangential and non-purist but always entertaining. That's how the Melbourne sound developed.

CHAPTER 7

WOMEN FOLK

STANDING AT THE CROSSROADS

Ask someone to name an Australian female pop singer in the early '60s and most likely they'll come up with Little Pattie, she of 'He's My Blonde Headed, Stompie Wompie, Real Gone Surfer Boy' fame. Sure, there was also Lynne Randell, Noeleen Batley and Betty McQuade, but for most part pop girls were kept in the background. As Marcie Jones wrote:

'Girls were harder to push in those days, because most of the kids that went to concerts and bought records were young girls, and they wanted to hear the boys.'[1]

In terms of pop, women definitely played second fiddle to men. As Patricia Amphlett (Little Pattie) has said, 'No matter how many hit records a female singer had, if she was appearing on a bill with male performers, she would never top the bill.'[2]

But in the early '60s, women were far more prominent in Melbourne's folk/jazz scene. In the early to mid-'60s, women performers such as Glen Tomasetti, Margret RoadKnight, Judith Durham, and Shirley Jacobs — and the previously featured Judy

Jacques — were often more popular than their male counterparts. These women were genuine superstars, not only in Melbourne, but also throughout Australia. But their preeminence didn't come easy.

Glen Tomasetti

Malcolm J. Turnbull ordained Tomasetti as the queen of the Melbourne political/ protest folk tradition of the '60s, think the politically charged protest material written in America by Bob Dylan and Pete Seeger (amongst others) and sung by the likes of Joan Baez and Judy Collins.

There's no doubt Tomasetti was all over the Melbourne folk scene. She was a singer that could do things to people, her contralto soared; and it helped that she was easy on the eye. More than just pretty, however, she was an organiser, beginning with those folk concerts at the Emerald Hill Theatre. She had presence, she was powerful, she was politically committed. She appeared weekly on Channel Seven TV to perform a topical political song after the general news broadcast, she sang on *In Melbourne Tonight,* and she became involved in the Save Our Sons organization, a group of women opposed to military conscription. This activism took an artistic turn when, in December 1965, she helped to organise the 'Songs of Peace and Love' protest concert at the Sidney Myer Music Bowl in Melbourne, described as 'the first major response of the folk scene' to Australia's military involvement in Vietnam.[3] She recorded two albums for record label W&G. The first was a collection of traditional nursery rhymes, *Folksongs with Guitar.* The second, called *Will Ye Go Lassie Go,* was with Martyn Wyndham-Read and Brian Mooney. Tomasetti's most famous song was 'Don't Be Too Polite, Girls,' a feminist call-to-arms which demanded equal pay, and was sung to the tune of 'Click Go the Shears'.

In 1967, Tomasetti was prosecuted for refusing to pay one sixth of her taxes, on the grounds that one sixth of the federal budget was funding Australia's military presence in Vietnam.[4] In court, she argued that Australia's participation in the Vietnam War violated its international legal obligations as a member of the United Nations, but the courts didn't see things this way. Her subsequent prosecution was 'believed to be the first case of its kind in Australia',[5] according to a contemporary news report, and Tomasetti was eventually ordered to pay the unpaid taxes.

Tomasetti was always moving; she directed fringe concerts for the Adelaide Festival, wrote music for short films and staged her own one-woman tribute to Bertolt Brecht. She also had a hand in founding the National Folk Festival, she organised the first poetry readings at La Mama and wrote two well-received novels, published by McPhee Gribble.

Her first book, *Thoroughly Decent People,* was described by critic Chris Wallace-Crabb as 'portraying ordinary suburban life without a supercilious sneer'. Her second book, *Man of Letters,* dealt with the subject of a womanising academic and was made into a film for television starring Warren Mitchell and Dinah Shearing.

Margret RoadKnight

'Her choice of material and at-ease delivery at times created an atmosphere of the music hall, you found yourself in a European Cabaret, she took us to folk clubs, the jazz bars and the rock'n'roll gospel halls.'[6]

Theatre Australia

In October 2018, in a fitting tribute to her over fifty-year career, Margret RoadKnight was given a lifetime achievement award at the inaugural Australian Women in Music Awards. Along with Renee Geyer and Patricia 'Little Pattie' Amphlett, Margret was recognised as a true pioneer in Australian music.

Margret certainly has contributed enormously to Australian music during her lifetime, as a recording artist, live performer, amateur musicologist and entrepreneur. She has presented the work of some of the world's finest songwriters, unearthing countless hidden gems along the way. Margaret has sung the songs of Paul Robeson and Odetta, as well as traditional English ballads, the blues of Bessie Smith, Ma Rainey and more. She's also bought into view the music of Malvina Reynolds and the power and glory of gospel.

The deciding factor for Margret in choosing material is lyrical content; it must be capable of communicating something worthwhile, because, as she has said, music has the power to inform and to educate. As she told Andrew Ford on Radio National's Music Show in 2019, 'It was through folk songs that I learnt about poetry, politics and history.'

I first saw her perform at anti-Vietnam War rallies in the late '60s and early '70s. I was always impressed with the power and expressiveness of her vocals, her humor, and her political commitment. I've followed her career ever since. As a woman working in a male-dominated industry Margaret, felt she has not so much suffered gender discrimination throughout her career, but rather, *genre* discrimination, because 'I've never wanted to be restricted to anyone category of performance.'

In 1962, Margret RoadKnight was working as a clerk in Melbourne's public service in Melbourne when a colleague suggested she might be interested in a Sunday afternoon concert series held at the Emerald Hill Theatre in South Melbourne:

> *The first act I heard as I walked into the theatre was Gerry Humphrys' little jazz trio, with Gerry playing clarinet, the trio was followed by Glen Tomasetti, the first woman I ever saw accompanying herself on guitar and singing. I was living at home in Reservoir at the time, listening to radio, harmonising gospel and the pop songs of the day with my sister, quite a contrast to the jazz, folk and poetry scene of the Emerald Hill Theatre.*

Margret eventually landed a three song spot on the bill at the Theatre, accompanied by Graham McClean, Gerry Humphrys' double bass player:

> *My first paid performance was at The Emerald Theatre on Mother's Day 1963. I had brought my mother with me to hear me sing, I remember one of the songs I chose to perform was 'Sometimes I Feel Like a Motherless Child', an interesting choice on my part for Mother's Day! I got a great reception that day as well as four pounds for my trouble.*

Margret got to work: she bought some basic instruction books and learnt a few chords, enough at least to accompany herself on guitar for her next performance. That performance included songs from her favorite performers, including, says Margret, 'Odetta, Mahalia Jackson and Harry Belafonte.' Clearly Margret was a quick learner; soon after she started playing guitar, she was offered a Thursday night residency at Tom Lazars' Reata's restaurant in Malvern, 'where I had heard my first folk singer in residence, Paul Marks'. But then something happened that would change her life forever:

In 1964 the Broadway and West End 'Black Nativity' theatre production described as, 'a gospel song play' starring Professor Alex Bradford (dubbed gospel's Little Richard) — came to town.

> *I was introduced to Alex Bradford, who invited me up to Sydney to record an album of folk meets gospel songs with the backing singers from the show. Well that was enough for me; I quit my job with public service and travelled north. Unfortunately 'Black Nativity' had a short run in Sydney, largely because it was a nativity production staged in February, needless to say, the album never eventuated. But I stayed and played Sydney's folk revival scene including appearances on Leonard Teal's Folkmoot as well as Dave (Kingston Trio) Guard's Dave's Place television programs.*

Around this time, Margret met the great Jeannie Lewis, who is still one of the finest jazz/folk artists in the country. This was the start of a long collaborative friendship that continues to this very day. Jeannie was politically involved on many fronts at the time, a proto-feminist who wasn't interested in singing traditional bush ballads because, as she argued, 'these were songs giving a male point of view.' After almost a year of living and working in Sydney, Margaret felt it was time to come back home:

> I realised Melbourne was more committed and genuine about nurturing folk music at the time. Sydney was more 'faddy'; venues came and went quickly and folk music television shows were all the rage for a while, then in a blink of an eye they were gone.

Margret RoadKnight has continued to prosecute the case for social change throughout her entire five plus-decade career, a career that has taken her from the jazz and coffee lounges of Melbourne, to the clubs, cathedrals, campuses and concert halls of the world. Margret has played everywhere, from Broome to Hobart, Beijing to Memphis, Paris to Auckland, Edinburgh to Tel Aviv, New York to Seoul, Amsterdam to Dublin, New Orleans to London, Vancouver to Nuku'alofa. RoadKnight truly has been everywhere, man, and everywhere she's been she has absorbed the local culture and incorporated its music, into her ever expanding, ever deepening repertoire.

I've only shared a bill with Margret once, at The Port Fairy Folk Festival in the early 2000s. Standing backstage with my band The Hornets, watching her perform, I understood why she was so loved as an entertainer. As the Canadian press observed, she was a walking, talking, singing folk festival in her own right,[7] and they couldn't have been more accurate. She sang folk, gospel, and blues, she told great stories, she had the crowd in the palm of her hand. Margret was simply magnetic. I realised that Sunday morning why Margret RoadKnight is one of the country's most important artists, a national treasure discovered and largely formed in Melbourne.

Judith Durham

Margret RoadKnight remembered the exact time Judith Durham set sail for England to become a superstar:

> *I'd replaced Judith Durham regular gig at Traynor's, when she joined the Seekers and was about to set sail to London and fame. I remember playing with The Seekers the week before they sailed. There were about twenty people in the room, most of whom were friends of the performers. I remember when Judy told me she was leaving with the band for the UK I must admit I had my doubts, clearly I was wrong. The next time I saw Judy was some years later in 1967 at The Myer Music Bowl when she played with The Seekers in front of 200,000 people, the biggest single attendance at an Australian concert in history.[7]*

Judith Durham emerged as the most successful of Melbourne's crossover artists, crossing from jazz to folk/pop and back to jazz. Durham was a jazz singer and piano player, and she held down a regular spot singing with Frank Traynor's band at Traynor's from 1963-64. It was at this time that Athol Guy — who along with Keith Potger and Bruce Woodley were part of a folk group called The Seekers – asked Judith to join the band on a cruise ship gig to England. According to her biographer Graham Simpson, when Juidth was asked to join the group, it was all a bit vague. The other members assumed she had fully joined the band, but in Judith's mind she was just sitting in for a while, a chance to have a paid holiday in Europe before sailing back to Melbourne.

But that's not what happened. Judith did indeed sail for England, but not for a short time, she stayed and over the next three years The Seekers, with Judith as their lead vocalist would become the first Australian pop music group to achieve major chart and sales success in the United Kingdom and the United States, and sell over 50 million records worldwide.

So how did a jazz singer from the affluent suburbs of Melbourne manage to join a folk group and conquer the world? It all came down to a series of accidents, the stars aligning. It was also due to Judith's talent and her willingness, for a while, to move out of her comfort zone. Though it all came at a cost.

Durham was a middle class, private school girl from Essendon who first planned to be a concert pianist, gaining a qualification of Associate in Music, Australia, in classical piano from the University of Melbourne Conservatorium. Even though she loved singing gospel, blues and jazz, she thought that maybe she would be a teacher in the future, get married and move to the suburbs. But then one night she had what amounted to a spiritual experience.

At the age of eighteen, young Judith Cock (her original name) was in the audience at the Memphis Jazz Club in Malvern and plucked up the courage to ask Nicholas Ribush, leader of the Melbourne University Jazz Band, whether she could sing with the band. Sure! She ripped into a Bessie Smith blues and some gospel from the 20s and 30s. It was as though she had this music in her genes. People were astonished, they applauded, they wanted more. She loved that feeling of affirmation, the rush of performance — she was hooked. All thoughts of a classical career and a life of the suburbs and babies was out the window; she burned for the blues.

By 1963, Judith was singing at The Memphis Club with Frank Traynor's Jazz Preachers, using her mother's maiden name of Durham and recording her self-titled first EP with Frank Traynor's Jazz Preachers, for W&G Records. But like a lot of young women in the public eye, Durham was unsure of herself; she thought she was dumpy, dowdy, unattractive. People loved when she performed, but

Judith didn't love herself. So she starved herself, going on crazy diets, and falling sick as a result. This insecurity would affect her greatly in the next phase of her life.

On Durham's first day as a secretary at the J. Walter Thompson ad agency, she met account executive Athol Guy, who was playing with The Seekers alongside Bruce Woodley and Keith Potger on Monday nights at the Treble Clef on Toorak Road, Toorak. They asked Durham to sing lead in the band as their original vocalist, Ken Ray, quit to get married, just as they'd landed a gig on a cruise ship bound for England.

Durham was second choice as The Seekers' female vocalist: it was Judy Jacques who was first approached by Guy to join. But Jacques graciously declined; she was, at the time, leaning more toward black American blues, gospel and jazz, according to Robin Ryan.

It was surprising that Durham had agreed to join Guy, Potger and Woodely on their slow cruise to Britain because, as David Nichols reports in his book *Dig: Australian Rock and Pop Music 1960-85*, Durham perceived the three other Seekers as daggy and herself, despite her insecurities, as very hip. She was, after all, a jazz singer running around town in skintight corduroys under fisherman's rib sloppy jumpers, making a huge impression as an electrifying singer and pianist. She wasn't moved so much to sing Australian folk ballads. Athol Guy no doubt recognised that this fresh-faced singer with a voice that could melt hearts would enhance the prospects of the band.

In the lead-up to the cruise, Judith played both sides of the road, singing folk songs like 'With a Swag All on My Shoulder' and 'Wild Rover' or 'Bound for South Australia' with The Seekers at the Treble Clef and hot jazz with Frank Traynor in funky town. To her, The Seekers were a sideshow, a paid holiday; Jazz and Traynor's was where it was at — in more ways than one, Frank Traynor and Judith Durham had a thing, goin on.

Frank, according to Judith, was a real bohemian and at the time he was setting up the folk and jazz club asked her to live with him. Unmarried couples living together was still a scandalous proposition, at least in straights-ville man, so Judith didn't accept Frank's invitation. But they remained friends; she continued to sing with Frank at Traynor's and fondly recalled him teaching her to play 'Pinetop's Boogie', on an old upright piano he had set up in the club.

But all this was all in the preamble to the next chapter in her life. She soon waved goodbye to Frank, his club and cools-ville to become absorbed into the insatiable behemoth that was the pop music industry of the '60s.

In early 1964, Judith and The Seekers stepped onboard the *Fairsky* and set sail for England and subsequent international fame, an achievement that came with a fair amount of ambivalence for Judith. As David Nichols wrote: 'Durham always assumed Seekers records would be credited to Judith Durham and the Seekers, but the paternalistic and single-minded Athol Guy opposed the idea.'[8]

In England, The Seekers met a young songwriter, Tom Springfield. Springfield had a hit record in the early '60s, 'Silver Threads and Golden Needles', with sister Dusty and their band The Springfields. But Dusty had gone solo, and Springfield was looking for artists to perform songs like 'I'll Never Find Another You'. When the Seekers recorded the song at Abbey Road in 1964, it went ballistic.

The band subsequently signed with W&G in 1963, produced two million-selling albums, and had worldwide hits including, 'I'll Never Find Another You', 'A World of Our Own', 'Morningtown Ride', 'Some Day', 'Georgy Girl', and 'The Carnival is Over'. The group was even named the 1967 Australians of the Year.

But despite the success of the band, Durham was burdened with thoughts about her weight; she continually dieted and deprived herself. As the focal point of an internationally successful band, she was deeply insecure about her appearance. She also became increasingly frustrated with her anonymity; people, she said loved her voice but at the same time didn't know who she was:

'I wasn't being myself. People really didn't know me. Many of our fans didn't know my name, but they recognised my voice. I might have felt differently if my name was up in lights, but I had this awful sense all the time of being a quarter of a whole. It occurred to me long after I resigned (from the band) that the boys believed The Seekers was the thing we should all have aspired to in life, that nothing should have attempted to take its place. But for the whole four years I was a member of the group, I had thought it was temporary ... that necessity to compromise all the time ... it takes its toll.'[9]

After four years, Judith became totally disillusioned with the whole melodrama that was the Seekers; firstly, her billing in the band, and then the management issues.

From 1964-1968, The Seekers' chart success was comparable to that of the The Beatles and The Rolling Stones, in Britain certainly. *The Carnival Is Over* single for example, outsold everyone including The Beatles and The Rolling Stones in 1965 reaching Number 1 in Britain in November and the album *The Best of The Seekers,* reached #1 in Britain in November 1968, knocking The Beatles "White Album" from the top position and staying on the British charts for an incredible 125 weeks.[10]

But whereas The Beatles played Shea Stadium in New York and raked in millions as a consequence, The Seekers were stuck on the variety circuit, sharing bills with bands like The Applejacks and The Honeycombs.

In fact, at the height of their career, The Seekers were booked to tour New Zealand playing small theatres for a flat fee of a thousand dollars a gig between them — no percentage! Any other group of a similar status would be on eighty even ninety plus percent of the door and would be playing much bigger venues, especially when those venues were sold out within minutes of concerts being announced, leaving thousands of people disappointed. But only Judith thought this was a problem. Whenever she raised her concerns with the other three members of the group, like her anonymity or the incomprehensible concert schedule, she was met with a stony silence. It all came to a head in the recording studio one day towards the end of 1967, when Judith exploded:

'I was consumed with frustration that things couldn't be done the way they were supposed to do … I was forever being forced to compromise because I was a member of a group…not a free agent. I never felt comfortable confronting the boys on something that was not agreeable to them.'[11]

It had reached a point, according to her biography, that she could no longer put up with the impenetrable wall that confronted her whenever she disagreed with the three boys.

'It just sort of came out, I was upset and just blurted out that I was leaving The Seekers and giving them the required six months' notice.'[12]

And so she left to pursue her jazz/adult music solo career, alongside her accompanist husband Ron Edgeworth. But she wasn't completely done yet with The Seekers.

Nostalgia is strange. People remember what they want to remember; not the compromises or the bad management, but those moments when it all flowed, when a young woman stood onstage and with nothing but the truth of her performance. Maybe that's why Judith agreed to all those Jubilee concerts, anniversary events, AFL Grand Final appearances and farewell tours.

Maybe she felt she owed it to herself and to her Seekers audience because, no matter what happened in the process, the band were Australia's first contemporary international superstars — way before AC/DC, INXS, any of 'em. The Seekers had achieved an enormous amount in a relatively short time and they had opened the door for a steady stream of Australian performers to follow. That's worth celebrating with the odd comeback concert and besides; every one finally knew her name.

It was Melbourne that nurtured Durham and shaped her as a performer; it was here that her voice became a soft weapon capable of blowing The Beatles off the top of pop charts of Britain. Melbourne helped produce an international superstar in Judith Durham, and no incompetent manager or bully-boy band mate could take that away from her.

Political Folk: Shirley Jacobs

Tomasetti was ordained by Malcolm J. Turnbull as the queen of the Melbourne protest folk tradition of the '60s, but she wasn't the only politically-minded folk singer on the scene. Peter Dickie and his friend Ian White sang Spanish Civil War songs made famous by Pete Seeger and the Weavers, Mick Counihan recorded an EP of local protest songs, and Trevor Lucas was vehemently anti-war, telling the Melbourne *Sun* in 1964:

'I believe I'd be a conscientious objector if total war came, and if I ever had time to make a choice. When I was in the school cadet corps, an instructor demonstrated the Bren gun, pointed to a group of kids playing in the park, and said: "This gun would stop them all within seconds". If social protest songs help rid people of ideas like that, then I'll keep on singing them.'

Shirley Jacobs was a Melbourne folk singer and social justice advocate who, as her obituary noted, was sure that she sounded better and looked more attractive than her fellow goateed, Irish-sea-shanty-singing male colleagues. She was right; Jacobs had sad dark eyes and long brown hair and a rich contralto voice that could break your heart. And she didn't sing sea shanties.

For Jacobs, a lot of the Australian folk material sounded tired, and she wanted to contemporise folk by making it more politically relevant. Initially she collaborated with Ade Monsbourgh setting a selection of Henry Lawson poems to music — her haunting version of Lawson's 'On the Night Train' can still be seen on YouTube. Eventually she moved into writing more contemporary material that dealt with the social and political issues of the time.

Jacobs was no pushover; *The Sydney Morning Herald* described her as, 'fiery and relentlessly defiant, refusing to back down if confronted by what she believed to be an injustice.'[13] And, despite her personal politics, Jacobs' talent and persistence finally led to a major recording contract with RCA records. This surely wouldn't happened in today's

corporatised, standardised, commercialised and sanitised world —
though maybe those sad dark eyes would've got her over the line.

With a recording contract in the drawer, Shirley continued to
write her own material, songs that dealt with subjects as diverse as the
West Gate Bridge collapse, the Skipping Girl neon sign when it looked
bound for the rubbish heap, and people with disabilities.

She published a songbook, played festivals, and sang at huge anti-
Vietnam War rallies. By the early '70s, Shirley was at the top of her
game, singing on kid's television shows and holding down a weekly
spot performing satirical songs on the ABC's current affairs program
This Day Tonight. On the eve of the 1972 election, Jacobs appeared as
warm-up at a gathering of Labor supporters at St Kilda Town Hall. As
The Sydney Morning Herald reported:

'The crowd went wild as she strummed a final chord and Gough
Whitlam strode onto the stage to give his "Men and Women of
Australia" speech.'[14]

Shirley's daughter Patti described her as extreme and eccentric;
maybe that's why she decided to present a weekly radio program
inside Pentridge Prison. It was there that she met, and fell in love, with
the notorious Painter and Docker Joey Hamilton. Hamilton needed
a platform to get the word out that he had been falsely convicted
for armed robbery in 1973, and the high-profile Shirley provided
that platform.

Unfortunately no one wanted to hear from Joey, and ultimately
no one wanted to hear from Shirley anymore either. Shirley Jacobs
spent the last nine years of her life in a Thornbury nursing home,
passing away in 2015. Joey visited her at the home every day.

I came across Shirley in the early '80s in my capacity as Fitzroy City
Councillor when she and Joey barricaded themselves in the Fitzroy
Town Hall after our regular Council meeting. They demanded of

the astonished council that we grant them political asylum, claiming persecution from Victoria Police. Their claim was not without merit — in 1978 the Beach Inquiry into corruption within Victoria Police had found that Hamilton had been falsely convincted of his robbery charge and was released with $26000 compensation in his pocket. But the coppers that put him there didn't like that. Soon after Jacobs and Hamilton were married in 1978 a bomb demolished the front of their Carlton house in Station Street. Crime writers John Silvester and Andrew Rule later wrote in *The Sunday Age* that a retired detective claimed two members of the consorting squad were responsible for the bombing.

In wake of the bombing, Hamilton and Jacobs fled to Waubra in country Victoria where, as Joey claimed at our impromptu council meeting, they slept with a railway sleeper at the bottom of their bed, fearing police would shoot at them in their sleep. Joey asserted that police had continued to harass the couple right up to 1982 which forced them to flee their Waubra hideaway and to seek shelter and protection in the Fitzroy Town Hall. Hamilton's idea was to hold up in the town hall for a week or two and organise a petition to serve on the newly-elected Cain Labor Government. It would call on the government to protect himself and Jacobs from police harassment; but he got a bit ahead of himself.

In his book *Chopper Unchopped*, Chopper Read claimed that Joey was a man who liked to talk; 'he talked to the Beach Inquiry, he talked to police, to politicians, he talked to reporters and he talked to other criminals.' Hamilton was also one of the most boring individuals Chopper ever met in jail; Chopper wrote that 'if I hadn't already chopped off my ears, I'm sure he would've tried to talk them off.'

That night at the Fitzroy Town Hall I discovered what Chopper meant. It was late when we'd finished our regular council meeting, maybe 10pm. We were all heading for home in preparation of resuming our full-time jobs the next day. The doors to the Council Chamber burst open and in stormed Joey and Shirley, who was carrying a guitar. Joey started his spiel; the police were gunna kill him and Shirley, he was Fitzroy boy, grew up in the suburb, a Labor man, he demanded our help. I pointed out that he should keep his voice down because the notorious Victoria Police Special Branch occupied the floor above our head and probably had the joint bugged. The Fitzroy Police Station was also located in rooms at the rear of the Town Hall. But Joey ploughed on, outlining in extraordinary detail incidents of police harassment and persecution. At some point around midnight Shirley broke out her guitar and gave an impromptu performance, singing songs of resistance and protest.

Finally at around one in the morning, exhausted councillors voted to grant that the couple could stay the night holed up in the Town Hall. We pointed out that we didn't have the power to grant the couple political asylum and that they should look to government for protection. We were surprised to see the Hamiltons on the following night's news, belabouring the door of The Premier's Office with a writ to place the Premier under citizen's arrest for failing to protect the couple against harassment from Victoria Police. Needless to say, Council's representations on their behalf had fallen on deaf ears within the Labor Party and within government.

CHAPTER 8

'DAMN RIGHT I GOT THE BLUES'

The blues slid under Melbourne's back door as far back as 1923, when one of the first touring bands from America, Frank Ellis and his Californians, played at Palaise de Danse in St Kilda. The band featured Australian Bob Waddington on bass plus three banjos, four saxophones and a three-piece rhythm section. They played blues numbers like 'Beale Street Blues' which was 'sung by vocalist Danny Hogan through a cardboard megaphone[1]

Australian dance bands such as Linn Smith's Royal Jazz Band had been playing a bastardised form of blues and jazz at venues like Carlyon's at the Hotel Esplanade for some years. But it took visiting American jazz bands to really get things started. Ray Tellier's San Francisco Orchestra — the first band to make a jazz record in Australia — got things going in Melbourne when they played the Palais de Danse from May 1925 until November 1926.[2]

But really these bands were all about getting punters up and dancing. Melbourne bands like Frankie Couglan and his Palais Royal

Californians who played the Green Mill at Princes Bridge were touted as a 'magnet for dancing feet'.[3] They played dance music, but it often came in the twelve-bar blues form.

It took people like Graeme Bell, Tony Newstead and Keith Hounslow to bring the blues to town through their hot jazz, New Orleans-inspired bands. But it wasn't until the '60s that the first full-length blues record was made in Melbourne, and it came from Dulcie Pitt, aka Georgia Lee.

Georgia Lee

Georgia was tall with dark hair and hazel eyes inherited from her Jamaican, Aboriginal and Torres Strait Islander heritage. Her hair was long and her voice was sultry — akin to the sound of Ella Fitzgerald, Sarah Vaughan and Della Reese, perfect for the blues. In the '50s, Georgia was recognised as 'Melbourne's Number One Female Singer'[4] and became the first Indigenous artist to record a full album, the now-legendary 1962 record *Down Under Blues* on Crest Records.

Georgia Lee, born Dulcie Rama Pitt in Cairns in 1921, grew up up in a family surrounded by music. On the verandah of her Cairns home she harmonised with her sisters, Sophie and Heather, accompanied by their brother Wally on guitar. They called themselves The Harmony Sisters and sang songs from the radio and Hollywood movies, like 'Swanee River', 'Blue Moon' and 'As Time Goes By'. The Sisters soon moved from the front verandah to the clubs of Cairns, and they got noticed.

When World War II broke out, Georgia packed parachutes by day and sang jazz at clubs by night. Then the Yanks arrived in town, bringing blues records, cigarettes, nylons and a need to be entertained. The Harmony Sisters got a gig playing USO shows and the segregated black clubs established for the African-American soldiers. The sisters' involvement with the Americans resulted in them being exposed to an audience beyond Cairns, and they were asked to be a part of the US Service Office Show. They shared the stage with US performers (like actor John Wayne) on tours of North Queensland. The Yanks loved them, so the sisters decided to try their luck down south.

After the war, Heather, Sophie, Wally and Dulcie (Georgia) moved to Sydney. Shortly after, however, the big city got to Heather, Sophie and Wally, and they hurried back home, leaving Dulcie living alone in Kings Cross. It was in the jazz and blues clubs of the boho post-war world that Dulcie Pitt changed her name to Georgia Lee and became an identity. She was picked up by JC Williamsons and played with Graeme Bell as well as The Port Jackson Jazz band at jazz clubs and hotels around town. She hung out with artists like Donald Friend, Margaret Olley and Russell Drysdale. At a concert in Sydney, Georgia introduced the soul-wrenching Billie Holiday classic 'Strange Fruit' to Australian audiences. The song, which dealt with the lynching of African-Americans in the US south, was thought to be too upsetting for our nation's delicate white ears, and was banned from Australian radio at the time.

Georgia came to Melbourne in 1951 and played a sold out Aboriginal music show at the Princess Theatre, put together by Koori singer Harold Blair for that year's Moomba Festival. Following her Princess Theatre performances, she held down long residencies at The Embers nightclub in South Yarra and Ciro's on Exhibition Street. Georgia's star was rising high.

Then, English promoter Harold Fielding picked her up and took her to Ceylon for five months, before offering her a show singing with the Ted Heath Orchestra at London's Geraldo's in The Dorchester Hotel. Georgia was a smash in London, playing with the Ray Ellington band and then touring Scandinavia.

In 1957, when promoter Lee Gordon offered Georgia the support for the Nat King Cole Big Show tour back in Australia, she jumped at the chance; but there were gathering clouds on her horizon. It was tough for a girl from Cairns alone on the road, the pressure to perform night after night became too much. She was isolated, cut off from her family and her support network and so sadly she had a breakdown and retreated to Cairns to reassess where she was going.

After a few months she came back to Melbourne, sang with Graeme Bell and appeared regularly on *Bandstand* and Graham Kennedy's *In Melbourne Tonight*, but it was tough, she was an alien in her own land. Her career was slipping away. But then in 1962, Georgia recorded the album *Georgia Lee Sings the Blues Down Under* and everyone sat up and took notice.

'Born to Be Blue', 'Down Under Blues', 'St Louis Blues', 'Blues in the Night', 'Basin Street Blues' were all recorded in one take with a crack band featuring Horrie Weems on guitar, Brian Martin and Ron Rosenberg on keys, Jack Glen, trombone, Ralph Melevende trumpet, Alan Turnball drums and John Fredrick bass. The song 'Yarra River Blues' summed up the feel of the album:

> *Oh the Yarra River took my baby from me,*
> *Yarra Yarra River took my baby from me,*
> *oh she swept him out to the deep blue sea ...*

Georgia Lee Sings the Blues Down Under was one of the first albums to be recorded in stereo in Australia and is now widely regarded as a classic of the genre. It was reissued in 2009 and added to the prestigious Sounds Of Australia register, which acknowledges it as a historically important Australian record. *The Encyclopedia of Women* quotes contemporary blues and jazz singer Liz Cavanagh describing the album as one that still inspires:

'One of the things [about] the album that was interesting ... is that it was [done in] a single take. That's the uniqueness about that time as well, they were brilliant musicians, and you get a glimpse of Georgia Lee without it being tampered with. It's a beautiful record'[5]

There was nothing fake about Georgia Lee, nothing manipulative; she sang songs that were real as flesh and blood, and the public wanted to hear more, but Georgia had had enough. She quit the Melbourne scene and retired to Cairns, her brave solo journey having come to an end.

As the *Women's Encyclopedia* also declares: 'Georgia Lee is generally acknowledged by musicians and musical historians alike as being at the forefront of Australian blues, her recordings had an Australian identity and themes, a first Australian leading the way.'[6]

Graeme Bell said of her, 'She had a really good jazz style and she could sing the blues'[7]

Her niece, Wilma Reading, who also had a major career as a jazz singer in London and who toured and sang with Duke Ellington, also reminded us that historically, she has three points going for her, she was a role model for other Indigenous performers in this country being the first indigenous person and the first indigenous woman, to record an LP and also the first recording to be recorded in stereo, 'which I think is a plus, plus, plus — so there you go'[8]

Georgia Lee died in Cairns in 2010.

Graham Squance and Ken White: Authentic Grit

By 1964, Georgia Lee had crept into the shadows and with her went the first blush of Melbourne blues. But if you knew where to look, you could hear another form of blues, not the New Orleans Dixieland style, but the raw sound of the Mississippi Delta played by Melbourne pioneers Graham Squance and Kenny White. They played their dark devil's music between the jazz and folk singers at Jazz Centre 44 or Traynor's, or maybe the Downbeat Club or the Green Man. The duo performed 'I'm Ready' by Muddy Waters, 'Walkin' Blues' by Son House, Leroy Carr's 'How Long' and Robert Johnson's 'Crossroads', playing with grit and honour to the music and those who performed it.

Both Squance and White had developed formidable blues guitar techniques by listening to Graham's blues record collection, described by Frank Traynor in *Go-Set* as 'one of the finest in the country.' They played primal blues, not the electric 'Sweet Home Chicago' style played in England at the time by The Rolling Stones and John Mayall. The Stones and Mayall were white boys playing electrified approximations of Howling Wolf's 'Little Red Rooster' or Muddy's 'You Can't Lose What You Ain't Never Had'. Squance and White played blues songs with the dust still on them, the songs as Alan Lomax would've first heard them way back in the '40s when he collected Delta blues for the Archive of American Song and the Library of Congress. For a couple of years Graham and Kenny played all over the country, featuring at the National Folk Festival, where they brought the rural blues of the Mississippi Delta to a wide, white Australian audience, inspiring a whole generation of musicians in the process.

It's obvious that Graham Squance and Kenny White were way before their time, but by the time the rest of the world caught up, they were gone. Squance was killed in a car accident en route to the Canberra Folk Festival in 1970. Frank Traynor said of Squance:

'Squance built a large following of blues fans interested in hearing the blues played in an authentic manner. This was before the present interest in the blues, and Graham was undoubtedly the cause of turning the interest of many folk singers to blues of the acoustic variety.'[9]

Kenny is still around, occasionally playing folk and gospel with his vocalist wife Fiona, or playing solo with material drawn from old familiar sources, Robert Johnson, Blind Willy Johnson, Muddy Waters and Elmore James. Kenny put out a solo record in the early 2000s, on which he manages some beautiful playing, despite losing a few fingers in a sawmill accident some time ago. Kenny is truly a blues man. He and Graham Squance were once hailed as the greatest blues duo in the country.

Ken was keen to tell me about another blues pioneer knocking around the cafés of Melbourne in the early '60s, an Aboriginal bloke named Allan Moarywaalla Baker from Port Hedland way. 'Black' Allan Moarywaalla, as he was known, described his music as Aboriginal grassroots blues. He wrote songs about Aboriginal oppression and rights, and he was probably the first Aboriginal acoustic blues man in the country, styling himself on Big Bill Broonzy. He was a travelling man, playing coffee houses and clubs up and down the east coast of Australia. People loved him, possibly because, as was written in his obituary, he was 'easy to get along with, highly sophisticated, full of twists and turns … for many he gave us a voice, a sense of togetherness.'

A committed environmentalist, Allan lived in Nimbin for a while and founded Greenpeace Australia, along with Gordon Mutch. He also had a hand in the formation of the Eastern Australian branch of the Greens. Black Allan only recorded one album, *Fire Burning*; it's hard to secure a copy of, but I'm told it's brilliant, and I'd love to hear it.

Dutch Tilders

According to ARIA Hall of Fame guitarist Wayne Burt, Dutch was the first person he saw play the blues live. He said that he was 'fascinated by his finger-picking style, his Big Bill Broonzy approach. Dutch was an original. Seeing him live kind of got me thinking about playing the blues myself.'

Many other early '60s musicians from Melbourne were similarly impacted by Dutch, Broderick Smith, for example. Smith described Tilders as 'loud, opinionated and bossy, and we listened to him because he seemed to know what he was talking about.'[10] Broderick first met Dutch when he joined the Adderley Smith Blues Band and the Dutchman took the band under his wing:

'[Dutch] introduced us to like-minded people on the folk scene such as Margret RoadKnight, Kenny White, Graham Squance and so forth. 40 years later he was still doing the same thing, helping young blues acts and telling them to 'keep the faith.'[11]

Born in the Netherlands in 1941, Dutch emigrated to Australia with his parents, four brothers and sister in 1955; his first year in

Australia was spent in the Brooklyn Migrant Hostel in Melbourne's west. By the age of fourteen he was already a blues-head, having been introduced to the form back in the Netherlands during and after the war. According to Smith:

'The Dutchman learnt the blues from American Armed forces radio (that broadcast to American troops stationed in Northern Europe at the time) ... he'd listen to them on a crystal radio set and (get access to records like Little Walter's 'Juke') relatively easily.'[12]

From the beginning, Dutch was devoted to the blues. It had opened a window to his soul, he felt its power, nothing else mattered; so he bought a harmonica and got to work. Night after night in the corner of a dingy hall in the Brooklyn Migrant Centre Dutch was learning to bend notes, playing and playing until his lips bled. At first it was hard going, like drilling through a brick wall, but then he broke through to the other side.

His very first paid gig, when just fifteen, was at the Collingwood Town Hall where he played the harmonica. On the same bill were Joff Allen and Johnny O'Keefe. Dutch was paid two pounds seven and sixpence, which at the time he was getting for half a week's wages at Broons timber yard in Brooklyn. 'It only cost two pounds and sixpence for the taxi home.'[13]

Dutch bought his first guitar in 1959, and by the following year he was playing in the trendy coffee lounges of Melbourne. He made up most his material as he went along, following his own road even then. He was forceful on stage, singing with a natural power that drew people like Wayne Burt, Kerryn Tolhurst and Broderick Smith.

Dutch got around to making his first record in 1972 with musicians like Brian Cadd, Phil Manning, Barry Sullivan, Barry Harvey, Laurie Pryor and Broderick Smith. He followed it up with two direct-to-disc recordings in 1975 with greats Jimmy Conway and Kevin Borich. Much to the horror of the purists, he put down his acoustic and picked up an electric guitar to front blues bands like the Elks, the Cyril B. Bunter Band and Mickey Finn.

In 1980, he formed the R&B Six, a band that included Charley Elul (drums), Peter Frazer (sax), Suzanne Petersen (flute and vocals), Mick Elliot (guitar) and Dave Murray (bass and vocals). They were constantly on the road. At the same time, Dutch worked solo and toured with John Mayall, Taj Mahal, Brownie McGhee and Sonny Terry.

I came across Dutch in the '90s when he held down a Saturday night residency at Ruby Reds, a blues club off Lonsdale Street. I played the graveyard shift after Dutch and his band, which featured young hotshot guitar player Geoff Achison. They were supposed to wrap up around 2am. It was a brutal gig but paid well. I had young kids at the time, so I'd put them to bed around 7.30pm and then tried to get some sleep myself. I'd get up just before 2am, pull on my pants, pick up my guitar and drive into the city. I'd park near the Library on Little Lonsdale Street and walk to the gig, trying to avoid the foxes rummaging through the rubbish bins on Swanston Street. Inevitably the club was packed when I arrived, the band firing off blue bullets with Dutch holding court. I was supposed to start at three, but with the place pumping, there was no vacating the stage for our Dutch. So I would sit at the bar and wait, the joint stinking of booze and smoke and sweat.

When Dutch had finally had enough, close to 3am, he'd sit on the side of the stage, signing records, drinking whiskey and talking shit. I once politely asked him if the drums could be pulled down and maybe the amps taken off stage so I could get on and play. He told me to fuck off. I never asked again, I just sat at the bar and waited for the time when Dutch was good and ready, all the while trying not to fall asleep, or throw up, I always hated the smell of cigarette smoke mixed with bad, bad whiskey, especially at three in the morning.

When I finally got to play, the club had invariably emptied, and my audience consisted of those too pissed to move or, sometimes, late night revellers wanting that one last nightcap before they went home. It was a dirty job but someone had to do it.

One night I looked up and there Dutch was, looking at me, smiling. I think I'd just played 'Sitting on Top of the World'. When I finished, he sidled up to side stage and said something like, *you sing like a black man, keep the faith.* He then shook my hand and walked out the door. I never spoke to him again. As Broderick Smith said, 'he had that way of making you think: well he seems to like what I do, so I guess I must be ok. Often that's all we need.'

The Four Days that Shook Melbourne

In 1964 in suburban Melbourne, it was the black-and-white era, a time Alan Howe described as, 'an era of test patterns', a time of the national anthem at the end of transmission. Though a lot was happening in the clubs and coffee houses of bohemian Melbourne, in the suburbs nothing, much had changed. As Howe points out in an article in the *Herald Sun*:

'Our prime minister, Robert Menzies — born in the previous century — had been leader for 15 years. Victoria's premier, Henry Bolte, had been there for nine. Australia was an isolated, British outpost. Not everyone owned a television. Overseas travel was prohibitively expensive, and so were international phone calls.'[14]

Melburnians, like the rest of the country, had an inferiority complex. Some called it the cultural cringe. When anyone famous arrived at Essendon Airport they were immediately asked what they thought of the country. 'Don't know, only just got here', was the standard reply. It was embarrassing; we were so desperate for affirmation by B-, C- or even D-Grade celebrities from England or America, we fell over ourselves to elicit their approval. As Howe points out, it was all a product of our *Tyranny of Distance*.

But then in June 1964 something happened that would murder that tyranny forever. The Beatles came to town and played six ground breaking concerts at the 'House of Stoush' Festival Hall; Melbourne would never be the same again.

Suddenly 'Hey Paula' and Cliff Richard's 'Summer Holiday' were knocked off the charts by 'I Saw Her Standing There', 'Can't Buy Me Love', 'A Hard Day's Night', 'All My Loving', 'I Should Have Known Better' and 'I Feel Fine'. To quote Howe: 'they had written them all. No band did that.'

By the time the Beatles flew out of Australia, they had inspired a generation of young musicians who would soon crowd our charts with home grown rock'n'roll — musicians like Billy Thorpe and The Aztecs, Bobby & Laurie, The Bee Gees, the Easybeats, Normie Rowe, the Master's Apprentices, The Twilights, the Loved Ones, Johnny Young, John Farnham and Russell Morris.

The Beatles had opened our ears to new sounds. Then The Rolling Stones, The Animals and later Hendrix, Cream and Peter Green's Fleetwood Mac often played electrified versions of the Delta and Chicago blues first introduced to our city by people likes of Graham Squance and Ken White. There's no doubt that a whole generation of young musicians were all ears, especially blues freaks like Kerryn Tolhurst and Broderick Smith.

CHAPTER 9

THE *BLUES HIGHWAY*

The Adderley Smith Blues Band

Melbourne's Adderley Smith Blues Band was formed in 1964. Like Graham Squance and Ken White, they were way ahead of their time. They were a serious, authentic, blues band; think Alexis Korner and Cyril Davis's Blues Incorporated or The Yardbirds. They played white boy blues only heard in places like the London Blues Barrelhouse or the Marquee Club.

That's not to say that Melbourne musicians weren't playing the odd electric blues number around this time. There were the The Rising Sons, fronted by Keith Glass, who would play early Stones tracks like 'King Bee'. Then came The Pink Finks, formed by the Rising Sons' occasional harp player Ross Wilson and his mate Ross Hannaford. In May 1965, The Pink Finks recorded Richard Berry's bluesy 'Louie Louie', which, reached #16 on the local 3DB charts. Later that year, the Finks recorded Muddy Waters' 'Backdoor Man' and 'I'll Put a

Tiger in Your Tank', quite risqué material for a couple of teenagers from Melbourne's bayside suburbs! Then there was The Spinning Wheels who made the charts with the Muddy Waters hit 'I Got my Mojo Working'.

While bands like The Pink Finks played the odd blues number, they weren't strictly a straight-ahead blues band — not like Adderley Smith. The band was formed by blues fiends Kerryn Tolhurst (guitar) and Mark Dindas (piano), and featured future high-profile Melbourne musicians like Broderick Smith and, later, Joe Camilleri. They took inspiration from the originals; Muddy Waters, Jimmie Rodgers, Junior Wells, Willie Dixon, Sonny Boy Williamson and Howlin' Wolf. Kerryn Tolhurst wrote their original material.

I met Kerryn early in 2019 in the renovated front bar of the Esplanade Hotel. The last time I was in this famous bar I had played a support gig with The Hornets for Ross Hannaford's legendary band Dianna Kiss. Ross and his band were at the butt end of an eleven year Monday night residency at The Espy and like the bar itself, the cracks were beginning to show. On this particular night, Hanna had been carted off to hospital when, after some slight overindulgence, he had over balanced adjusting an effects pedal at his feet and fallen from the stage.

As I looked around the distressed walls of the unrecognisable front bar, I saw a framed photograph of Hanna fixed to one of those brick exposed expanses and wondered if he were alive today what he would think of the room where he spent so many Monday nights in the '90s and early 2000s. I reckon it would be probably something like …

'Yeah cool man, but where is the stage?'

I found Kerryn alone at a table overlooking Port Phillip Bay. He wore sunglasses and was drinking a beer from the vast selection of boutique beverages that lined the sidewall of the bar. Not a Carlton draught in sight! After pleasantries we got down to business; I wanted to know about his childhood and how he got into music.

Tolhurst was born in Williamstown and went to school in the semi-industrial suburb of Fawkner, north of Melbourne. Luckily the mother of a close friend was a bit of a bohemian and had an extensive record collection, which transported young Kerryn away from the limitations of his surroundings:

> *She was a bit of a Bolshevik, had a lot of left wing folk music, Woody Guthrie that sort of thing. But she also had Muddy Waters records, Ray Charles and this young singer-songwriter called Bob Dylan.*

The dominant myth of the day was you could do anything you wanted; as long that 'anything' involved a steady job and wasn't too outrageous, like becoming a musician. This was the early '60s, when most of the bands Kerryn saw live were instrumental outfits like The Strangers, Thunderbirds, Lincolns, Cherokees and The Monarchs. As Kerryn said:

> *This was the first music I heard live and it always stayed with me. They used to play at various suburban town halls like Coburg and Moonee Ponds. Often they were 50/50 events featuring a 'dance band' for those who preferred ballroom dancing followed by a 'modern' band like The Strangers. I remember a band called the Flies that featured Ronnie Burns on vocals, they were a proto-mod outfit, probably the first long hair band in Melbourne and they created their own scene. But once the Brits invaded many of those instrumental bands added a lead singer and like The Flies, grew their hair. Ray Columbus and the Invaders, Billy Thorpe and the Aztecs, were a couple of examples.*

But what specifically inspired him to take up the guitar?

> *Back in 1963 I had just left school and I had joined the Department of Labour and Industry in Exhibition Street in the city and started hanging out at places like Traynor's, where I*

heard the acoustic blues played live for the first time. It was Dutch Tilders, he played a lot of Big Bill Broonzy and Brownie McGhee. I was hooked.

It was while he was working at The Department of Labour and Industry that his life changed:

Our offices were opposite the Southern Cross Hotel and then one day in June 1964, the Beatles checked in for a couple of days. The streets were filled with screaming girls and I thought, hmmm that's a good job; think I'll give it a go. So I walked up to Clements Music Store in Russell Street and bought a guitar.

With his brand new git, plus a Jimmy Reed chord book and a bunch of FolkWays, Blue Note and Chess records bought at Discurio music shop, Kerryn got to work:

In those days folk, blues and jazz crossed over in Melbourne, especially at places like Traynor's where you could hear all three genres on one night. It was a great education. After about six months I got competent enough to join a band as the guitar player, the band was called Vacant Lot and included Mark Dindas on bass. We played the usual Stones covers, Them, that sort of stuff. But I was into the blues and one day I found out that Mark played piano. Fantastic! I introduced him to Otis Spann and others from the blues repertoire and he took to the whole thing with vengeance. Pretty soon, the pop stuff was out and the blues was in.

But Kerryn was a serious blues fan and, as he told me, the name 'Vacant Lot' wasn't bluesy enough; he wanted to change it. One morning, on the train from Fawkner to his job at the Department of Labour and Industry in the city, Kerryn looked outside towards Festival Hall in West Melbourne. His attention was drawn to the name of the street on one side of the hall: Adderley Street. As Kerryn remembers:

I thought 'Adderley' sounded cool but what would go with
that name...something simple 'Smith' for instance... and so
'Adderley Smith' became our bands name.

We paused here and ordered another beer. It came delivered by a
young woman whose left arm was covered in a sleeve tattoo. Kerryn
and I shared a knowing glance and smiled. He took a sip from his pot
and took up the thread of our conversation. Apparently all was not
well with the band:

Our singer, John O'Brien, was great but he wasn't quite right
for us, we needed a more bluesy approach. We persisted for
a while and things started to open up for us, we got gigs at
places like the Catcher, the Queensbury Hotel and a club called
Chicago — which was over the road from the Queensbury pub.
At Catcher we played dusk till dawn on Saturday night, we
were the fill-in between bands. It was a tough gig, but a great
way to get ourselves together. But I still felt we needed a singer
who could really sing the blues.

Then, one day, a young bloke walked into the Queensberry Hotel and
asked if he could sit in with the band. His name was Broderick Smith.
Kerryn recalls:

He could play harp and sing like a demon, the first song he
played with us was Sonny Boy's 'Help Me'. And suddenly he
was in the band right there and then, Brod was exactly the
singer we had been looking for.

With a line-up solidified the band got to work learning more material
and dive deeper into the blues. They hung out at Tony Standish's
record store upstairs at Traynor's, Kerryn says:

Everyone hung out at Standish's, Ross Wilson, Keith Glass,
David Pepperell, Kenny White; we'd all fight over the vinyl,
swap ideas and exchange music. It was a very competitive

space, you know … 'my blues record is more obscure than your blues record', lots of one-upmanship. Despite all of that, we picked up a lot of obscure stuff at the store, some of which found its way into our repertoire, things like Willie Dixon's, 'The Same Thing', Eddie Floyd's 'Five Long Years' and Junior Well's 'Chitlin' con Carne', stuff like that.

As their repertoire grew and the band got tighter, they were soon playing more prestigious venues, like Q Club and the Thumpin' Tum, plus a few University gigs as well:

We even set up our own club in Little Bourke Street over a Chinese restaurant, the building owned by a dodgy Yugoslavian bloke who wanted to attract more people to his café, so he gave us use of the top two floors for free. We set up a listening type venue on the first floor, where folk singer and acoustic blues players performed and the top floor was for bands. The club lasted for six months or so and was going well until the Yugoslav shot someone in the café and at that point we thought it was time to move on.

As band member Broderick Smith has written, this was a time when the Vietnam War was raging and the Australian government was kidnapping young men to serve in the army, many of whom were shipped off to the killing fields and the burning, alien jungles of our northern neighbour.

During conscription, numbered marbles were pulled out of a lottery basket. The date of the twentieth birthday of young men corresponded to the drawn numbers, and those drawn were marched off to prepare for war at a Puckapunyal training facility north of Melbourne. Bad luck befell both Broderick and Kerryn, whose numbers came up in the lottery. But it was not the end of The Adderley Smith Blues Band.

More beers were ordered as the late afternoon light streamed into the front bar illuminating, not only the assembled bearded and tattooed patrons, but also memories from Kerryn's past.

Brod was shipped off to sit out his time in far off New South Wales, while I was stationed in Melbourne, so I was still able to keep the band going. We found a singer Paul (Langford) Lever, to replace Brod and life went on as normally as it could be. We even booked a gig at The Dallas Brooks Hall to showcase our new line-up, but Lever for whatever reason left the band on the eve of the show so we got in Joe Camilleri to play the gig.

The place was packed with our friends and fans. This was a very important gig. We were on stage dressed in our denim playing the intro to our first song when Joe bounced on stage wearing a lime shirt, pink trousers, Cuban heels and shaking castanets. He was doing his whole Mick Jagger shtick ... I was so embarrassed. You see I was a very serious young man, way, way too serious; but at the time I saw it as my mission to bring the blues music to the people...this was serious stuff as far as I was concerned, it had nothing to do with show business.

Suddenly Lever jumped up on stage, he was very upset and started screaming that this was 'NOT THE BLUES' and pushed Joe out the way and started to sing. He was as horrified at Joe's antics as I was, but pushing Joe aside ... the whole thing was excruciating. (Though according to Camilleri the audience went wild!!!)

After the show I pushed Lever up against the wall and screamed at him never to do anything like that again, I also told Joe he was sacked for embarrassing me in front of my friends.

Joe still managed to hang in the band for a year before he left for the jazz and be-bop mayhem of Lipp Arthur and the Double Decker Brothers, followed by an adventure playing behind a stripper in the wild, mining towns of Western Australia. Joe himself said he was 'the wrong singer for Adderley Smith Band'; however Kerryn said that, 'yep, he just might have made us famous'.

Sometime in 1970, Adderley Smith had run its course. Kerryn (and Brod) joined Keith Glass in his band Sundown, playing covers of country rock artists like Neil Young and The Byrds. Then, sometime after playing with Sundown, Kerryn was asked to join Greg Quill's Country Radio. Kerryn remembers:

> I told Quill's manager that I could play guitar and mandolin because that's what they were looking for, trouble is I'd never played mandolin in my life. So I borrowed one and worked out a few chord changes on the road to Sydney to record with Country Radio. Greg loved what I played in the session and suddenly I was in the band and turning my hand to writing songs. The first thing I wrote with Greg was 'Gypsy Queen' which was a hit in Australia — a turning point in my career. I was now taking song writing seriously, Greg was a huge influence on my writing and it was Greg who unwittingly exposed me to songs with Australian references.
>
> We were travelling through Forbes in New South Wales and Greg played me the Australian folk song… 'The Streets of Forbes', which was about the death of bushranger Ben Hall. The song resonated with me, I thought now here is an opening for a bright young man. Maybe I needed to establish a band with an American country/rock approach but write songs with an Australian narrative.

This was a time of the Whitlam Government when Australia was undergoing a cultural renaissance. It was an era when government enthusiastically supported all sectors of the arts, from theatre to cinema, from literature to publishing and painting, all in an attempt to promote a unique Australian identity and to kill off forever the country's debilitating cultural cringe. Kerryn Tolhurst picked up on the zeitgeist.

'I was inspired to write songs in the spirit of Lawson and Patterson, songs about the land, the dust and desert, songs about ordinary Australians, 'Way out West' was the first.'

Tolhurst had the audacity to form a band with Broderick Smith on vocals, Chris Stockley on guitar, John Bois on bass and John Lee on drums — and call it The Dingoes! The band had that country/blues feel — think The Band or The Byrds — but their songs had Australian, working class themes that also resonated with international audiences. Songs from their self-titled debut album included 'Boy on the Run' (written by Chris Stockley and Brod Smith), 'Sydney Ladies' (Tolhurst, Smith), 'Pay Day Again', 'Goin' Down Again', both written by Tolhurst.

The band played a legendary Saturday afternoon residency at The Station Hotel in Prahran, where three hundred people packed into a space that could comfortably handle a hundred. When The Dingoes played that bar-room, it crackled with energy; it was loud, smoky, raw, wild. And a bloke named Billy McCartney picked up on the whole vibe.

Billy, a roadie, was a regular at The Dingoes' Station Hotel session. He was back home for a short stint having relocated to the US to work for Elvis, Lynyrd Skynyrd, and the Stones. When Billy returned to the US he took The Dingoes' first album with him and played it for Lynyrd Skynyrds' manager, Peter Rudge. Rudge loved it. He invited the band to America and signed them to a record deal with A&M Records in Los Angeles.

The Dingoes had the world at their feet. On top of being signed to a major label by a powerful figure in the US music scene, they had Neil Young's producer Elliot Mazer signed up to oversee their first album, plus session musicians Nicky Hopkins (keyboard player with The Rolling Stones, The Kinks and The Who) and The Band's Garth Hudson ready to play on the records. There were promises of support slots for Lynard Skynyrd, and a tour in their own right, but there was also a lot of hanging about and drinking and partying, for months, years. Too long.

The official history is that The Dingoes' career crashed with the aeroplane that took down Lynyrd Skynyrd one October night in Gillsburg, Mississippi in 1977. It killed singer Ronnie Van Zant, as well as band member Steve Gains, his sister Cassie, the pilot, co-pilot and road-crew, and seriously injured the rest of the band.

'That's all bullshit,' said Kerryn. 'We were given it all on a plate and we blew it'.

> *I should have been writing more songs, we should have gone home to Australia to consolidate our home audience, it would have invigorated us, but we didn't. We just hung about and went crazy. You only get one chance at success and we had it but didn't grab it with two hands. Sure when Lynyrd Skynyrd went down in the plane crash and the tour supporting them was cancelled — it sure didn't help, they were our cash cow. But what was more important ... we simply dropped the ball! We didn't work hard enough, didn't take the opportunity given to us seriously enough.*

The Dingoes persisted in the US, recording, touring, hanging out in Woodstock, but it was all a long goodbye. Stockley left in early 1978 and, finally, after recording their album *Orphans of the Storm*, they disbanded in 1980. Says Kerryn, 'I can't listen to the records we recorded in America, too many bad memories.'

From the '80s, Tolhurst divided his time between New York and Australia. He played with Richard Clapton, was a session musician in New York, played in bar bands. Notably, he wrote the hit song 'Man on Your Mind' with Glen Shorrock and recorded by The Little River Band, as well as the international hit 'All Fired Up' for Pat Benatar. He also produced records for the Black Sorrows, Paul Kelly, Goanna and Chris Wilson, just to name a few.

Kerryn Tolhurst has written some of Australia's most enduring and articulate songs. He is a pioneer; like Australian author George Johnson before him, Tolhurst was able to encapsulate a transformative moment in our history when it seemed possible that a confident, reinvigorated Australian artistic vernacular was about to conquer the world.

Travelling the Blues Highway

Kenny White, Graham Squance, Dutch Tilder, the Adderley Smith Blues Band: these musicians opened a lot of doors, blues-wise, in Melbourne. One of the many musicians who walked through this door to see what was on the other side was Phil Manning.

Phil had come over to Melbourne from Tassie and helped form the band that became known as Chain in late 1968, with Wendy Saddington as the singer. Chain took their inspiration from the American greats but also were influenced by the British blues of the '60s, like a lot of bands at the time. Phil, on the Phil Manning, Chain website describes the band's take on things at the time as working class:

'We performed songs that represented the feelings of the anti-Vietnam War movement…we were more suited to the alternative life-style people of the late '60s/early '70s than the mainstream pop world.'

The band built a dedicated, following which went ballistic when they added Brisbane singer and harp player Matt Taylor into the mix. With Taylor in the band it took on a tougher, bluesier edge that was captured when the band recorded the song 'Black and Blue' in a Sydney recording studio. The song was destined to be an Australian rock classic; as Manning writes, it 'smashed the charts and went to number one in Melbourne' with its 'totally original take on blues/rock.'

More singles followed. 'Judgment' went to #2 on the national charts, and the band's debut album, *Toward The Blues*, went gold. It was an unprecedented achievement for any blues-playing band in Australia at the time.

This line-up only lasted for eleven months for the band before singer Matt Taylor went solo and recorded an album of his own songs, with the help of the other Chain members. He had huge hit with 'I Remember When I Was Young'.

Chain was — and occasionally still are — a great Australian

blues band. The thing about Chain is they have maintained their commitment to their working-class roots, they are not pretentious or over-blown, they are just a great, tough blues band and a band never afraid to admit to their Australian-ness. Chain established a subgenre of the blues — let's call it 'Oz Blues' — which was a bona fide stylistic variation of its American father. In creating this, they immeasurably influenced a whole generation of Melbourne-based blues musicians.

Chris Wilson

One of the many blues babies Chain fathered was the late, great Chris Wilson. Wilson added new textures and imagery to Chain's tough Oz blues formula. Throughout his career, Wilson played harmonica, saxophone, guitar and sang with an incredibly powerful baritone voice. He was simply an amazingly present performer, a man capable of controlling rooms with the strength of his personality.

Wilson first came to notice playing saxophone and harmonica with Harem Scarem in the early '80s. It was a band McFarlane felt 'few alternative bands of the day could ever hope to match for muscular bravado and sheer instrumental firepower.' In the '90s Chris played harp with Paul Kelly and The Coloured Girls, and fronted the Crown of Thorns. *Rhythms* reported that, in March 1996, Wilson collaborated with Johnny Diesel (aka Mark Lizotte) for the 1996 album *Short Cool Ones*, which became one of the biggest selling blues albums in Australian music history. Wilson was a dominant presence in Melbourne's blues scene for decades., He was passionate, authentic, he sounded like he had paid a price to sing the blues.

A young woman at Ruby Reds paid me a huge compliment one night when she mistook me for Chris. She'd been coming to my gig for a few weeks, sat at a table right up front. We'd chat between sets, nice girl; I couldn't understand why she was always there alone. She said she loved how I sang the Dylan song 'It Takes a Lot to Laugh, It Takes a Train to Cry', and that she had my version on a cassette that she had played constantly on a recent road trip around New Zealand. I was confused; I'd never recorded the song. I got even more confused when she asked me home that night!

When I remembered that it was Chris who had recorded a version of Dylan's song for one of his releases, everything became clear. I thanked the young woman for her very flattering invitation, then told her that my wife would probably be upset if I accepted.

'Plus,' I said, I would have slept with you under false pretenses. You think I'm Chris Wilson, don't you?'.

'Well, aren't you?' She replied.

'No, I'm Craig Horne … Chris is the bloke you need to speak to!'

The look of horror on her face is hard to erase from my mind. She picked up her bag and ran out the door, and I never saw her again.

Ian Collard

I want to single out the great Ian Collard for special mention. Ian played harp on The Hornets second album, *Can't Live with You, Can't Live Without You*. He came into the studio carrying a bullet harmonica mic, a couple of practice amps and a box full of harps. He sat the amps down, slaved them together and turned the volume to window-shattering. Ian had never heard the songs before, but he wasn't fazed. He sounded like a mixture of Miles Davis and Little Walter; melodic, fluid, stunning. He blew a masterful line on my song 'Bob Dylan at the Palais Theatre' which pulled the song together, and he underpinned the feel of 'Changes' with a perfect riff. I'd never heard anything like it — If I had hair it would have stood on end. I immediately differentiated what Ian did from everybody else I'd ever heard.

Over the years I've seen Collard play in bars and at festivals, and played on the same bill as him. I love his voice; there's something kinda Clarksdale Mississippi about it. He's an original at home in Melbourne's blues scene, which has evolved a million miles away from the delta. It's a scene that is as legitimate and as original as those in Chicago or Memphis or even Clarksdale.

Kerri Simpson — Crossing the Divide

Kerri Simpson has a mystique about her. Her voice can be a howl or a whisper, sometimes a croon and sometimes the sound of a sweet gospel bell. Her approach is eclectic and intelligent, with a real philosophical basis. She's lived in New Orleans and travelled to Chicago and New York, where she saw Etta James, Koko Taylor, and Ruth Brown, all the while absorbing the essence they transmitted from the stage.

I met Kerri recently at her home in the northern suburbs of Melbourne, where she had just arrived home after a hard day of teaching at an eastern suburban secondary school. Tea was poured and we settled onto her large and comfortable couch. We sat in her lounge room, filled with collections of objects from her musical past, a photo of Chris Wilson, voodoo memorabilia, records, lots of stuff. I started our conversation by asking her the standard question of how she got into music.

Kerri got caught up in music at a young age. She was raised on the northern outskirts of Melbourne, where she played the accordion and listened to her Aunt Jean play blues and swing on the piano. When she got hold of Bessie Smith's three record set, put out by Columbia, she was hooked. She heard the power of the blues through Bessie, a singer who had a different way of looking at things. From that point on, so did Kerri. She now knew what she wanted to do:

I dropped the accordion and started to play guitar and bass, joined a high school band, we wrote originals, played covers, Top 40, rock — the usual.

When she was old enough, she ventured down to Fitzroy's The Royal Derby Hotel on Brunswick Street to see the Steve Purcell and Ken Farmer's band The Echo Vampers. She ended up sitting in with them and they loved what she did. It was like she had been born and raised to sing the blues.

If you were a musician in the early '80s, Fitzroy was the place to be. Rents were cheap and gigs were plentiful; Martinis, The Aberdeen, The Derby. And you could catch the tram to The Espy, Bananas or The Venue. Kerri was singing with the Swinging Sidewalks, various jazz outfits, Kia Kaha and Sophisticated Boom Boom with Jenny Tubbs, Louise Taunt and eventually Vika Bull. According to Kerri, Sophisticated Boom Boom 'sang early '60s girl group stuff like 'Be My Baby' by the Ronettes, The Shirelles and stuff like that'.

And then Kerri took off for America. She lived in New Orleans for a while, hung out at gigs, got invited to sit in and sing, made herself known. Later she went to London and sang with Henry Maas' funk, soul and jazz/rock band, The Bachelors From Prague. The blues was at the base of everything she did, but she was stretching herself, moving across genres and learning what it meant to be a performer. Heading back to Melbourne after a stint singing in jazz clubs in Barcelona, she formed a salsa band with percussionist Ray Pereira.

There had been a steady influx of musicians into Melbourne: Steve Purcell and Vernon Gibson from Brisbane, Ron Tabuteau, Ken Farmer from Adelaide, Dean Hilson and Paul Cummings from Perth, Steve Dagg from Sydney. Gigs had dried up interstate, but the Melbourne scene was thriving. Kerri was working for Henry Maas in his Black Cat Café and was the regular opening act at his legendary nightclub The Purple Pit, later joined by Vika Bull when the Pit morphed into The Batch Box. Kerri, as she told me, was on the right road, memorizing songs, learning melodies, and receiving firsthand knowledge from musicians arriving in Melbourne from all over the country:

There were musicians like Steve Purcell, Doug Kelly, Dai Jones, Steve Dagg, Jeff Raglus, Dean Hilson and Paul Cummings, all of us busking on the streets, gigging, jamming, sitting in, doing what we could to master our respective instruments. Everyone met in Bourke Street on a Friday night and busked down at the Mall. We played R&B, swing, jazz, name it, up-tempo, music to move by. Steve Purcell was such a great front person; he drew in the crowd, got a reaction. We always did really well busking; at the end of the night we'd divide up the proceeds then all go our separate ways to our regular gigs later in the night.

That loose gathering of musicians became the Swingin' Sidewalks and variously included people like — Steve Purcell (double bass), Pete Martin (guitar), Dai Jones (guitar), Paul Cumming (guitar), Doug Kelly (drums), Dean Hilson (sax), Steve Dagg (sax) and Jeff Raglus (trumpet). Kerri told me that she remembered those days fondly:

I learnt so much about singing and performing in that band, I honed my craft, expanded my repertoire learning literally hundreds of songs. But I learnt more, I learnt how to get up and sing — anything. I learnt to improvise, listen, how a rhythm section worked, how the horn sections worked, how players complemented the each other, all unbelievably invaluable lessons.

The Swingin' Sidewalks were hugely successful; they played long residencies at various clubs, appeared regularly on television, and toured. They were the archetypical good-time Melbourne outfit. Eventually, the band evolved into its current incarnation: The Pearly Shells Orchestra. Kerri then teamed up with longtime musical associates Ron Tabuteau, Mark Grunden, Ben Grayson and Dean Addison, and later Andrew Ogburn, Chris Rogers, Shannon Bourne and Dean Hilson, on a number of blues-based projects. She also ventured into Cajun territory with Andy Baylor, and gospel with Chris Wilson, all the while carrying the blues in her luggage. 'I love the blues,' says Kerri; 'it informs all modern music, you can express how you feel singing the blues.'

Along the line Kerri journeyed back and forth to the US, travelling through Chicago, New York and New Orleans, where she hung out and wrote songs with The Caesar brothers and Jason Neville in New Orleans.

Kerri kept crossing the divide, falling head over heels into recording hard rock albums, eliciting the comparison of 'Patti Smith with a glass of scotch in one hand' by critic Andrew Masterson. She was featured alongside Beth Orton on Fritz Radio in Berlin, when her album *The Arousing* went to #1 on their charts. She lit some fireworks when she recorded some techno tracks with Ollie Olsen and put out a couple of Patti le Belle/Chaka Khan-esque dance records, 'Higher' and 'Kiss Her Goodbye'. As a result, Kerri toured Australia supporting Kylie Minogue. But somewhere there, Kerri needed to understand the truth of things; she travelled to Haiti and New Orleans making field recordings of Voudoun rituals for her *Vodou Songs Of The Spirits* album.

Working with Ray Pereira back in Melbourne, Kerri wrote and produced, *Vodou Songs of the Spirits* an album which featured over a hundred musicians from every continent on the planet. This trip also led to her *Confessin' the Blues* album, recorded with some of the country's finest roots musicians. The album went crazy, receiving airplay throughout the US, Canada and Australia, where it was nominated for multiple ARIA Awards. On the back of this album, she supported The Blind Boys from Alabama, Dr John, and Keb Mo on their national tour.

In 1999, Kerri was invited to perform with her old New Orleans mates Norman and Ricki Caesar as well as Jason and Aaron Neville Jnr at that year's Jazz and Heritage Festival. making her one of the few Australians to appear at the prestigious festival, and the first Australian female to perform there.

Back in Australia Simpson explored vast musical worlds through her *Knockin' at The Backdoor* album suite, recorded at Thirty Mill Studios, where she is one of the house producers. Along the way she has dabbled in ska and other eclectic live projects. These inlcuded The Ears (post-punk), The Majestics with Kylie Auldist and Nichaud Fitzgibbon (ska 'n' soul), The Gospel Belles with Kelly Auty, Marisa Quigley and Diana Wolfe, Alt-country with Suzannah Espie, Ali Ferrier and Barb Waters, let's all take a deep breath at this point.

This was, according to Kerri, how it is in the industry in Melbourne; 'as a working musician, just by its very nature, you have to diversify to make a living.'

Finally how has it been for a woman like Kerri Simpson was also working in the very male dominated world of the blues and roots musical scene of Melbourne. Did she, like Judy Jacques, have to learn how to fight drummers? Did she need to go to gigs with an axe in her hand? Says Kerri:

> *You know, I only ever play with people I admire. I've never had much trouble from band members; I've always been shown respect. The audience however has been a whole other thing. I've had horrible incidents occur both physical and verbal. I've been stalked, shoved against walls, grabbed onstage and dragged around offstage. Something about performing makes you fair game for a certain type of person.*
>
> *It is harder for middle-aged female musicians but ultimately I tend not to buy into that kind of male vs female thinking, I find it distracts from the playing, after all the music that has inspired me over the years has been played by male and female musicians.*
>
> *I also think it's got a little easier for women playing music in Melbourne these days. When I started out there were a few women in the scene. Renee Geyer, Jeannie Little, Jane Clifton and Robyn Archer, probably that was about it. Then gradually more women started appearing, people like Chris Farmer and The Mojos broke a lot of ground in the blues scene. I think it is a whole lot healthier now; it's no longer unusual being a woman singing or playing the blues anymore.*

Country Music — The White Man's Blues

We now journey from Melbourne's gritty inner-city blues scene of the late twentieth century back to a more rural musical environment. To this we have to travel back in time to the early twentieth century.

America's Jimmie Rodgers has been called the father of country music. His recording career lasted from just 1927 to 1933, but in that time, he recorded over one hundred songs. During his career, right up to his death from tuberculosis in 1933, at the age of 35, he redefined country music as white man's blues. He accomplished this by incorporating worker-oriented, railroad-themed songs with rhythmic yodelling, blues and jazz forms, Hawaiian guitar and vaudeville style entertainment. It was a formula adopted by our own version of the 'Singing Brakeman' (as Rogers was known), Melbourne's Smoky Dawson. So how did America's white man's blues find its way down south?

Australia's white man's blues then has its origins in Britain's ballads, sung by convicts incarcerated under the washed-out decks of convict ships that arrived in Botany Bay. Following the folk tradition, the new settlers soon adapted these songs to the new land they found themselves in, a situation dominated by the axe, the plough, the whip, chains and guns. As Peter Beilby and Michael Roberts wrote in their book *Australian Music*:

'Settlers took their (English and Irish) songs with them into the bush and later into the gold fields... the life of the new country was reflected in songs about bush-rangers and drovers. Later, shearers joined convicts and miners as song heroes — or anti-heroes — and fuelled the camp-fire anthems with such underdog fodder that the songs soon took hold back in the city.'[1]

As G.M. Ellis rightly points out in his blog *The Story of Australian Country Music*, 'these bush anthems were all accompanied by a mixture of fiddles, banjos, concertinas, mouth organs, penny whistles and tea chest basses.'

One topic the songs didn't broach was the nauseating land clearing of whole nations of Aboriginal people, when clearing meant men, women and children were gunned down by white men out for a jolly Sunday hunting party. Nor did the bush ballads deal with the shame of whole Aboriginal clans wiped out by white man's disease and alcohol. The songs certainly didn't mourn the loss of Indigenous language and culture, a culture rich in understanding of this beautiful land, a culture that was at least sixty thousand years old. What the songs did deal with were the hardships, isolation and injustices felt by white men in what they perceived as a harsh new country. It was these topics that formed the basis of Australia's early country music.

Later, in the 19th Century, Henry Lawson and Banjo Patterson established the tradition of the bush ballad that flowed through the country genre (as well as folk). Patterson's 'Waltzing Matilda' was the most famous of the form.

The song is a perfect example of the folk tradition in action, wherein a popular tune is adapted to fit a contemporary narrative — in this case, an incident from the 1891 shearers' strike in Queensland. Legend has it that Banjo Paterson wrote the words to 'Waltzing Matilda' in January 1895 while staying at Dagworth Station, a sheep and cattle farm near Winton in Central West Queensland owned by the Macpherson family. The words were written to a tune played on a zither by 31-year-old Christina Macpherson, one of the family members at the station.

Macpherson had in turn originally heard this tune, 'The Craigielee March', played by a military band at the Warrnambool steeplechase horse racing in Victoria in April 1894. She played it back by ear at Dagworth. Paterson decided that the music would scan well with the lyrics, and completed the song during his stay at the station, and then nearby Winton.

The march itself was based on the music the Scottish composer James Barr. He composed it in 1818 for Robert Tannahill's 1806 poem 'Thou Bonnie Wood of Craigielee'. In the early 1890s it was arranged as 'The Craigielee', a march for brass band by Australian composer Thomas Bulch.

The bush ballads were taken up and sung by rural workers around campfires, on front porches, in country halls, as a form of self-expression. But the introduction of new technology changed all that. The radio and the gramophone bought American country music to our shores and, through a process of cultural appropriation, the bush ballad morphed into what soon would be recognised as Australian country music.

Just as the introduction of radio and the gramophone the radio and the gramophone brought jazz music and the flapper to the masses in the '20s, so too did the same technology bring the music of Jimmy Rodgers, Wilf Carter and Hank Snow to rural Australia. It was this music that inspired young, New-Zealand born showman Robert Lane (better known as Tex Morton) to take up the guitar, write songs and eventually become universally acknowledged as the 'Father of Australian Country Music.'

Tex was not only a singer, he was a showman incorporating hypnotism and sharpshooting into his act. He recorded original material on Columbia's Regal Zonophone label, songs laden with Australian bush themes: 'Old Blue, The Black Sheep', 'The Orginal Ned Kelly Song' and 'Wrap Me Up in My Stock Whip and Blanket'. It was these songs that influenced the careers of seminal Australian country artists such as Buddy Williams and Slim Dusty.

Slim was born David Kirkpatrick in the Macleay Valley near Kempsey in New South Wales. He was one of Australia's most successful recording artists and, according to the *Slim Dusty Centre*, country music's best selling artists with seven million units sold. He rode the country music boom throughout the '40s and '50s, recording over one thousand songs across a fifty-five year career. This included Australia's first single to gain a gold record 'Pub with no Beer' and reaching Number 3 on the British charts in 1957, 'The Rain Tumbles Down in July', and the '80s smash hit drinking ditty, 'Duncan'. As

Beilby and Roberts wrote, 'Slim's act was traditional country, but saw nothing wrong with taking a bunch of rock musicians on the road with him;'[2] musicians like Melbourne band Saltbush (Bernie Obrien, Ross Nicholson, Paul Pyle and Harold Frith) or Andy Baylor's little brother Donal. As a result of Slim's willingness to move with the times, by the end of his long career he was one of Australia's most enduring and most loved entertainers.

Aside from Slim, there were country performers like Johnny Ashcroft, who had an Australian wide hit single with 'Little Boy Lost'. Lucky Starr had a major national hit with the Geoff Mack song 'I've Been Everywhere Man', a song subsequently recorded by everyone from Hank Snow to Johnny Cash to Asleep at the Wheel. Let's not forget the later contributions of Reg Lindsay, Buddy Williams, Aboriginal country star Auriel Andrew, Christie Allen and Jean Stafford.

Herbert (Smoky) Dawson

It was the hard streets of Melbourne's inner city working class suburb of Collingwood that produced, arguably, Australia's first internationally famous country star, Herbert (Smoky) Dawson. Dawson, whose mother died when he was five years old, lived in a violent household, enduring beatings and bashings by his invalid, alcoholic father, himself the victim of post-traumatic stress syndrome resulting in time on the killing fields of the Gallipoli Peninsula. Like many young people born into violent and dangerous circumstances, young Herbert found truth and liberation in music.

He made up hokum about being born in the Never-Never and that he spent his life travelling through smoky towns and dusty, winding roads. In fact, later in life he may have spent time living on Wakanui Street in Northcote, just around the corner from where I grew-up on the corner of Swift and Kellett Streets.

That's what I was told as a little boy listening to *The Adventures of Smoky Dawson* and his horse Flash on his radio show. It didn't matter to me if it was all hokum; Smoky showed me the red dust and the blue-forested mountains of my country. He showed me in story, and song, what the world could be beyond the cobbled lanes of Northcote; it's what poets do. Dylan, for example, said he came to New York in a boxcar, via a travelling circus and a stint playing piano with Bobby Vee; what he *did* do was escape a middle-class, vanilla life in the US northwest and travelled across country to Greenwich Village in a '57 four-door Impala. In the process he created not only a new persona but also a whole new way of looking at music.

Smoky Dawson too created a persona — Australia's first singing cowboy. He was a singer, a yodeller, a guitar player at local dances in Carringbush and a busker outside the Princess Theatre in Spring Street. He and his brother Ted teamed up in '32. Smoky playing steel guitar — he is credited with playing the first electric steel guitar heard in Australia — and dobro, wihle Ted played acoustic guitar and bass. They played as the Coral Island Boys on radio 3KZ with Peggy Brooks as lead singer, and on *The Smoky Dawson Radio Show*, which was sponsored by Pepsodent. It was the first live country music show on Australian radio.

In the lead-up to World War II, Dawson went on the road playing hillbilly music at rodeos and theatres, adding whip-cracking and axe- and knife-throwing to his repertoire. He recorded extensively, including, in 1948 the famous 'My Heart Is Where The Roper Flows Tonight', and wrote a series of songs and stories based on his own experiences for radio show *Inlander*, broadcast by the ABC.

By 1951, the boy from Collingwood had taken his country act to England, where BBC Television covered his performance live (including the knife-throwing) at the Festival of Britain. Dawson toured the USA — for a time with a kangaroo called Zip, until the roo got lost in New York City — on behalf of the Australian government. He recorded eighteen songs in the US, including his popular versions of 'The Man From Never Never' and 'The Wild Colonial Boy'. He travelled to Nashville in 1952, working with a pioneer of American country music Ernest Tubb, famous for writing and recording the hit song 'Walking the Floor Over You'. Smoky also promoted the film *Kangaroo,* that starred Maureen O'Hara and Peter Lawford and appeared on Broadway with his whip and knife act in *Kiss Me Kate.*

Back home, his Kelloggs-sponsored radio show *The Adventures Of Smoky Dawson* (accompanied by his wonder horse Flash) had become a national institution. The show ran for ten years, finally ending in 1962 not because of public reaction, but simply because the actors had had enough.

But Dawson still had plenty to prove. It's that working-class thing: ya just gotta show people you aren't a hophead, you're the real deal, you're worthy. He opened Smoky Dawson Ranch just north of Sydney, hosted country music shows, opened an amusement park, a holiday camp and a stunt school. Between 1973 and 1979, he made daily appearances on Channel 9.

In 1978, he joined two other Australian country pioneers, Tex Morton and Buddy Williams, when he became the third artist to be elected to the newly-created Country Music Roll Of Renown (Australia's equivalent to Nashville's Country Music Hall Of Fame). That same year he flew to Nashville to receive a special award for services to country music and returned the following year to star on the All Time Greats Show, receiving a pioneer award from the American Country Music Association.

Dawson was an Australian country music legend that refused to let poverty slam life's door shut in his face. He waved goodbye to the slums of inner Melbourne, the beatings by his damaged father and stepped out onto the dusty roads of Australia and beyond to find what he was looking for. Whatever that was, Dawson transcended the limitations that life threw at him to help put Australian culture and Australian country music on the world stage.

CHAPTER 10

MELBOURNE, AMERICANA, MAINSTREAM & INDEPENDENT

THE MARVELLOUS MELBOURNE MUSIC SCENE OF THE '80S

I t was the early '80s, and the living was easy-ish. At the very least people *acted* like everything was wonderful; the Vietnam War was over and Australia was emerging from the recession brought on by the first oil crisis of the mid-'70s. Even though unemployment sat at seven per cent and Melbourne's manufacturing industry was slowing down, life was pretty good if you were young. Those of us from industrial suburbs had been educated for free courtesy of Gough Whitlam and the Labor Government of 1972-75. As a consequence, we had jobs; we were teachers, public servants, scientists, engineers. And we owned homes — in my case, a terrace in Fitzroy bought with a deposit partially financed by playing a year of country footy, and partially from a loan serviced by my base-grade public sector wage. We could confidently afford to take on mortgages because our jobs were permanent; we had career structures and superannuation.

In the early '80s egalitarianism was not a fading memory; it was a reality. Sure, Big Mal Fraser was Prime Minister and Rupert Hamer was Victoria's Premier (replaced by The Cain Labor government in 1982), but schools, hospitals, and public housing units were being built. Hamer had doubled the number of Victoria's national parks, built the Arts Centre, decriminalised homosexuality, abolished the death penalty and introduced tough environmental protection laws. Federally, we welcomed tens of thousands of Indo-Chinese refugees as they arrived in boats on our northern coastline. They came, they were housed in migrant centres, and then they were absorbed into the great Australian multicultural mixing pot.

But there were clouds on the horizon. Ronald Reagan and Margaret Thatcher were in power in the US and Britain respectively, together preaching the gospel of deregulation, lower taxes, free trade, privatisation of government services and the smashing of trade unions. This was a seductive gospel that resonated with powerful elites, and it would eventually find its way down under. But for now, we had the weekend, Bob Hawke and a living wage.

Melbourne's musical landscape in the '80s reflected the decade's confidence and diversity. It was a tale of two cities; on the one hand, there were the mainstream commercial bands that played the beer barns like the Burvale, Matthew Flinders, The Pier Hotel, Sentimental Bloke and Southside Six. All were full to brim with fist pumping fans worshipping at the feet of The Hunters and Collectors, Australian Crawl, Paul Kelly, The Sports, Crowded House, The Black Sorrows and Mondo Rock. It was high commerce underpinned by Premier Artists and Mushroom Records who promised and delivered big budgets, big rigs, big overheads and big egos.

Running counterpoint to the high risk, high reward commercial mainstream were the independents. These were also the DIY years, when some bands shunned commerciality for art. It was a time when a Melbourne form of punk flourished, especially in St Kilda venues such as the Crystal Ballroom, the Palace and the Esplanade Hotel, not to mention the Aberdeen, Tiger Lounge and Ivanhoe, soon to be the Tote. It was a scene encouraged by Keith Glass and his record label Missing Link, and by Bruce Milne's Au Go Go Records and underpinned by community radio stations such as RRR, PBS and 3CR. Emerging from this scene were bands like The Birthday Party, Essendon Airport and The Moodists.

In many ways, the '80s was a decade when Melbourne cemented its reputation as the nation's live music capital. It was the decade when you could hear not only pedal-to-metal hard rock, but also, for the first time, those little known music genres like Western Swing, zydeco, Tex-Mex or Cajun at inner city hotels.

Joe Camilleri and his two most well-known bands, Jo Jo Zep and the Falcons (initially formed in the '70s) and The Black Sorrows, encapsulated the commercial mainstream of the era, while Andy Baylor and his Dancehall Racketeers typified Melbourne's DIY independent scene. In their own idiosyncratic ways, both Camilleri and Baylor introduced Melbourne audiences to obscure Americana forms like Western Swing, reggae, power-pop-blues and zydeco, up until then an obscure genre born in southwest Louisiana by French Creole speakers that blended blues, rhythm and blues with French and Native American Indigenous musical forms. They presented these forms in a way that would come to be defined as the Melbourne method.

Paul Neuendorf, multi-instrumentalist and singer from such bands as The Dancehall Racketeers, Zydeco Jump and Texicali Rose, was one of the key musicians to first play this new music in Melbourne. We met in Paul's eastern suburban home and sat at his dining room table where he described a method of 'cross-referencing' which came to define the Melbourne approach to this new music:

> *Melbourne bands put their own flavour into the pot. We listen to everything from Charlie Parker to Delta Blues, Beatles, Bob Dylan, Chuck Berry, Tex-Mex, Western Swing, reels and rags. We aren't precious or purist about any style, we respect it, but we put our own take on the music. We don't slavishly follow one*

musical form, Texas blues, Lafayette Cajun, Jamaican reggae, we listen to everything and incorporate bits and pieces into our sound. We throw a Duke Ellington lick into a Jimmy Liggins tune, Charlie Parker might wander into a Bob Willls number or on any night you might hear a Chuck Berry song played by a cajun band. It's whatever it takes to get the people moving and what ever puts a smile on their faces. More importantly it's whatever keeps 'em drinking and coming back for more.

Joe Camilleri understands the Melbourne's cross-referencing musical process very well — it has defined his career for the past five decades.

Joe Camilleri: from the fringe to the mainstream

I've known Joe from afar for many years. I used to see him scuffling around the hard streets of Carlton in the early '70s when he was playing with Peter Lillie, Johnny Topper and Stephen Cummings in the Pelaco Brothers. A skinny little bloke with a wild dress sense, he crackled with energy. Our paths crossed at gigs and in rehearsal spaces at that time, I think I referred to him as The Maltese Falcon, not terribly original I know. He had an enormous presence, he dressed in suits, wore turbans, played crazy sax. At that time he often spoke in song titles … 'Hey man, *Move it on Over*, I need some space,' or when you asked how he was he might answer, '*I Can't Get No Satisfaction*, man', don't know why. Maybe he didn't want to get too close and so he just deflected people like me with jive, or maybe he was just shy and didn't want to reveal anything about himself. I didn't find out the answer until much later.

I reconnected with Joe through Jeff Burstin. They played together for over eighteen years in Jo Jo Zep and the Falcons and The Black Sorrows and it was Jeff who arranged for me to meet Joe early one Friday morning at his favourite café in South Melbourne. He ordered a steak, sausages, eggs, mushrooms, maybe some avocado, lashings of toast and a coffee. Over the next hour he demolished the lot as we talked about his life in music.

In the mid-'50s, Joe was a young man finding his way through the brutal, working-class streets of Port Melbourne in 1955.

Back then there was not a latte or bruschetta in sight — just painters and dockers, wharf labourers and toughs drinkin' hard at the Pier or Prince Alfred until they were chucked out at 6pm, known universally at the time as six o'clock closing.

But it was after six in the evening that Bay and Pickles Street got particularly dangerous. At that time there was no one walkin' and talkin' with the lord, and if you happened to be in the wrong place at the wrong time it was as though you were standing naked. In the '50s, Port Melbourne streets were dark, despairing places. People carried knives and, some people, guns so you kept your head down and your eyes on your feet, especially if you were a little different; a boy from Malta for instance. Joe told me that he was 'called a greasy wog and beaten with pickets off those wooden Victorian fences. I tried to be invisible…at the start anyway.' Joe, as a Catholic attended the local Catholic school and school was tough, and he ended up leaving early.

At this time, Elvis and Buddy Holly, Little Richard, Jerry Lee and Johnny O'Keefe ruled the airwaves. Joe explained that he and his mates took solace in this music; not his brother's piano accordion or the tuba played by his father but 'Hit the Road Jack' by Ray Charles, and eventually the songs of Bo Diddley and Chuck Berry.

Chuck was Joe's first role model in incorporating different music forms and creating something new and exciting. It was through the latter that the first hint of Western Swing hit Melbourne. Listen to Berry's 'Maybelline' and you can hear Bob Wills' 'Ida Red'; it's Wills' feel that races the Cadillac and Ford down Chuck's idiosyncratic highway. But hey, Berry was working firmly in the folk tradition, he borrowed stuff and added his own thing and that thing opened a lot of minds to a lot of possibilities, including Joe's.

Melbourne-based teenagers like Joe certainly picked up on those possibilities in Berry's lyrics, which were as much a motivating force as his duck walk and his signature double string slur. Joe Camilleri heard the message as he told me:

> We formed a band called the Drollies, I sang and tried to play bass. It was a time when if you liked the look of drums, you were the drummer in the band. So there we were, learning our instruments, trying to play Chuck Berry songs and Little Richard's 'Lucille' — we failed badly.

But Joe was doing something right; soon, he was headhunted by the bluesy King Bees as their singer. The band included Peter Starkie, soon to be a founding member of Skyhooks, and Dave Flett, who would go on to Captain Matchbox. Joe told me that 'Dave was a big influence on me, he introduced me to blues and jazz.'

It was the mid-'60s, so the King Bees were playing radio hits by the Beatles and the Stones; but they were spreading some country-infused bluesy goodness all over those radio songs. It was a great education in cross-fertilisation for Joseph, and the band was really getting somewhere. But it all came crashing down when Dave and Peter went off to university; says Joe, 'I was lost for a while.' Soon after, however, he was asked to fill in for Broderick Smith as the singer for The Adderley Smith Blues Band while Broderick was away in the army, as has been been previously discussed. Joe remembers:

> I was the wrong singer for that band, I was a bit more adventurous with my clobber ... I lasted about a year in the Adderley Smith Blues Band. It was fun, and it was great to connect with Kerryn Tolhurst ... But my tastes were changing; I'd gotten into Miles Davis' 'Bitches Brew' and John Coltrane's 'A Love Supreme'.

Joe then teamed up with Peter Starkie, Dave Fleet, and Jane Clifton in Lipp Arthur and the Double Decker Brothers. By joining Lipp Arthur, it was as though Joe had entered a musical hothouse:

*I heard Eric Dolphy and decided I wanted to play the
saxophone. It was 1971, I was 23, and I was in the city, bored.
Russell Street had a lot of music shops in those days, and I
walked into Clements, they had a sax in the window for $32. I
bought it. I got it home and it was really dirty, so I chucked it
in the bath, ruining all the pads. It was shiny, but unplayable.
I've still got that sax.*

Joe laughed at the memory and told me that it was while playing with
Lipp Arthur that he began to flourish as a musician:

*We played avant-garde pop songs and Robert Johnson blues
with a John Coltrane twist. It was a wild free band that had
Captain Beefheart's Trout Mask Replica as our bible.*

*We treated music as an art form and the scene was
receptive to that, the T.F. Much Ballroom in Fitzroy was
perfect for us; a big stage, fire-eaters and jugglers between the
acts; you could buy dope or incense in the foyer. Daddy Cool,
Captain Matchbox, or MacKenzie Theory were all on the bill,
and the audience were freaks — a great place to play. Campus
audiences loved us too. It was a culture thing — they got off
on the Ornette Coleman and Beefheart. I also learnt about
presentation around that time, I was an apprentice tailor and
used to make these crazy suits to wear on the weekend, green,
orange, didn't matter, they only lasted a couple of days then
fall apart.*

Then came the Pelaco Brothers, a band fronted by Joe on sax and vocals
and including Stephen Cummings on vocals, Johnny Topper bass,
Peter Lillie guitar, Chris Worrall guitar, Karl Wolfe drums and later Ed
Bates on guitar. The band, which lasted just eighteen months, played
an amalgam of styles such as rockabilly, country swing and R&B, all
with a fiercely Australian outlook. Of the band, Ian McFarlane wrote
that 'they virtually defined a scene that encompassed a new musical
aesthetic.' Joe described the approach:

We couldn't play that well, at first we were like $2 chicken on a $3 plate, but we worked it out by playin' six nights a week. We swapped licks and learnt from each other, we wrote our own songs; played universities and the word spread.

The word spread all the way to Ross Wilson.

As I wrote in *Daddy Who?*, my biography of Daddy Cool; at the end of 1975, Ross Wilson was sitting out a contractual dispute with his record company. The contract was due to expire in 1976, but he wanted to produce a one-off single for Mushroom Records — a version of Chuck Berry's 'Run Rudolph Run' — to coincide with a Mushroom Showcase gig at the Sidney Myer Music Bowl. Legally Wilson wasn't able to perform the song himself, so he recruited his old mate Joe Camilleri, whom he first met when they both played the Mentone Mod (short for Modern) dance in 1964 in their respective bands at the time, Ross with The Pink Finks, and Joe, The King Bees. Wilson also recruited bass player John Power and guitarist Jeff Burstin, with whom he had worked when producing tracks for their band Company Cain's album, *Dr. Chop*.

This is the agreed-upon version of the formation of Jo Jo Zep and the Falcons, though there is an alternative courtesy of Wayne Burt. Burt claims he saw Joe playing around town and recruited him to join Jeff Burstin, Power and himself as sax player and back-up singer in a new R&B band that eventually became Jo Jo Zep and the Flacons. Whatever the process the band really hit their straps when Gary Young joined the band as drummer. Wilson went on to produce their debut album, *Don't Waste It*, which included R&B-flavoured songs written by Burt including 'Beating Around the Bush', 'Dancing Shoes' and 'King of Fools.' Wilson also produced their second album *Whip it Out*. Joe said that at the time:

I wasn't meant to be the lead singer of the band. My whole idea was to play the saxophone. I wanted Stephen Cummings to be the singer, 'cause we were really great mates but for whatever reason he bowed out after just a couple of rehearsals. We had a full list of songs by Wayne Burt and that made the difference for us. I wasn't writing any songs really and I thought Wayne was a much better singer than me as well but he didn't want to be the lead singer, so we sort of shared it around for a little while.

I saw the Falcons play many times at the start of their career at places like the Kingston in Richmond and Martini's in Carlton. They were amazing and authentic, playing the rhythm and blues we first heard played by The Stones, Animals and The Beatles. Songs like the Louis Jordan penned 'Saturday Night Fish Fry', 'Boogie in the Barnyard', 'Choo, Choo Ch'boogie'; in fact Melbourne's roots music legend Andy Baylor in an interview with the author (see below) remembered the Falcons playing a full set of Louis Jordan songs at The Kingston, saying: 'they had the horn parts down, mainstream pop music seemed insipid in comparison to what the Falcons were playing at the time.'

But Burt wasn't happy. He left the band after the first album; he told me he hated playing discos: 'More of the audience got up to dance when the DJ played records between sets than when we played live, it was such a demoralising experience.'

Perhaps the reason was a little more complex than that. Having played in The Hornets with Wayne for many years, it is my observation that Wayne hates the limelight; he is uncomfortable as the focal point of the band. He's more comfortable in the sideman role, albeit one that still writes blues classics like 'Dancing Shoes' and 'Beating Around the Bush'; a sideman in the Lowell George mould, a sideman who can sing as well as any frontman. Wayne just doesn't want the attention, responsibility or aggravation of leading a band. As the main songwriter of The Falcons, he was under pressure to deliver; ultimately the pressure of 'lead' was a pressure he could live without.

After Wayne left the band, Tony Faehse joined on lead guitar, which gradually moved the band away from its R&B roots towards more of a ska/reggae feel. This culminated in *Screaming Targets*, their biggest selling album, which bore the hit single 'Hit and Run.' It would prove to be the record that broke the band internationally. Joe didn't think 'Hit and Run' would do anything but that maybe the lick was infectious enough — 'though as a song it was a bit stupid — but it got us a deal all over the world.'

The Falcons went on to a successful eight-year career that went from the deep roots of Chicago blues to Jamaican reggae and London ska. As their late bass player John Power is quoted in *Drum Media* in 2007 describing the Falcon's approach:

'We started off with no idea at all. We pretty much threw all the stuff in the pot and went on playing. It was a case of demand driving it. It took off like a rocket. We got more work than we could travel away, but the thing took on a life of its own. The thing with the Falcons, we never actually changed our style that much. We just accumulated new ones. It turned into a stratified thing 'cause we were mixing everything together all the way through. There was no plan.'[5]

What John was describing is the experience of a band finding what worked with the crowd, pleasing them, but also pleasing themselves. It's the alchemy of mixing art with commerce — finding that golden formula that keeps the band interested, the crowd drinking and the people coming back for more.

The Black Sorrows: from the DIY Fringe to Mega Mainstream

With the demise of Jo Jo Zep and the Falcons in 1981, Joe was working at the Queen Victoria Markets, making coffees at Café Neon and brewing an idea for a new band, a zydeco band he would name The Black Sorrows. I asked him how it all began:

I got a bunch of desperadoes together, including Steve McTaggart on violin, George Butrumlis on piano accordion, Paul Williamson on clarinet, Wayne Burt on guitar, Jeff Burstin *guitar, Wayne Duncan on bass, and Gary Young on drums. We did a couple of gigs and said, Hey, let's make a record. I remember playing birthday parties and weddings, just so I could get enough money to make a record. We made the first Black Sorrows album, Sonola, for $1300. I just wanted to have some sort of documentation that we existed.*

Initially the Sorrows were operating on the same turf as other Melbourne independents. Joe hustled for gigs, self-funded albums, and designed covers and publicity material himself. But then *Sonola* sold enough copies to warrant another trip to the well, and so *Rockin' Zydeco* followed. Once again the album was a self-financed zydeco affair, the whole thing recorded in a day. It had some great moments; the song 'The Shape I'm In' received airplay and kept the band on the road and working.

But Joe was searching for that alchemic formula. Their next album, *A Place in the World* showed some colour, but it moved the band away from their Americana origins. It still featured Butrumlis' accordion, but it was a bit more country, rockier, with a kind of Ry Cooder feel to it.

The alchemic mystery was revealed with the band's next venture into the studio to record their album, *Dear Children*. The zydeco flirtation was jettisoned for a more mainstream, blues-based/rock/country/soul feel, a move that paid-off in gold records and houses full of adoring fans.

The Black Sorrows' then-drummer, Peter Luscombe, who had joined the band for the *A Place in the World* album, can possibly throw some light on how and why the change took place. After a couple of false starts Peter and I finally met at Mario's café in Fitzroy and as some background, Peter told me that he had grown up with some unusual influences, such as The Monkees, for example:

I wanted to live in a house with my band and play music, get up to mischief, it looked like fun; the reality was of course, when I actually came to live with a bunch of musicians on the road, somewhat different.

As he lived in America as a child, another key influence was the various guests of the Ed Sullivan Show. There was also Peter's jazz drummer dad. Eventually, Peter — who would go on to play a major role in the Paul Kelly band, both as a drummer and talent scout — learnt jazz drum technique from Glen Bayliss. As a result, he spent years playing several nights a week with Australian master jazzman Vince Jones. 'But once I had proved to myself that I could hold my own to a degree in the jazz world,' Peter recalled that, 'I wanted to play rock'n'roll.' This led to a six-month stint with Tinsley Waterhouse. As Peter says: playing eight gigs a week … 'I learnt to hit hard in that band, really play the groove, it was something I needed to be able to do for what followed.'

What followed was playing with The Black Sorrows and Joe Camilleri.

It had been a slow build for Joe and the Black Sorrows. A couple of self-funded albums had allowed the band to tour. It was a case of: record album, release the album, play gigs and stay in vans and bad hotels, record another album that led to more gigs. As a result of this cycle, an audience slowly formed. According to Luscombe:

It was a hard-rocking band by this stage; we toured interstate, drove long miles, all the country towns and Brisbane, Adelaide. You could feel the band was building, especially when we played the Crowded House tour. On that tour we were playing to big audiences and getting our point across.

Then came the turning point as Luscombe recalled:

The Dear Children *album was when it all took off; Sony/CBS liked the record and signed the band to a distribution deal.*

Suddenly there was no need for Joe to take out a second mortgage to fund the next record; Sony/CBS would take care of that. With the deal came a few line-up changes; Mick Girasole replaced Johnny Charles on bass, and most importantly, Vika and Linda Bull came on board as backing singers. The band had finally found their formula for success, and in many ways the Bull sisters were the key ingredient. Says Luscombe:

> *Signing that Sony deal meant the money thrown at the band was ridiculous, $100,000 for the next record,* Hold on to Me. *Venetta Fields and Lisa Edwards had been singing back-ups on some tracks and I was hearing a kind of* Exile on Main Street/ *soul and R&B vibe for the record. We needed to replicate that sound, not only on record, but also at our live shows. I'd seen Vika sing somewhere and was knocked out. I knew she had a sister, which meant their voices would naturally blend. So I suggested to Joe that we get them in, rehearse some stuff and see how it goes. He was reluctant at first, the whole … 'Don't want no chicks on the road thing'. So we agreed on a six-week trial.*

But the probation period for the Bull sisters proved to be very short:

> *When we played the first gig with them, the audience went nuts. The sisters sang well and they had that whole Tongan dance moves thing going on; Joe was knocked out, the band had not only found two incredible singers but also gained a whole visual component to the show! Pretty soon the sisters had their own solo spots and were causing a sensation wherever and whenever they performed. Together with Vika and Linda, Wayne Burt also re-joined Joe in the band, adding another element to the sound.*

Wayne replaced Nick Smith on guitar, Nick no longer wanting to tour, preferring to stay home with his young family and concentrate on song writing with Joe. Luscombe recalled Burt's impact on the band at that time:

Wayne was the loose cannon, he would jump up on a table and peel off some amazing lead break, or play a crazy slide thing, it was a whole new sound.

The band had gone from playing inner-city pubs to selling out stadiums and major concert venues. The *Hold On To Me* album went triple-platinum, the band toured Europe four times in twelve months, and there was international anticipation for the band's next offering.

In 1990 Jen Anderson was added on violin and Richard Sega replaced Girasole on bass guitar. The band then went into the studio with a massive budget — around $300,000 from Sony/CBS — and recorded what would be their biggest album, *Harley and Rose*. The album peaked at #3 in Australia and remained in the top 50 for 51 weeks. It also sold well in northern Europe, reaching #5 in Norway and #36 in Sweden. The album produced two top 30 singles; 'Harley and Rose' and 'Never Let Me Go'.

But something was not right. Despite the massive amounts of money thrown at the band by their record company, and despite them playing huge, sold-out gigs throughout Australia and overseas, the musicians were earning only workers' wages. According to Wayne Burt:

I think I was earning maybe $120 a gig, sure we played eight or nine gigs a week when we were on the road, so it was a reasonable weekly wage — just. As the band became more successful, the quality of the accommodation certainly improved and we flew everywhere rather than drove, so the conditions of employment also improved, but the money stayed the same.

The problem was that once we came off tour the money dried up so we had to scramble around for other work before the next run of gigs. It was a hand to mouth existence for us even though we were playing in one of the most successful bands in the country at the time.

I must say however, I was given a $10,000 advance on royalties from the record company for my song 'Calling Card' *that appeared on the 'Harley and Rose' album. That advance couldn't have come at a better time; I had a young family and lots of bills to pay.*

This was not uncommon for musicians playing with mainstream bands in Australia in the '80s and early '90s. The budgets were huge, but the overheads were massive, the associated risks enormous, and the ultimate rewards for musicians relatively small. It would soon prove to be an unsustainable situation for many bands.

'80s Rock'n'roll — everyone is rolling in cash right? Wrong!

Joe Camilleri's two bands, Jo Jo Zeo and the Falcons and The Black Sorrows were deep in the white-water of a musical torrent, mammoth bands tumbling through the chaos of '70s and '80s mainstream excess. This was the *Countdown* era, where megastars like Mondo Rock, Little River Band, INXS, Divinyls, Paul Kelly, AC/DC, Hunters and Collectors, Australian Crawl and Midnight Oil appeared weekly on the nation's TV screens. It was a scene dominated by the capital-M 'Music Industry' — Michael Gudinski's Mushroom Records and its live music arm, the Frontier Touring Company.

Compared to today, there were fewer bands but working more often in a demarcated music scene. Jo Jo Zep and the Falcons played the beer barns (like The Pier Hotel in Frankston, The Ferntree Gully Hotel, Sentimental Bloke Hotel in Bulleen, Waltzing Matilda Hotel in Springvale and the Matthew Flinders in Chadstone) up to six nights a week. This was on top of touring elsewhere, recording, and appearing on television. Most gigs were booked through major agencies, and guarantees of over $3000 per show were normal, according to Falcons guitarist Jeff Burstin. The Falcons also got a percentage of the door take once the guarantee was reached. Burstin remembers walking into a hotel room and seeing a pile of money on the bed:

Shows were booked on the basis of guarantees, so we knew we
would cover our costs and the band would be paid on the basis
of the guaranteed payment from the venue on the night. But
we also took a percentage of the door, so if a ticket cost $15 we
might take $12 and the venue $3. I think that night there would
have been tens of thousands of dollars in cash piled up on that
hotel room bed.

So where did all that money go, promoters, booking agents, maybe
it was used to pay debts incurred by the band recording the albums?
Maybe. Sarah Taylor, sums it up in her excellent article for the *Cordite*
Poetry Review:

'In the early '80s live music was a reliable workhorse, offering a
life of regular gigs but punishing overheads, powerful agencies, beer
barns, drunk drivers, and unabashed arse-licking hierarchies.'[6]

Joe Camilleri explained to me that, in 1979, The Falcons grossed
over $1 million in the year, but he took home just $15,000. Jeff Burstin
also remembered that at that time, the band was paid around $100
per gig per musician, which was adjusted to a fixed weekly wage of,
he thinks, $300 per week. This was whether they worked or not —
but they always worked. 'There was so much administration', as Joe
put it, and that administration consisted of hiring a massive public-
address system, a van for transport, and a small army of roadies and
technicians to lug and operate the monster. In the Falcons' case, they
had Graeme Fraser mixing, Jeff Lloyd lugging, someone operating the
lights, a foldback or stage monitor mixer — and a drinks mixer. Yes,
a drinks mixer. 'My drink of choice was bourbon and coke and after
a couple of those I'd lurch off stage completely legless,' remembers
Burstin. But $1 million in 1979 was a lot of money, so someone was
getting screwed.

In retrospect, the '80s were really the start of the end of the rock
music boom. The biggest acts pulled massive crowds with their raucous
rock'n'roll, but that was all about to change, with the introduction
of random breath testing, fire regulations and, in Sydney's case, the

introduction of 99,000 pokies into venues across Sydney. Beer barns like the Bondi Lifesaver, which closed in 1980, were under threat. Sarah Taylor quotes an unnamed Sydney musician reminiscing about this time:

'I've always felt in retrospect that we were at the tail end of what we'd call the golden era of rock in Australia. The venues were just starting to change and something was different. People were changing their behavior; poker machines were coming in, the breathalyser.'[7]

With tougher drink-driving laws, the suburban beer barns in both Sydney and Melbourne were unviable. Taylor writes that 'suburban circuits quietly shrank and the golden age of Australian pub rock, for all its debatable pros and cons, was definitely one thing: past tense.'[8] It is a decline in the live music scene in Sydney has continued to this very day.

In Melbourne the live music scene flourished, especially in the poker-machine-free, public-transported inner city, where we could jump on a tram and be anywhere in minutes. As a result, Melbourne was the place were low-budget bands like the Dance Hall Racketeers came to spread their western swing gospel.

Andy Baylor and the Dancehall Racketeers

The Dancehall Racketeers were the first band in Australia to explore the western swing genre, a sub-genre of American country music that incorporates elements of blues, rock'n'roll and string band sounds. This was an interesting development given Australia's isolation from the genre's homelands of Fort Worth and Tulsa in Texas. Luckily for the Racketeers, Melbourne's alternate music audience understood what the band was trying to do. They gave them licence to try and sometimes fail. That's what you do with important music; you listen to the story and you pick up on the narrative.

The Racketeers were a hard band to pigeonhole; they played stuff by Duke Ellington and Bessie Smith, Doc Watson and Johnny Nobel. Big Joe Turner was in there and Jimmie Newman, Bob Wills, a bit of Hokum, Leroy Carr. You could call it western swing mixed with a bit of Cajun, bluegrass and hillbilly obscurity. I heard rockabilly mixed in as well, and a bit of bluesy vocal goodness courtesy of Paul Neuendorf. It had a wildness, and weirdness, and Melbourne loved what it heard.

I seemed to have met most of my sources for this book in eateries of various kinds around Melbourne. In this case I caught up with Andy at a groovy little Brunswick café, when he was down from his new New South Wales base to play a few gigs around town. His story, as I found out, is a fascinating one.

Baylor is the son of Jack Freeman, a Socialist Realist artist, and Gracia Baylor, who was one of the first women to be elected to Victoria's Legislative Council in 1979. Baylor lived in Healesville, attended Geelong Grammar and completed an Arts Degree at Monash.

Andy started playing guitar at around thirteen, inspired by The Beatles and the Stones, and later, when he delved deeper, Chuck Berry. He hung around The Eltham Supershows held in the Research Hall and attended other blues shows in pubs around Eltham, Research, St Andrews, Panton Hill and the Christmas Hills, listening to bebop jazz. Around this time he also heard Lightning Hopkins who was a revelation and led him to folk music at the Commune cooperative in Clifton Hill. He haunted Traynor's and the Green Man, listening to Paul Wookey, Margret RoadKnight and Dutch Tilders.

Jo Jo Zep and the Falcons introduced him to Louie Jordan and he found import record shops like Archie and Jugheads in the city, plus Readings in Carlton, which imported the latest blues and jazz from the US. Sue Matthews, the inaugural station manager at radio 3RRR, encouraged Andy to present a foundation blues and roots show on the station. This became the long-running *Chicken Mary* show, eventually presented by hosts Gary Young and Jimmy Beck. The show tangentially led Andy to form his funky soul and rhythm and blues outfit, The Honeydrippers. Says Andy:

We did the whole mainstream Premier Artist thing. We owned a PA, had a truck, had roadies and we played eight nights a week! We wanted to broaden the public's idea of what modern black music was about. We didn't rely on volume, we had no hit single — it was all about musical ideas — it's feel and soul. But the band was out of it's time … we supported Cold Chisel at The Manhattan Hotel and got full cans of beer thrown at us. We had a similar reception when we supported Midnight Oil at The Pier Hotel in Frankston. I guess what audiences lapped up in Melbourne's alternate scene; the mainstream didn't won't to hear.

After the Honeydrippers, Baylor did a complete turnaround. He began playing fiddle and steel guitar with the 'ocker-billy' outfit the Autodrifters, where he met his long-time musical partner Rick Dempster. Johnny Topper also played in the band. Andy says:

The Autodrifters was originally Peter Lillie's band but by the time I joined he had moved on, but his influence was palpable. He was an original who wrote songs with references to locality and place, very rare at the time. His dry Australian humour, his cutting satire was a huge influence on Melbourne song-writing and song-writers. He was a mix of Henry Lawson, Banjo Patterson, Chuck Berry and Merle Haggard. He showed how you could be roots Americana and Australian all at the same time.

When the Autodrifters' sojourn came to its inevitable end, Baylor moved to Sydney to play with country outfit Hit and Run. Andy listened to the country wing of Commander Cody and his Lost Planet Airmen, Dan Hicks and his Hot Licks, and the pedal-steel-driven Asleep at the Wheel. Then, somewhere along the way, he heard Bob Wills' album *For the Last Time* and he was hooked on that whole western swing thing.

In 1981, Andy Baylor and his former Autodrifters bandmate

Rick Dempster were sitting on the rooftop of a seven-storey building hard by Sydney's Railway Square. According to Dempster, the retinue of junkies and musicians who frequented the building referred to it as 'Marlboro Country' because of the huge billboard that stood outside the kitchen door on the roof. They were practising fiddle and harmonica duets, preparing for another day of busking on the streets of Sydney. Rick had just arrived back in Australia following his months-long musical pilgrimage through the US, armed with a new steel guitar and a head full of ideas. Andy in the meantime had been earning a living playing six nights a week at the Bourbon and Beefsteak up at the Cross. But it was proving too hard for the two friends to stay in Sydney by 1981, the introduction of poker machines into pubs and various planning restrictions meant that gigs dried up, it was time for a rethink. So that day sitting on that Sydney roof-top they decided it was time to go home. It was a mutual decision between Andy and Rick that they form a western swing band when they got back to Melbourne. According to Andy:

> Rick was a very knowledgeable, an interesting and charismatic figure at that time, a huge influence on my career and the development of my musical philosophies. He knew a huge amount about various historical styles of Americana, country music, rockabilly, hokum, Hawaiian, you name it, Rick had the ability to translate this knowledge to musical ideas when we were getting the Racketeers together, I learnt a lot from him at that time.

They recruited brothers Mike and Steve Andrews, on piano and drums respectively, Graeme Thomas on bass, as well as vocalist and multi-instrumentalist/guitarist Paul Neuendorf. Andy explained:

> Right from the start, we were very different to anything else at the time. Western Swing is essentially a jazz/swing with folk roots style of playing, but due to a number of factors it was almost hunted to extinction.

At first it was hard for the powers that be to understand what The Racketeers were trying to do, as Andy Baylor's brother Doral explained in his blog:

'The '80s decade was becoming a period of highly processed pop music, androgynous popstars and electronic music was now taking over from guitars and we were the antithesis of that. The music journalists back then had a difficult time working us out, they were always looking for an angle 'cause we were (in comparison to what was happening in the mainstream), pretty edgy. To us, we were just playing and enjoying the music we loved and were trying, somewhat idealistically, to make a living from it.'

Luckily the band were immediately welcomed by the inner-city music loving public. As Donal Baylor, who was not part of the original Racketeers but subsequently joined the second version, wrote on his blog:

'The Dancehall Racketeers couldn't have picked a better city in Australia to play western swing... with such a vibrant live music culture, [Melbourne] was one of the best places to locate bands and musicians who were faithful to many musical styles that had been neglected, discarded or modified beyond recognition.'

Paul Neuendorf, who was in the thick of Melbourne's alternative live music culture at the time, explained to me how the Racketeers were able to establish their eclectic repertoire and distinctive sound:

Melbourne was unique in the early 80's, we'd all hang out at Hound Dog's Bop (record) Shop in North Melbourne and when we could afford it, buy the latest imported jazz, country swing and country and blues records from America, obscure stuff. We'd then learn songs and glean ideas from the records we bought. It was a great time, we were young and we had the time to grind out arrangements, work out three-part harmonies, figure-out steel guitar, fiddle and guitar parts. We were learning on the job, hungry to try stuff and as a result developed our own unique sound. Andy loved Bob Wills and as a singer I tried to channel Bob's vocalist Tommy Duncan as well as Big Joe Turner and Fats Waller.

Another key factor in the Racketeers' success was Melbourne's lively and influential community radio network. Paul Neuendorf says:

I'm not sure if Gary Young and Jimmy Beck also hung out at the Bop Shop but somehow this Americana music seemed to find its way to them and they would play it on their Chicken Mary radio show on 3RRR. Rick (Dempster) also had an Americana music show on 3CR for years called Vinyl and Shellac and did the same. It was community radio that turned Melbourne audiences on to the West Texas low down stuff we were playing.

But how had they gone about getting what they were playing down on vinyl? Studio time was prohibitively expensive and vinyl reproduction was ridiculous, but the band had an ace up their sleeve in the form of their bass player Graeme Thomas who happened to own his own recording studio. Graeme, according to Baylor:

… was an electronics nut and had recording equipment set up in his lounge room. We recorded all of our first recordings at Graeme's place, all our EP's and singles, we couldn't afford to put out an album. Rocket 88 was the first EP we put out on Graeme's label, the infamous … Preston Records.

Rick Dempster wrote in the liner notes to The Dancehall Racketeers' album *The Preston Years* that the whole venture fell into place over seven months. It sounded as good as the band envisaged, but a great sounding band and a cult following was ultimately not enough to keep all of the Racketeers members focussed and happy. According to Dempster, 'It was too good for this world, after seven months and a whirlwind of gigs it fell apart.' The Dancehall Racketeers went into temporary recession.

Baylor hinted at a possible reason behind the breakup: the temptation of the ubiquitous stimulants used to fill long nights on the road, medicine that distracts from the work and leads to irreparable cracks in the united front of the band.

Despite this hiatus, the western swing seed had been planted, and there were plenty of other Melbourne bands ready to take the place of The Racketeers. Paul Neuendorf, for example, went on to play with the Melody Sheiks, a little café, jazzy outfit that played regularly around town, before hooking up with his old mate George Butrumlis to play with the hugely successful Zydeco Jump in the late '80s. Paul remembered the band's beginning:

> We played Bob Starkie's venue The Club in Smith Street Collingwood and held down long residencies at The Espy in St Kilda as well as Max Fink's: 'The Smith Street Bar and Grill' on Friday night. We played dance music, waltzes, polkas, music of the southern Louisiana bayous of the Cajuns, the Creoles and the Afro-Americans. It was music to move people, music that kept the punters dancing and drinking; and it was great music to play.

The Zydecos variously featured founder George Butrumlis on accordion and vocals, Paul Neuendorf on guitar and vocals, Toots Wostry on backing vocals and saxophone, Gerry Hale on fiddle, Alan Wright on vocals and bass, as well as Gary Samolin on drums. The band played festivals, toured Australia and appeared on television, including the ABC's *Big Gig* and Channel 7's *Tonight Live* show. They also toured with the legendary Buckwheat Zydeco; a *bon temps* band if ever there was one.

More rhythmic southern border bands followed for Neuendorf, including the much-travelled Tex-Mex outfit Texicali Rose with Sally Ford, Patrick Cronin, Paul Pyle and Hugh Waylan. Then came the Louisiana swamp, Chicago blues and boogie outfit Blues Before Sunrise, with Mike Andrews on keys and the extraordinary Ian Collard on blues, harp and vocals, and Alan Wright bass and Doug Kelly on drums. Then there was a stint with Dave Hogan's Meltdown

and a period playing banjo in a New Orleans all-brass outfit The Blow
It Out Ya Brass Band. Paul described why he loved to play this way:

> *I love being part of bands that have a strong identity and that*
> *play music from different musical regions, that's what makes*
> *it interesting for me, learning and discovering music that has*
> *flavours and colours, music that seemed deeper than the pop*
> *scene. The blues of course is embedded in everything I ever did*
> *and that ultimately is the music that I love to play.*

Sounds like a pretty good approach to me — an approach that has
kept Paul working for over forty years.

After the first incarnation of The Racketeers had collapsed, Baylor
and Dempster had formed a Hawaiian trio that played Tin Pan Alley
material in cafés and bars around the city. At the same time Andy was
a guitar-slinger-for-hire playing with various jazz musicians including
jazz drummer Allan Browne. Browne, with Baylor on board, held
down a regular gig at The Lemon Tree in Carlton and The Victorian
Jazz Club, and played the odd special opening or corporate event —
the usual fare of the working musician.

Then after a year or so came The Dancehall Racketeers Mark II
— officially named The New Dancehall Racketeers. It included Andy's
two younger brothers: Peter on guitar and Donal on violin, with Ed
Colbourne and Ian Hayes completing the line-up. According to Andy:

> *We were a working band, playing a set list of mixed styles.*
> *There was more Americana records available at the time, so*
> *we were able incorporate material into our set that had been*
> *unheard in this country before and mixed it up with a bit of*
> *jazz, like Herman's Woodchoppers Ball folk, even a bit of early*
> *R&B; but we played what worked, we played to the crowd. I*
> *was conscious of my responsibility to my two brothers, so I*
> *worked tirelessly during the week to find gigs that — at the*
> *time — I was able to do. At our peak we played over 250 shows*
> *a year! We played Tamworth, toured Sydney and supported*

American yodeller and crooner Slim Whitman as well as Slim Dusty and Chad Morgan. It was full on.

It was a hard life operating outside the mainstream, with no agent, no management…every day was a struggle… always thinking and finding ways to make this thing work and the means to make a living in a world that largely tuned into 'Wake Me Up Before You Go Go' on the radio.

Then Gary Young from Daddy Cool and Jo Jo Zep and the Falcons joined on drums and shifted the feel of the band, we got rockier, tougher. Gaz loved the band, all those string ties and cowboy shirts, he made a real difference, he is such a musical drummer, he really added colour to our whole sound.

At their gig at Sydney's Graphic Arts Club, The Racketeers had a brush with fame. It occurred when Richard East brought Led Zeppelin's Robert Plant along to hear the show, Andy told me:

Plant loved what he heard and offered us a support gig at the Old Swimming Pool in Olympic Parade in Melbourne. We got talking backstage about old blues songs and records and about what I was trying to do when I was with The Honeydrippers … a very pleasant conversation.

The big day arrived. The Racketeers drove up in their station wagon full of equipment, only to be confronted with Plant's semitrailers worth of gear, as Andy said:

Plant was all high volume and rock'n'roll shtick, I remember Richie Heyward, Little Feat's drummer, was in the band. Here we were playing with rock royalty with all their amplified accoutrements — Marshalls, massive PA's the whole catastrophe — and here we were just a little band from Melbourne playing through our home-grown Goldentone amps. When we walked out on stage resplendent in our string ties people laughed, but we weren't fazed, we played what we played … Roy Brown's

'Good Rockin' at Midnight', stuff like that, down-home rhythm and blues and eventually we won over the crowd.

After the show, we're backstage hanging out with Robert Plant who really liked what we played. I had a great conversation with him. Then our roadie Frank came into the room ...' 'Hey Andy do you know they recorded your show?' ... 'yeah? Really? I'd didn't really think too much about it ... until a few years later when Plant put out this record ... The Honeydrippers Volume 1, the band was made up of Jimmy Page, Nils Rogers and Jeff Beck. The record featured our version of Roy Brown's 'Good Rockin' at Midnight', same riffs, same key change ... an exact copy ... go figure.

Now all this may be just coincidence, but a few years later Plant and Page reached an out-of-court settlement with Willy Dixon, who claimed the pair plagiarised the music from Dixon's song 'Bring it on Home' and the lyrics from his composition 'You Need Love'. And there are many more examples, most notably the long-running court battle about the true authorship of the music for 'Stairway to Heaven' ... you be the judge.

Andy is very proud of the New Dancehall Racketeers explaining that the band:

ended up playing over a thousand gigs, we played Aboriginal settlements in the Northern Territory, festivals, it was a wild ride!!! Then Donal was headhunted to play fiddle with Slim Dusty's band, Peter also left to do his thing so the Racketeers went into recession once again.

Never one to stand still for very long, Baylor moved on:

I travelled to the United States for about six months, did the whole music pilgrimage thing. I met and played with my musical heroes, legends like David Grisman, Flaco Jiminez, Cajun great Dewey Balfa and fiddle player, Johnny Gimble.

The Uptown Club in full cry, L–R: Cy Watts, trombone; Pixie Roberts, clarinet; Ade Monsbourgh, trumpet; Keith Cox, banjo; Russ Murphy, drums; Lou Silbereisen, bass; Bud Baker, guitar and Graeme, piano. Roger Bell absent. Seated down front, L–R: Max Marginson, pianist Rex Green and trumpet player Ken Owen. Photo courtesy: Graeme Bell

top: Traynor's in the early '60s. Photo courtesy: Australlian Music Directory 1st Editon

middle: Ms Georgia Lee. Photos courtesy: the Australian Jazz Museum

bottom: Graeme Bell band wiggin' out. Photos courtesy: the Australian Jazz Museum

top: Judy Jacques
sophisticated lady. Photo
courtesy: Judy Jacques

bottom: Judy sining out
with the Yarra's. Photo
courtesy: Judy Jacques

The Loved Ones with Ian Clyne (standing centre) with Gerry Humphries front right.
Photo courtesy: Australlian Music Directory 1st Editon

top: Glen Tomasetti. Photo
courtesy: Sarah Tomasetti

bottom: Glen Tomasetti
with Trevor Lucas at
Traynors. Photo courtesy:
Australlian Music Directory
1st Editon

top: Jeannie Lewis. Photo courtesy: Australlian Music Directory 1st Editon

bottom: Garry Kinnane at Traynors. Photo courtesy: Australlian Music Directory 1st Editon

top: Unknown artist Jazz Centre 44. Photo courtesy: Australlian Music Directory 1st Editon

bottom: Dutch Tilders. Photo courtesy: Margret RoadKnight

Margret RoadKnight leads the band at The Outpost Inn.
Photo courtesy: Margret RoadKnight

top: Margret with the Jazz Preachers at The Troubadour. Photo courtesy: Margret RoadKnight

bottom: Margret at the Dallas Brookes Hall. Photo courtesy: Margret RoadKnight

top: Judith Durham, 1966. Photo: Robert Whitaker, courtesy: Graham Simpson

bottom: Margret at a meeting of the clan, L–R: Margret, Mattyn, Wyndham-Read, Trevor Lucas, Glen Tomasetti, David Lumsden, Danny Spooner and Frank Traynor. Photo courtesy: Margret RoadKnight

top: Smoky Dawson. Photo
courtesy: Australlian Music
Directory 1st Editon

middle: Smoke and Flash. Photo
courtesy: the author

bottom: On the road with
Smoky Dawson. Photo
courtesy: the author

top: Ol'55 with Frankie J. Holden in full flight, Photo courtesy: Wilbur Wilde

bottom: Jo Jo Zep and the Falcons from the rear, Tony Faehse, Jeff Burstin, Joe Camilleri, Wilbur Wilde, John Power and Gary Young. Photo courtesy: Wilbur Wilde

top: Flying Circus on the Arcadia embarking for US, Feb 1971, L–R: Colin Walker, Doug Rowe, Jim Wynne, Terry Wilkins, Sam See (the pretty one). Photo courtesy: Sam See

bottom: The Dingoes, L–R: John Bois, John Lee, Brod Smith, Kerryn Tolhurst and Chris Stockley. Photo: Kevin MacLean

Vika and Linda Bull. Photo courtesy: Vika and Linda

top: Blues Before Sunrise, Fitzroy Gardens, L–R: Ian Collard, Paul Neuendorf, Doug Kelly, Al Wright and Aaron Choulai. Photo courtesy: Paul Neuendorf

bottom: Kerri Simpson. Photo courtesy: Carol Milton

top: Dancehall Racketeers, Aberdeen Hotel, 1981, L–R: Mike Andrews, Andy Baylor, Steve Andrews, Rick Dempster, Graham Thomas and Paul Neuendorf. Photo courtesy: Paul Neuendorf

bottom: The Hotsie Totsies: Jim Conway, Mic Conway, Sue Bradley and Paul Neuendorf. Photo: Sue Jones

top: Andy Baylor, traveling man.
Photo courtesy: Andy Baylor

bottom: Paul Williamson. Photo
courtesy: the author

top: Chris Wilson. Photo courtesy: the author

bottom: At the launch of *Daddy Who?* L–R: Jeff Burstin, Chris Tabone, the author, Ross Wilson, Andy Scott, Gary Young obscured. Photo: Ellen Cheng

Then I came back to Melbourne and freelanced, playing with people like Slim Dusty and Kerri Simpson, The Moovin' and Groovin' Orchestra, Swingin' Sidewalks and at the same time formed the Cajun Combo.

An interesting interlude was playing with both Redgum and Kevin Bloody Wilson. Redgum were very corporate, mainstream, it was all about the business, which I found rather odd for a band that prided itself on its left-wing credentials. Kevin Wilson on the other hand was a cottage industry. He was a western suburbs boy — knew what his audience wanted and his audience loved him for it. Sold records by the truck-load at his gigs, as a consequence he was generous to his band and couldn't have been easier to get along with, such an interesting insight into the music business at the time.' Then came Andy Baylor's next band, the Cajun Combo.

The Cajun Combo

The Cajun Combo, according to Baylor, played a hybrid of Louisiana-inspired Cajun dance music, blues, and original tunes delivered with a definitive Australian roots flavour. It featured the cream of Australian musicians — Daddy Cool's rhythm section of drummer Gary Young and bassist Wayne Duncan plus Sam Lemann on guitar and Peter Linden on steel guitar. As Andy explained:

It was such a treat working with Gary and Wayne, they were Australia's Duck Dunne and Al Jackson from Booker T and the M.G's. they played simple, straight ahead feels, but they knew how to dress-up a song, with that quintessential Duncan/ Young groove.

The band again played festivals like Tamworth and held down the Tuesday night slot at Fitzroy's Rainbow Hotel that lasted over ten years. It was probably a golden age for independent bands in Australia, as Andy recalled:

> It was a time when digital recording first came into vogue. It meant that we didn't have to hire studios and cut expensive vinyl records. It truly was a great time for independent artists. Gary Young in fact put up the money to make our first CD. We sold it through Shock Records and it went well, shifted over 5000 copies.

The Combo supported a range of international acts including John Mayall, Screamin' J. Hawkins and Queen Ida, and acted as backing band for Cajun legends like Louisiana Red. Andy remember that night well:

> Red played a cordless guitar and liked to walk out into the audience, playing and mixing with the people. He could do it because of an aerial that sat on top of the amp and caught the signal from his guitar. It was all going swimmingly until Wayne hooked the aerial onto the headstock of his bass, he didn't know what to do. The look of utter terror and confusion on his face was precious; Gary of course laughed his head off.

Then the Cajun Combo got the call every independent Melbourne band dreamed of — the gig supporting Bob Dylan. Andy explained to me how it all happened:

> Peter Noble, he of the Byron Bay Blues Festival fame, was touring Bob Dylan in the early '90s. Peter let it be known to our booking agent at the time, Suzette — who also happened to be President of the Australian chapter of the Barbie Doll fan club, she looked like Barbie as well, long blonde hair, willowy, with a pinched waist — that Bob wanted a support band that was non-mainstream, a little different, authentic. Twenty bands sent Peter their CD including the Cajun Combo. You

wouldn't believe it but Bob chose us as his support. But he was only offering $500 for the whole band, for which we had to find the airfare to Sydney, hotel rooms the whole thing, so we simply couldn't do it. The next band off the rank to win Bob's nod was my brothers Donal and Peter's Western Swing band … The Baylor Brothers Band, so what was I gonna do? I flew to Sydney to play with my brothers.

It was the time that Bob had had a bit of trouble with an Australian exotic dancer, Gypsy Fire, she claimed an affair with Dylan, which caused trouble at home. He was also hanging out with Brett Whiteley possibly taking some powerful medicine, not a goodtime perhaps for him to be playing a string of concerts at Sydney's State Theatre.

Before the show I hung out backstage with Bob's bass player and Musical Director Tony Garnier and apparently, he had sent a message to the band via Tony that he didn't want anyone to speak to him or look at him before the show.

When Bob finally arrived, he was wearing a hood over his head, shades, Mr Incognito. The band followed instructions, no one looked at him 'til show time. But when the Bob band finally played it was a little ragged, maybe too much medicine? Whatever it was all those pregame instructions hadn't helped that much.

Post show we were all backstage again, taking full advantage of the hospitality, the wide variety of food, the odd drink, very pleasant. Bob was paying special attention to Suzette, he took her aside, talked intimately; there was a lot of chemistry going on. Then Bob's manager walked into the room, took a look around saw what was going on and hit the alarm button, ordered the room cleared, everybody out and out now!

Suzette was literally dragged off Bob and thrown onto a couch as the rest of the backstage entourage were ushered out of the room. I was concerned about our agent; she was on the couch sobbing, so I sat with her. I looked around and saw the bodyguards arrive, big boys, big shoulders, not to be messed with. Now Bob Dylan is a diminutive man, so he was easily picked up by his minders and carried out of the room, his legs off the ground, his feet kicking in mid-air. I couldn't believe what I was seeing. They carried him down the corridor and marched him into the goods-lift. The last time I saw the spokesperson for a generation he was being held under the arms by his bodyguards, feet off the ground and thrashing around, demanding that he be let go ... 'let me down, let me down!!!' But they didn't let him down, the doors to the lift closed and he was gone.

Just like Bob Dylan, Andy Baylor is still on the move, travelling the back roads of popular culture, drawing inspiration from many forgotten music forms and playing everything from the blues to Bebop, Cajun to Western Swing, Tex-Mex to Rockabilly, R'n'B to New Orleans jazz, Country to Rock, Folk to Funky. Like Keith Glass has said: 'Andy Baylor is one of Melbourne's greatest musical treasures ... he lives by his trade and his trade is music.'

CHAPTER 11

MELBOURNE'S
NEW WAVE

THE VIEW FROM THE EDGE

T he Dancehall Racketeers were just one strand of Melbourne's independent music scene of the '80s. It was a scene that produced bands like The Birthday Party (fronted by Nick Cave), The Models, I'm Talking, Men at Work and Dave Graney and his expressionistic rock visage. This was a scene supported by a relative abundance of the venues I've already mentioned, plus independent record producers, a lively street press and community radio network. It was the confluence of all of these factors that has allowed Melbourne to nurture such a dynamic and unique independent music scene right up to the current day. I knew this scene well; as a member of several independent bands in the '80s, I was able to observe how the system worked. In fact, I saw first-hand the transition of one independent band from the dingy, inner-city pub circuit to what seemed to be overnight international success.

Attila and the Panelbeaters

In the late '70s and early eighties, I played Melbourne's independent music circuit with Attila and the Panelbeaters. They were a band that certainly didn't boast a drinks mixer — we operated very much outside Molly Meldrum's, and *Countdown's*, gaze. Like most independent bands, we were a small cottage industry; we wrote our own songs, directly approached venues for gigs, produced our own publicity material and funded our own recordings. We could be found at venues like The Albion Hotel in Carlton, The Sarah Sands in Brunswick, The Aberdeen and Metropol in Fitzroy, and The Prince of Wales in St Kilda. Along the way we managed to build up an enthusiastic following, perhaps not one as large as that of others on the scene, but enough to warrant, say, a Thursday night slot at The Sarah Sands. It was there that I witnessed first-hand a transitional moment in Melbourne's music history.

We shared the bill that night with a quirky little band from Fitzroy North that consisted of a guitar player/singer and a little blond leprechaun of a flautist/saxophonist. They were an act that kept you on your toes and they seemed to transcend genres; a bit of folk, a bit of jazz, some rock'n'roll, and many Australian references. The singer told a great story on stage, You could tell that, not for him the primeval inner-city musical jungle, he wanted to capture the world's attention. The singer was Colin Hay, the leprechaun was Greg Ham and the band was Men at Work.

I remember the fee for the night was a grand total of $200 between both bands. The pub owners had gone out of their way to publicise the gig, with giant posters, hand-bills and — as the headline act — our names emblazoned in lights on an illuminated billboard attached to the pubs' Brunswick Road wall. It read: ATTILA AND THE PANELBEATERS with men at work. We filled the rear room of the pub with dancing, drinking panelettes, the name for our regular followers, and the M@W crowd.

After a few weeks the venue owners who were, shall we say, very much part of the pre-#metoo generation, decided that strippers and topless barmaids would pull in an even bigger crowd on a Thursday than a bunch of tribal rock dogs from Fitzroy. *We're not sackin' ya mate, you stay on play your set then back the strippers, waddya reckon?* This was the offer. *I'll give youse the whole $200, can't do better than that mate.*

I knew that Peter Starkie had quit Skyhooks to play guitar with Dave Fleet and Joe Camilleri in Roger Rocket and the Millionaires — a band that backed stripper Mary Doody Scott Pilkington on a tour of mining towns in Western Australia in the '70s. But backing strippers? Nah! We moved on.

A couple of months later I was walking around the Plaka in Athens when I heard a familiar riff pouring out of cafés and bars all over the city. What was that riff, it sounded so familiar? I sat down in a bar, ordered a coffee and ouzo and waited. When I heard the first notes of Men at Work's 'Who Could it Be Now' burst through the house speakers I nearly choked on my olives and grilled octopus. What the fuck had happened? Men At Work had achieved what had previously seemed impossible: they had come from the pubs, clubs and bars of urban Melbourne and gone on to achieve a worldwide #1 single and album. When I got back to Melbourne I drove past the Sarah Sands and smiled when I saw the billboard still sporting 'THE PANELBEATERS supported by men at work'. I have a shot of it somewhere ...

For Attila and the Panelbeaters it was back to playing Melbourne's more niche venues. On a good night we might command $200, but often it was less. That's $200 split seven ways, six musicians and one roadie. At least we owned our own PA, an old clapped-out piece of shit we made ourselves out of thumping speakers stuffed into blackened, chip-board W bins. Speed, our roadie/sound man, lumped that thing into bars and up stairs and onto stages for six years. Every band we knew did the same thing. It was the punk ethos of do-it-yourself, an ethos that worked against the grain of the monolithic, commercial music business. We got to play exactly what we wanted, and we got to choose where we played.

But the independent ethos has its costs. There's the administrative work associated with keeping the band going, the media releases, the posters, the hustling for gigs, and more. It was punishing, it took up hours of time, and this was then time not spent rehearsing, writing or practising. In many ways, independence meant cocooning oneself in known environments and endlessly playing the venues you know would receive you favourably. If you moved outside of your supportive enclaves you were often met with resistance from people who failed to understand what the fuck you were doing. It was often a brutal experience and, if an independent act happened to land a gig supporting a mainstream band, it could be humiliating. The audience may boo or throw things like full beer cans and coins. The audience paid their money to see the Hunters and Collectors or The Oils, and dance to the hits they heard on the radio; they didn't come to listen to a bunch of hippies from Fitzroy play the songs they'd written but no one had ever heard. There's only so much of this stuff you can take as an independent band before the creative process shatters and musicians disappear into distractions like cheap alcohol, regular work, families and golf. In the Panelbeaters' case we reached that point after six years, going into hiatus in the early '80s. But I wasn't done yet; my next outing was with a band directly inspired by Melbourne's unique experimental electronic underground, oh, and Australian Rules football.

The 'Ken Brothers and the Little Band scene

Panelbeater guitarist Simon Goss and myself formed a little duo called the 'Ken Brothers (as in fuc*ken* brothers, get it? Gawd we were funny). We'd written a bunch of football-themed songs, very much aimed at the country/suburban footy fan rather than big business AFL, or VFL, as it then was. In other words, we wrote the songs for our own amusement and the amusement of our friends and loyal Panelbeater fans. The songs were a bit of a laugh, but they also, hopefully, made a subtle point about the working-class origins of Australian Rules football, a code developed from an amalgam of rugby and an Indigenous game played with a possum skin stuffed with grass called Marngrook. Although the hybrid game was initially played by elite cricketers as means of keeping fit in winter, Australian rules was subsequently played by young men (and some young women) in a team-based competition. The players were largely drawn from Melbourne's industrial inner suburbs and both the game, the players and their suburban teams were enthusiastically embraced by their local communities, so much so that Australian Rules football outstripped cricket as Melbourne's most popular sporting code.

The 'Ken Brothers' songs looked back at the suburban history of the game, with titles like 'Pre-game/No Wuzz,' 'Footy Utopia,' 'Bruce Doull's Gotta New Pair of Boots,' 'The Day the Flick-pass Died,' 'Footy Finals Fever (it gets ya in the head like a meat-cleaver)' — you get the picture.

Our approach in many ways was inspired by Melbourne's Little Band Movement; a music collective and the brainchild of members from the Primitive Calculators band, amongst others. It was based in the halls and lounge rooms of Fitzroy North from the late '70s. The movement was made up of a host of primitive musicians, as well as non-musicians including poets and painters, who applied a Dada-ish approach to making music. Julian Knowles from the Sydney Conservatorium of Music described the movement as 'a mixture of epileptic drum machine rhythms, stabbing synth lines and creepy/witty lyrics making for oddly compelling results'.

The Little Band scene was a modernist participatory Bolshevik artistic movement, where bands shared not only equipment but also members. 3RRR DJ Alan Bamford brought the movement to wider attention when he recorded Little Band gigs using a reel-to-reel tape recorder and a Shure microphone, and then broadcast the results on his midnight-to-dawn shift program. Bamford subsequently collaborated with Max Robenstone, owner of Climax Records in Fitzroy, and together they released the *Little Bands* (1980) EP featuring studio recordings by Morpions, Ronnie and the Rhythm Boys, The Take and Too Fat to Fit Through the Door. A little later, Richard Lowenstein (son of Wendy Lowenstein, the left–wing musicologist we met earlier) wrote and directed the feature film *Dogs in Space*, which was loosely based on the Little Band scene and featured many of its principal players, like The Primitive Calculators and Marie Hoy.

The 'Ken Brothers shared the democratic, participatory mind-set of the Little Band movement. We thought it would be interesting to take its post-punk approach and apply it to our wildly chaotic suite of footy songs. Over one Saturday afternoon at Richmond Recorders, we recorded four tracks using an 808 drum machine. We had access courtesy of the Panelbeaters' roadie mate Speed, who was studying a sound engineering course at Richmond; he got to practise on us and we got an afternoon of free recording. We named the EP *Footy Rock*, mastered the whole thing ourselves, and had a mate design the cover. Then we pressed a hundred or so vinyl copies and staged a launch at The Sporting Club Hotel in Brunswick, expecting a few of our mates to turn up for a laugh. That was the extent of our vision for the band.

Good plan, only I got my journalist mate Gib Wettenhall involved. A media release was written, a dance devised, a character invented: Professor Von Flickin-passer, played by Fitzroy Councillor, professional punter and ratbag Kevin Healy, who doubled as emcee for the event. We also inveigled Melbourne/Essendon ruckman Crackers Keenan to formally launch the record by handballing a footy through a target with a *Footy Rock* logo spread across the bullseye (his critique of the record centered on the phrase *hmmm it's a bit different*)!

What could possibly go wrong? Actually, it went well, too well, *overwhelmingly* well. A gaggle of journalists from every television news channel turned up to the launch, plus journos from radio as well as the Fairfax and Murdoch Presses. A very young Sarah Henderson, the future Member for Corangamite and Federal Senator but then a journalist with Channel Seven, appeared at the pub sporting a Melbourne footy jumper and a pair of very short shorts (still have the footage Sarah, just sayin'). Sarah, with fellow conspirator Gib Wettenhall, proceeded to demonstrate the subtleties of the *Footy Rock* dance in front of massed TV cameras and a crowd of flogger-waving, streamer-throwing, specky-taking hippies.

That night, vision of the whole surrealist onslaught was flashed across the nations' television screens.

Whadyya think that's all about Cheryl?

Buggered if I know Bert, they're all on drugs! Look at that long hair!! Have … an iced Vo Vo dear.

Offers poured in for TV appearances, footy club shows, newspaper interviews and radio spots — but we weren't a band, we were a drum-machine. Plus we were infirmed, I stuttered and Simon — or Squid as he was known- was partly deaf from years of standing in front of his Fender twin amp turned up to 11; plus he played hockey at school and knew fuck-all about football — hardly a formula for mainstream media exposure. So what do you do when a post-punk concept became a *multi-media phenomenon*? You ride it out and see where the whole thing takes you.

We scored a regular spot on a 3CR community radio footy show called *The David Rhys-Jones Football Show*, and one of the songs from the EP became the theme for Victorian Football Association footy segment on 3RRR's *Coodabeen Champions*. Then the whole thing went apeshit when radio host and future Senator Derryn Hinch played our songs on his 3AW AM show for a couple of weeks. Suddenly we knew how Charles Goodyear felt when he accidentally dropped sulphur into latex and invented vulcanised rubber. Demand for the record was ridiculous; Max Robenstone from Climax Records contacted us with the news that every independent record shop in Melbourne wanted a copy of the *Footy Rock* EP. Fuck! We'd only pressed a hundred!

A highlight came when we played a *Melbourne Times* newspaper event, attended by legendary Carlton halfback, Bruce Doull, the namesake of of our song 'Bruce Doull's got a New Pair of Boots'. As a lifelong Blues supporter I could hardly contain my excitement when he bought several copies of our record, featuring a cartoon of the man himself on the cover, 'for the wife', apparently. Mike Fitzpatrick, Carlton's captain at the time, also turned up to the event and bought several copies. I had reached the top of the mountain as far I was concerned, but then the whole thing got a bit wobbly, and we fell.

A major promoter offered us a series of gigs supporting Paul Kelly and the Dots, plus the ska band No Nonsense, at The Venue, a rock dive on the Esplanade in St Kilda. We grappled with our founding punk — anti-establishment ethos, an ethos that was the very antithesis of the monolithic mainstream music business we were being encouraged to join. It simply wasn't what we had in mind when we started the whole project. But we had struck a nerve and thought maybe we should see where it took us, not stopping to consider that maybe a couple of electric guitars — one of which was played very badly by me — plus a drum machine and one vocalist was not the standard formula for mainstream rock stardom. But we had a plan.

For the show we bought an old ironing board as a stage prop for the drum machine, draping the whole thing in team colors. We then enlisted our Panelbeaters bandmate Phil King to dress as a goal umpire, doubling up as sound-mixer and raffle-ticket salesperson (we planned to raffle a chook during the show). Great. But we didn't count on the expectation that support bands were supposed to not only perform for almost nothing, but also act as unpaid members of the road crew.

Simon and I arrived at the venue an hour before showtime. We walked into the foyer of the cavernous Venue only to be immediately accosted by the promoter:

'Are you the 'Ken Brothers?'
'Speaking.'

'Where the fuck have you been?'

'Sorry?'

'You were supposed to be here at 1.00pm to help load-in the PA?'

'What ARE you talking about?'

'You're the support act, so part of your role is helping the roadies load-in.'

'Sorry mate we have day jobs, couldn't get off work.'

'Well I'll try and smooth it over with the crew, you'll just have to hang around 'til after the show at around 2am and help them load out.'

'Hmmm sure, well … maybe not!'

We both mumbled under our breath.

We found our allocated space in the Green Room and watched what was like a scene from *Trainspotting* unfold. There were dealers dealing smack and skinny, pale, leather clad spider-men cooking it up, shooting it up and throwing up. This was not where we belonged, but we were there and we needed to see this thing through. We quickly changed into our footy gear and waited for the call: *ladies and gentlemen, The 'Ken Brothers!* The curtains pulled back to reveal an ironing board, and Phil hit play on 'Eye of the Tiger'. We let the dramatic song run for a while as we handballed a plastic football back and forth. Squid fired up the drum machine and it sprang into action, and suddenly the New Orleans beat of 'Footy Finals Fever' filled the room:

> *Sittin' in a doctor's surgery*
> *Doctor, doctor what's happening to me*
> *He said son it's plain to see*
> *Ya got footy finals fever in the nth degree*

Puzzled looks from the stovepipe-trousered hipsters greeted us at the end of the song. We ploughed on, the preprogrammed shuffle beat of 'Bruce Doull's Got a New Pair of Boots' punched through the cigarette smoke, but we were going down like a deflated footy.

Eventually it was time for the raffle draw. I picked up a thawing chicken from an esky, reached into Phil's hat and announced the winning number. I was met with a mixture of groans and a scream of delight. I handballed the dripping chook to the prize winner, who raised it triumphantly above her head as she ran back to her seat, carried by a wave of cheering and applause.

That show was the end of the wild, hysterical mess for us; the reality of the music business was too dangerous. The 'Ken Brothers were destined never to raffle a chook again.

HOUSE BANDS,

SIDEMEN & SIDEWOMEN

OF MELBOURNE

THE MELBOURNE SOUND

K eith Richards said it best:

As a sideman, it's your job to be invisible; you should be heard and not seen. You've got to know who you are and where you stand in the hierarchy. The hard thing for a sideman is that the better you are at your job the less people notice you, and that's the whole point.[1]

Side musicians perform in the shadows. You may not know their names, but they are the sound of the band, bringing the vision of the writer to light. You'd know their work, if not their name. Everyone knows that Joe Camilleri was the singer for Jo Jo Zep and the Falcons, but only fans would be aware that Gary Young, Jeff Burstin, Tony Faese, John Power, Wayne Burt and Wilbur Wilde variously made up the band and played on the records.

John Farnham is one of Australia's best known singers, but only geeks know his show is augmented by Stuart Fraser and Brett Gorsed on guitar, Angus Burchell on drums, Craig Newam bass. Chong Lim plays keys and acts as John's musical director and Lindsay Field, Lisa Edwards, Susie Ahern, Rod Davis and Michelle Serret-Curiso sing backup. Paul Kelly's band — Ash Naylor and Dan Kelly on guitars, Peter Luscombe on drums, Bill MacDonald on bass, Cameron Bruce on keys and Vika and Linda Bull on backup vocals — is one of the best in the business.

These often anonymous 'sidies' help establish the reputation of the front man or lead. In some ways it's a good gig, all care, no responsibility; if the band stuffs up, it's the reputation of the singer that suffers. But there are considerable downsides — the pay can be minuscule, and sometimes a side-musician can be as disposable as toilet paper.

You might see saxophonist Paul Williamson playing with his outfit, Paul Williamson's Hammond Combo at the Rainbow in Fitzroy, then later in the week he'd be touring with Dire Straits. Maybe on the weekend you'll see him backing Vince Jones or playing baritone with Big Jay McNeely or tenor with Cornell Dupree at the Palais. That's the life of a gigging Melbourne musician like Paul Williamson; have sax will travel.

Then there's Melbourne bass player Stephen Hadley. Stephen has been a Black Sorrow, played in the Paul Kelly band and had stints with Vince Jones, Men at Work and Kate Ceberano. He's been the musical director for *The Man in Black,* a Tex Perkins theatre show dramatising the life of Johnny Cash, and toured with Stevie Wonder. He also bailed on a Hornets gig when he was asked to fly to Los Angeles on short notice to screen test for a role as a young Keith Richards. I don't think he got the gig, but it was the best excuse for not playing a show I've ever heard.

Then there's guitarist/keyboard player James Black. He's played keys with Mondo Rock and Men at Work as well as being part of the RocKwiz Orkestra and has owned a record label. Let's not forget Shane O'Mara, Ash Naylor … the list goes on and on. These are musicians I know of largely because I've either played with them or known them personally for many years. I could have chosen dozens of individual players whose sound encapsulates the approach that is unique to the city, but the book would have been twice as long.

Melbourne House Bands

Let's look briefly at the history of Melbourne House Bands and session musicians. Within the 'sidies' category are session musicians. When we think of session musicians, we might think of America's famous Wrecking Crew. They were a loose collective of session musicians based in Los Angeles who played on thousands of studio recordings in the '60s and early '70s, including several hundred Top 40 hits. The Wrecking Crew musicians were not publicly recognised during their era, but were viewed with reverence by industry insiders. They are now considered one of the most successful and prolific session recording units in music history.

Most of the players associated with the Wrecking Crew — including Dr John, Leon Russell, Glen Campbell, drummers Jim Keltner and Hal Blaine, bassist Carol Kaye (the only female member), keyboardist Larry Knechtel, guitarist Tommy Tedesco — had formal backgrounds in jazz or classical music. They were the de facto house band for Phil Spector and helped realise his Wall of Sound production style and subsequently became the most requested session musicians in Los Angeles.[2]

They played behind Jan and Dean, Sonny & Cher, the Mamas and the Papas, the 5th Dimension, Frank Sinatra and Nancy Sinatra. They were also the 'ghost players' on records such as The Byrds' 1965 rendition of Bob Dylan's 'Mr. Tambourine Man', the first two albums by the Monkees, and the Beach Boys' 1966 album *Pet Sounds*. Arguably the Wrecking Crew developed their own 'sound' that came to define that era of LA pop.

The Wrecking Crew as an entity rarely toured, though members such as Dr John, Leon Russell, and Glen Campbell became stars in their own right. Melbourne had its own versions of the Wrecking Crew in the '60s in the form of The Strangers, The Thunderbirds and The Lincolns, with all three adding their own Melbourne twist to the genre. The Strangers in particular can be seen as the closest to Melbourne's version of the Wrecking Crew.

The Strangers

Melbourne's The Strangers were the crème de le crème, the most important Australian house band from 1963 to 1967 and possibly beyond. They also had a distinguished career in their own right. During the early to mid-'60s The Strangers were everywhere: onstage, on television, and constantly recording studio. The band were consequently acknowledged as one of the most versatile and musically accomplished bands in the country. As the *Milesago* website postulated, The Strangers played a vital role in shaping the sound of Australian Sixties pop.

The original members were an early Melbourne super group: Laurie Arthur on guitar, Peter Robinson on bass and vocals, Graeme Thompson on drums and Fred Weiland also on guitar. They had all worked with most of the top Melbourne dance bands of the day, including The Thunderbirds, The Planets, and The Chessmen. But it was in late 1964 that The Strangers' career really took off. Laurie Arthur had gone and was replaced by a hot shot eighteen-year-old guitarist/singer, John Farrar (Farrar went on to marry Melbourne singer Pat Carroll and wrote and produced a string of international #1 hits for Olivia Newton John).

With Farrar on board The Strangers were now in furious demand, both as session musicians and playing backup for top solo artists. To quote *Milesago*:

'To handle the punishing workload and bookings, the group started their own Entertainment Agency managed by old friend Ron Fletcher, and they also formed a private company, Magnum Productions Pty. Ltd. (under the wing of Elmo Moss & Assoc.) to handle their business affairs'.

The group were voted top instrumental/vocal group of 1964 and as a result in 1965, it was reputed that The Strangers had only 15 days off in the whole year and in March 1966, manager Brian de Courcy, claimed that they had worked 'twenty-nine hours a day, fourteen days a week, four hundred and seventy-two days last year.'[3]

The Strangers were then hired as the house band for new Australian pop TV show *The Go!! Show*, backing the numerous solo singers who appeared on the program. As a result, the band became a household name throughout the country. The Strangers were almost constantly in the studio as the main in-house band for W&G's stable of solo acts. They also freelanced, backing solo singers signed to other labels.

The Thunderbirds

In the late '50s and early '60s The Thunderbirds' classic lineup included drummer and founder Harold Frith, Murray Robertson on piano, Charlie Gauld on guitar, Henri Bource on sax/flute, and Gordon Onley on bass. Like the Strangers they had a dual role, firstly as the house band at a number of local dances such as Earl's Court in St Kilda and the Preston Town Hall. And they were also studio musicians who backed solo singers for various labels around town. But they also had a solid career in their own right, recording a clutch of classic instrumentals in the pre-Beatles era of the early to mid-'60s including, 'The Rockin' Rebels', 'Wild Weekend', 'The Theme from the Rat Race', 'New Orleans Beat', 'Delilah', 'The Riptides', 'Machine Gun', 'Teen Scene', 'Royal Whirl', 'Yippee Hoedown' and 'Dardanella'.

It was the combination of their own recordings and their freelance recording session work that cemented the band's reputation as one of Australia's premier backing bands of their time. Rock historian Ian McFarlane is quoted in the *Milesago* Music website rating The Thunderbirds' version of 'Wild Weekend' as one of the best and most successful Australian instrumental singles of all time.

As the *Milesago* site highlights, the band's stint as house band at dances such as the Preston Town Hall made the Thunderbirds an all-purpose band with an ability to play a variety of styles and genres. It was this ability that led the Thunderbirds to back artists like Roy Orbison, Jack Scott, Ray Peterson, Dion and Johnny Chester on a nationwide package tour. Similar tours followed, headlined by their idols Cliff Richard & The Shadows, with The Allen Brothers, Andy Ellis and Judy Stone. They also appeared at Festival Hall, backing many visiting overseas and local acts including Jack Scott, Dion, Ray Peterson, Fabian, Helen Shapiro, and Australia's own Col Joye and Johnny O'Keefe.

The Lincolns

The pre-Daddy Cool band of Gary Young and Wayne Duncan, The Lincolns (which also featured Roger Treble on lead guitar and Ed Nantes on rhythm guitar) also came into their own as the backing band for solo singers.

In my book *Daddy Who?* I quote Gary describing a typical night playing the legendary rock'n'roll dance of the early '60s at The Preston Town Hall:

> *Back in those days pop music was dominated by singers like Johnny O'Keefe, Normie Rowe, Merv Benton, Johnny Chester and Lynne Randell; so a typical night would see three or four singers on the bill, each would sing a clutch of songs, we'd rehearse those songs through the week. Stan Rofe was the MC at the dance so and would announce to the audience ...*

> *And now ladies and gentlemen, with his national Number 1 hit … 'Shakin' All Over' Johnny Chester! Johnny would run out, Roger Treble (the guitarist in the band) would play the riff, then off we'd go. After Johnny's three songs we'd play an instrumental like The Shadows' 'Apache' before Stan announced the next act … Merv Benton and his hit single … 'Yield Not to Temptation'. And on the night would go, one singer, three songs, sometimes four, followed by an instrumental … followed by another singer.*

The Lincolns eventually morphed into The Rondells when, in 1965, they became the backing band for national pop sensations Bobby & Laurie. The duo had a major career in Melbourne in the mid-'60s with hits such as the Laurie Allen-penned 'I Belong with You,' and 'Hitch Hiker'.

In 1966 The Rondells were thrust into national prominence when they formed the core of the backing band for the ABC music program *Dig We Must* co-hosted by Bobby & Laurie and which also featured Judy Jacques as a co-host and regular performer. Others to appear on the show included Ronnie Burns, Normie Rowe and Lynne Randell, almost the regular bill at The Preston Town Hall!

The Rondells came into their own as a tight, versatile band that developed an ability to adapt to any style or genre of popular music. They also evolved a unique sound based on The Rondells' iconic rhythm section of Wayne Duncan, with his distinctive loping, warm bass sound and Gary Young's driving, expressive drum style. This combination would go on to be a defining feature and major contributing factor to the success of Daddy Cool years later.

From the Shadows to the Spotlight:

Vika and Linda Bull

'I reject the notion that the job you excel at is somehow not enough to aspire to, that there has to be something more. I love supporting other artists ... some people will do anything to be famous. I just wanted to sing.[4]

This is a quote that could easily apply to Vika and Linda Bull.

I've known and worked with Vika and Linda for a number of years, shared a stage with them at the odd school fund raiser, played an intimate Fitzroy North café owned by Linda's partner and — with The Hornets acting as her backing band — performed a series of shows with Vika entitled *Vika Sings the Blues,* at a number of venues and festivals during 2011.

Whenever I have shared a stage with Vika and Linda I have been amazed at the ease of their harmonies, the grace of their presence and the power they have over audiences. They are the most loved vocal duo of their generation.

I recently visited the sisters at Linda's home in Clifton Hill to talk about their life in music and life in general. They'd asked me to help them write a speech they were to give at an International Women's Day breakfast event held at The Esplanade Hotel in St Kilda and hosted by One Of One, an organisation that puts the 'spotlight on women in the Australian music industry.' The theme for the speech was 'Our Life in Music and Together', so it was a perfect opportunity to help my friends with their speech and get some material for this book, win-win!

Not many musicians who started life at the side of the stage supporting a headline act went on to become headliners in their own right, but Vika and Linda achieved just that and they did it through the weight of their talent and ambition.

Vika and Linda have performed with everyone: Joe Camilleri, Paul Kelly, Ross Wilson, John Farnham, Iggy Pop, C.W. Stoneking, Archie Roach, Deb Conway, The RocKwiz Orkestra, Renee Geyer. For much of their career, Vika and Linda stood twenty feet from stardom. But they also successfully took, to paraphrase Bruce Springsteen, that long complicated walk to the front of the stage, both individually and together.

Vika and Linda grew up in the '60s in white-bread, Anglo-Saxon Doncaster — an outer northeastern suburb of Melbourne — to an Australian father and Tongan mother. Vika and Linda's mother arrived in Australia in 1959, during which the White Australia Policy was in effect. The Policy meant immigration to this country was strictly limited to people from European origins, and prohibited what it referred to as 'alien coloured immigrants'. As a result, their mother had to get special dispensation from Australian and Tongan authorities to settle in this country.

Vika described the sisters' life at school where they experienced the full blast of Australian racism, experiences that continue to this very day:

> My nickname at school was coke (and) we were referred to as boong and nigger in the playground. We've had to go in the back door at our own gigs because of the colour of our skin and we've been spat on and completely ignored in queues. But our fiercely independent Tongan mother and our gentle greenie father taught us from an early age how to stand up for ourselves and to not take a step back when you know you are being treated unfairly.

Standing up for themselves included learning how to use their fists on occasion. As Vika explained:

> I decked a kid once for a racial slur, broke his nose and put him in sick bay… luckily when his mother arrived at school she privately confessed that she knew that he was in the wrong.'

But the apology didn't make up for the relentless questioning of their cultural heritage. All through their childhood the sisters were constantly asked where they came from; 'Everyone used to always ask if I was Greek and if Linda was Chinese,' remembered Vika. Very few understood the rich cultural heritage in which the sisters were born, a heritage that has both informed and sustained them as performers and as individuals all through their lives. Vika explained:

> *Tongans by nature are fun, always laughing, always eating, always singing and always praying. The church played a big role in our lives; it was where we learnt how to sing because the Tongans are great harmonisers. Everyone sung, it was expected. The church choir was our teacher. The first song we ever sung in public was in church, a song hand-picked by mum called 'Everything Is Hunky Dory Children Of The Lord' and some of our first memories included our mother teaching us to harmonise.*
>
> *Mum has a beautiful voice, one we love listening to but she only sings for Jesus! On long family drives she would listen to us singing along to the radio and critique from the front seat. Linda hold your note! Vika take the high part, Linda you the low, Vika cut your note off! It's advice we still use to this day. She was fundamental to us becoming singers.*

Their father had a big part in their development as well …

> *A big music fan himself he loved listening to the Tongans sing and made sure we went to church every week. He'd suffer along with us because Church went for hours but it was worth every minute just to hear those beautiful harmonies.*

The other major force in the sister's development was ABC's *Countdown*. Vika explained:

> *We loved Countdown. Every Sunday night we'd turn on the ABC and sing along to all our favourite bands. We loved ABBA, Cheetah, Renee Geyer, The Divinyls. We learnt their songs and sang them in our Doncaster bedroom, hoping that one day we could be like them.*

'Then school was out, and all hell broke loose', according to Vika. She got a job at shabby-sheik HQ — Henry Maas's Black Cat Café on

Brunswick Street in Fitzroy, where:

Every shift we'd play Aretha, Etta James, Ruth Brown, Dinah Washington. It was a magnet for musicians, artists and creative people. Fitzroy was such an exciting place to be then, there were gigs everywhere and so we started the unhealthy practice of hanging out with musicians and guesting in various bands.

Linda was still at university, so Vika joined Sophisticated Boom Boom, a band that included fellow talented Melbourne women Jenny Fenton and Kerri Simpson. The band was named, rather appropriately, after the song by the all-girl band the Shangri-Las:

We were three women up front singing all the classic girl group hits from bands like the Shirelles, The Chiffons, The Ronettes, it was great training. Then Linda quit uni, joined me in our own band The Honeymooners and we were off!

They played most nights of the week in the bars and clubs of inner Melbourne, hanging out, chasing the 'speed and sound of music' as Allen Ginsberg put it. It was at this time that the sisters came across Peter Luscombe. He was, at the time, the drummer for Joe Camilleri's Black Sorrows, and according to Vika, gave the girls their 'first big break by recommending us to Joe Camilleri as backing singers.' Through Joe the sisters were suddenly thrust into the complicated life of an internationally touring band. It was an amazingly momentous time, as Vika explained:

If ever we were going to need each other it was now because we were young and green and unbeknownst to us things were just about to take off in a big way.

Joining the Black Sorrows took us from our lounge room into pretty much everybody else's. It was a sudden and shocking rise. One minute we were playing to fifty people at the local pub and then after the release of Hold On To Me in 1988, we played stadiums and stages all around the world. What started as a 6-week tour turned into 6 years of constant touring 6 days a week. It was where we got our rock'n'roll training, touring the Australian Pub scene, a tough male dominated environment.

We had to learn fast because Joe, bless him, decided to put us up front. We thought geez we're the upfront backing singers now so what the hell are we gonna do, we fell back on what we knew best, Tongan dance moves and harmonies which was a risky move in a rock band but we figured it was better than standing there staring at our feet — and it worked!

Touring that relentlessly was tough but it was where we cut our teeth. We worked hard on our sound learning how to sing to an audience and then bingo! We hit the jackpot because we met Venetta Fields. Venetta sang on most of the Sorrows albums. She was an original Ikette, one of Ike and Tina Turner's backing singers and had sung with The Rolling Stones, Boz Scaggs and Aretha Franklin just to name a few. What an Angel sent from heaven she was; sassy, relaxed, professional, an incredible singer and an incredible woman. She took us under her wing and really showed us how to sing, be quick, be good, be in tune. Venetta was really the key. Teaching us to be professional backing singers. We were new to the industry, we had never sung on records before and there she was an Ikette teaching us to sing.

We idolised The Ikettes, The Raylettes, The I-Three, Darlene Love, all of those legendary female backing singers who paved the way for people like us.

According to Linda, being part of the Black Sorrows also introduced them to the business side of the music world: 'We watched and listened to all the stories about who to avoid, how to manage money and how to survive in a very tough industry. We were still only 20 and 21. It turned out to be invaluable advice.'

This was especially when the Bull sisters left the Black Sorrows to form their own band. But we're getting ahead of ourselves.

The meteoric rise of the Sorrows meant that suddenly the sisters had a profile, as Linda explained:

We were performing regularly on Hey Hey it's Saturday, video clips on MTV, and appearing on Rock Around the World with Basia Bonkowski and Rock Arena with Suzanne Dowling two very rare female hosts. We didn't think there were a whole lot of mixed-race kids out there taking notice, particularly young girls. But they were wrong.

We have recently been very moved by a story Mojo Ju Ju [a young female artist with both an Indigenous and Filipino heritage] told us of her first time seeing us on telly and how that made her feel. To think that we have had an impact on others in a positive way means a lot!

By the mid-'90s the sisters were, in Linda's words, 'working our arses off.' She remembers:

We'd left The Sorrows and Paul Kelly our dear friend and mentor produced our debut album — which thanks to Mushroom and Paul — went double platinum. We added management and were touring the world ourselves, doing an album at Peter Gabriel's studio in Bath, a duet with Iggy Pop, sessions as backing singers, opening for Billy Joel, Sting and Joe Cocker and travelling to Tonga to sing for the King. Life was crazy, we needed to slow down a bit so Vika found a solution, pregnancy!

Pregnancy slowed both Vika and Linda down a little, both wanted to be home more. They opened a children's clothes shop on St George's Road in Fitzroy North, and Vika held down a regular day job as a legal secretary. But around this time, things went off the rails because, Linda says, '*we stopped taking care of our career.*' In her words:

Delegating the control of key aspects of our career to the wrong person nearly destroyed us both as artists and more importantly as sisters, causing a rift that very nearly tore us apart. For the first time in our lives we had stopped communicating and working together. We hurt each other and we hurt our mother who had sacrificed so much for us only to have her two daughters nearly come undone after a lifetime spent together. Fed up she stepped in with Dad and they did what they do best, told us to 'cut it out' and in her words, 'not to leave the room until you sort it out.' We did. I realised I had made a huge mistake. I underestimated the strength of our bond and didn't trust my instincts but rather made decisions based on obligation. I took my hands off the wheel and my foot off the brake.

During this time, Vika continued to perform sporadically, while Linda largely concentrated on her retail business and with time and a lot of talking the sisters got back to sharing a stage. Then, in 2015 a chance meeting with artistic manager Lisa Palermo changed everything. Linda gives Lisa the credit for resurrecting the career of Vika and Linda. Said Linda: [Lisa was] 'a perfect fit.' The first gig Lisa secured for them was 'singing in front of 100,000 people at the AFL Grand Final in 2016. Not a bad effort.'

With the help of Lisa, The Bull sisters' career was back on track. According to Vika:

After thirty-five years we feel we are just hitting our stride. We have never been in a hurry to get to the top; that has never been a goal, longevity has … We are about to record our first album in eighteen years!

Through all this we've learnt to be honest with ourselves, work as hard as we can, to take on only what we know we can handle, to take full responsibility for our decisions both good and bad and to most importantly get the job done and to enjoy ourselves. We have been very lucky to have had such a strong community of wonderful people around us.

Vika told me that the International Women's Day speech at The Espy went well, as she said the audience laughed and cried and you can't ask for more than that. In many ways the title of their presentation could have been 'The Story so Far' because really the sisters, although already household names, still have a few more milestones to tick off both for themselves and for other women in the Australian music industry, as Linda said in her International Women's Day speech:

> We need champions and advocates and Vika and I have had lots of those, male and female. Going forward we need more role models, women who are authentic, women who are powerful, women who are just very good at what they do. We will be very lucky if we can do that for someone going forward. That's what we strive for. The boundaries are shifting in our favour. We're not there yet, but we're getting there.

As Kurt Cobain once said … 'the future of rock belongs to women'. It does, especially when women like Vika and Linda Bull have the desire and the courage to take that future into their own hands.

Aaron Choulai

Melbourne's various university music programs have produced a whole new generation of musicians, who are gaining world recognition for their unique take on their chosen instruments. Keyboard player Simon Marvin for example is a recent graduate from Monash University and, along with his soul funk band Hiatus Kaiyote, has earned a Grammy Nomination for Best R&B Performance, for the band's release *Tawk Tomahawk*.

But it was a graduate from Melbourne's other music program, the Victorian College of the Arts that I kept hearing about from my son Alex, a former music student himself. Trusting Alex's taste, I decided to investigate. I caught up with Aaron at a Collins Street Café, a few hundred yards up from Melbourne Books.

Aaron I discovered is an artist who paid his dues in Melbourne before moving overseas and gaining an international reputation for his unique approach to jazz keyboard. This is his story.

Choulai was born in 1982 in Papua New Guinea. He spent his early years playing in the village, fishing, and eating mangos, coconuts and mud crabs. When he was twelve he moved to Melbourne with his family where he took piano lessons and discovered the blues, amongst other styles. Choulai became a true child prodigy — at fourteen, Choulai was accepted into the Victorian College of the Arts and studied under Paul Grabowsky, who became his long-term mentor.

Within a year he was playing regularly in blues clubs around town in bands like Blues Before Sunrise, The Swingin' Sidewalks and The Dancehall Racketeers with the likes of Paul Neuendorf, Andy Baylor and Ian Collard. As Aaron said of this unique experience: 'I think the duality of living in contrasting musical worlds on a daily basis at a young age taught me a set of skills that would help me through a career in music as an adult.'

Choulai finally graduated with a Bachelor of Music and things took off. He was playing keys in his critically acclaimed quintet, alongside fellow VCA students, at various clubs around town and jazz festivals like Wangaratta. It was at one of these gigs where he was approached by legendary drummer Allan Browne. Browne wanted to recruit Aaron to join his band for a Monday night residency at the Bennett's Lane Jazz Club in Melbourne, how could he say no? Running parallel with the Bennett's Lane residency, Choulai spent time as Musical Director for Kate Ceberano, both touring and recording with her.

Aaron was on to his second coffee at this stage and warmed to his topic, even though outside the café a chilly wind was blowing down Collins Street. He revealed that New York saxophonist Tim Ries happened to be in Melbourne working with The Rolling Stones. According to Aaron, Reiss was at a loose end one Monday night and he drifted into Bennett's Lane, where he heard Aaron playing with Browne. Ries was obviously impressed, because he encouraged Choulai to come to New York to record with some of that town's finest, musicians like bassist James Genus, drummer Clarence Penn and Scott Wedholdt.

The move to New York resulted in 21-year-old Aaron signing to Sunnyside Records. He lived and worked there for five years, returning to Melbourne regularly to perform, especially with Browne and Grabowsky.

In 2007, Choulai began a four-year stint as producer and music director for the production *We Don't Dance For No Reason*, which included a 16-member choir from PNG, a small jazz ensemble from Melbourne, and a set of short films about Port Moresby. Originally commissioned by Paul Grabowsky — who was the Director of the Queensland Music Festival at the time — the production went on to be performed at the Melbourne International Arts Festival, Port Moresby National Theatre, WOMADelaide Festival and the Australian World Music Expo. Not bad for a bloke who, at the time, was in his mid-'20s. 'Young Jazz Artist of the Year' at the Australian Jazz Awards, followed in 2006.

The rise and rise of Aaron Choulai continued with performances at international festivals in the Antibes, Israel, Tokyo and Italy, and a stint performing in the Jazz/Noise and improvised music scenes of New York and Tokyo. Did I mention the large-scale multimedia festival commissions in Australia and overseas, as well as collaborations with artists such as Ben Monder, Jim Black and Joel Frahm?

Around 2008 Aaron completed a two-year artist-in-residence position in Japan and decided to stay on. He is currently based in Tokyo, moving into the beat hip-hop world, a world he describes as 'deep waters'. 'I recently released a collaborative album with Japanese hip-hop artist Dalchi Yamamoto'. '*Willow* and toured it for six months or so all around the world. When it comes to beat making Tokyo is really one of [the world's] creative centres.'

According to Aaron, he learned his eclectic chops age fourteen:

… sitting in as a sideman with bands like the Swingin' Sidewalks
and local roots legends like Andy Baylor, Paul Neuendorf, Ian

Collard and Rick Dempster and playing a long Monday night residency at Bennett's Lane with Allan Browne's band.

It was in the clubs and pubs of Melbourne that Aaron was able to not only develop his piano style — acknowledged as unique by his international jazz musician colleagues and bandleaders — but also allowed him to move seamlessly between jazz, blues, R&B and now beats and hip-hop. Aaron explained how Melbourne's jazz and roots scene moulded him as a musician, and how the city contributed to his development as a performer:

It's to do with harmony and chord changes, I learnt so much playing with those western swing bands back at the Rainbow, or blues guys like Ian Collard at Muddy Waters or where ever. I learnt to break down chords to their root notes and to transpose keys. I learnt the classic blues, country and jazz repertoire. It was an intense apprenticeship, but I learnt to deal with situations. I learnt to approach bar owners. Nowhere else is like Melbourne, in the bright lights and big cities of New York, bars are largely owned by faceless corporate entities, musicians can't rock up to a venue and ask to play a gig. It's all emails and bullshit. Whereas here I played long residencies and learnt how to build an audience. I learnt to listen. Sure, I can compose and play complex art pieces like Umi No Uzu which I did recently for the Australian Art Orchestra at The Arts Centre, but then at the end of the show I headed off to Claypots in St Kilda to blow off some steam playing trad jazz with Eugene Ball; only in Melbourne.

Don't get me wrong the scenes overseas can be great for a while and of course the musicians are outstanding, but they don't have that Melbourne take on things, in the US for instance the younger dudes don't know about Louis Armstrong, they haven't got a repertoire and they don't know their own history. We know more about America's musical legacy than many Americans.

It's also very social in Melbourne; the music is connected to the community and what's going on. In New York for instance it's all about individual expression, where as we have a different way of looking at it here, in Melbourne we honor the song.

Aaron Choulai is still evolving and playing what he loves. As one of Australia's greatest jazz/contemporary exports, he credits Melbourne's music scene with giving him the technique and the confidence to take on the world and conquer it.

Wilbur Wilde — A Real Wild Child

I've known Wilbur for a while, played with him occasionally and laughed at his jokes backstage at many gigs; he's a big presence. I arranged to meet him one autumn morning to get to know him better at 'musicians' corner' Mario's café in Brunswick Street Fitzroy. There was Colin Hay at a table at the back, Jane Clifton sat at another and of course host Mario Pasquale, former proprietor of the legendary Melbourne venue The Continental in Prahran, seamlessly presiding over proceedings. Wilbur and I shook hands, he ordered breakfast and I asked him about his early life.

Wilbur Wilde (or Nicholas Aitkin to his mum) is the archetypical journeyman musician made good. Formally trained, with the ability to adapt, Wilbur has the chops to mix it with the best in the country. But he has something else, it's an optimistic chutzpah that's taken him on a wild ride from Ivanhoe to *Hey Hey it's Saturday* and all parts between.

For Wilbur, becoming a musician started young when he was holed up in bed, sick as a dog:

I had a collapsed lung from really bad bronchitis when I was ten. My family doctor said maybe I should play a wind instrument to make my lungs stronger. The next year I started at Ivanhoe Grammar with the clarinet, and then moved to the saxophone a bit later ... the chicks loved it. I went on to study music for my HSC and took more lessons. I couldn't get into the Melbourne Conservatorium at the time however, they didn't accept saxophone as an instrument!! So I enrolled in an Arts course at Monash and took music as an elective. I had a vague idea that maybe I would teach music, maybe play a little bit on the side.

Who knew that playing the saxophone 'on the side' would take Wilbur on a journey that saw him sharing the stage with some of the greatest musicians in the world. Wilbur played in some of Australia's most successful bands, and became a much-loved radio and television personality. Says Wilde:

My horn teacher first got me into playing live gigs; it was a rock'n'roll band at the Rosebud pub in August 1973 when I was 17. We also did Friday nights at The Pier in Frankston. I thought, hmmm, I'm getting paid, we've got beer and there are girls, hey this is a good job!

A little later in the year Wilbur got a gig at The Spanish Eyes Club: 'The band was made up of older musicians, playing stuff like 'Lady is a Tramp' but also 'Hi Heel Sneakers' and some blues, the full cabaret shtick, all good experience.

In 1974 the first Oil Crisis hit Australia, fuelling inflation and discontent within the community. Conservative forces were massing, with the Queensland Premier Joh Bjelke-Petersen describing the Whitlam Labor Government as 'the alien, stagnating, centralist, socialist, communist-inspired ... Federal Labor government', a very measured assessment I'm sure you'd agree. The nation's smouldering conservative unrest turned into a raging flame when Lance Barnard declared Australian independence in foreign policy. He told that Australia would no longer be a junior partner in a strategic alliance and asserted its determination to assess its national interest in matters of defence, an extraordinary development in the context of Australia's post war foreign policy up until that point, and beyond. When Cyclone Tracey hit Darwin on Christmas Eve, it seemed to be a portent for the political maelstrom in November of the following year.

For young 18-year-old-Wilbur, 1974 was significant for other reasons. He was looking for what many others sought in Australia's tropical north — freedom, the chance to get lost. Like a Beat poet, Wilbur took to the road to see what happened. Wilbur had received an open invitation to come up and stay from a saxophone-playing mate, so he got his mum to drop him and his saxophone out at the Ford Factory on Sydney Road, and then he stuck out his thumb. Two days later he set his bag down in a spare bedroom in his mate's place in Surfers Paradise and lay on the bed. Soon after arriving, the phone rang — it was a used car salesman promoting Roy Orbison's northern Australian tour, and they needed a sax player.

Pretty soon he was in the promoters' Cadillac cruising down the highway with Roy in the back, bound for Rockhampton, Toowoomba and Brisbane's Festival Hall. Says Wilbur:

> I only heard Roy speak on the tour twice, the first time was on stage when he told the audience ... 'We've had a request; but we'll keep playing anyway' ... and the second time was in the car. I'd never seen such a luxurious car before; I was playing with the electric windows and pushing my seat in and out and tilting my backrest, up and down. Roy, who was sitting right behind me and yelled ... 'Hey kid stop screwin' with the seat you're crushin' m'legs man!

On the Gold Coast, Wilbur landed a six night a week gig at The Mouse Trap. He lived in an apartment attached to the club, ate steak every night and was paid $60 per week. On his nights off he'd play at one of the other clubs on the strip.

This was the routine for most of 1974 until Wilbur moved down to Sydney to play with Ray Brown and the Whispers, who 'were older musicians who had lived the life,' he says. He also felt that it was time to get back to more serious musical education:

> *I was really into jazz; Parker, Getz, Sonny Rollins, Diz. I was accepted into the Sydney Conservatorium Jazz Program. The first person I met there was Eric McCusker, in fact I was driving with Eric in his father's car when I heard an advertisement on radio 2JJ from a band called Ol' 55 who were after a sax player. The auditions were held at some club in East Ryde. So I went along ... what the?*
>
> *Frankie J Holden was dressed in a gold lame suit and the rest of the band was in their full on cartoon rocker gear, V8 belt buckles and Brillcreamed quiffs. My hair was long and I knew everything because I was studying jazz and my head couldn't have been further up my backside.*
>
> *I played a couple of tunes with them and was instantly drawn to Frankie's enormous spirit of fun. After the gig I said, that I liked what they did and I'd join the band. They were taken aback at my confident declaration ... 'well' I said 'I'm the only bugger here so you haven't any choice have you?' Good argument, so I was in!*

The first gig Wilbur played with Ol' 55 was live-to-air on 2JJ. This was also the 'birth' of the name Wilbur Wilde, a name he borrowed from a mate.

After a string of gigs at university union nights, TAFEs and high-school lunchtime shows, the band recorded their double-platinum album *Take it Greasy*. The album picked up on the whole *Happy Days/ Daddy Cool*, '50s-era fashion at the time. But Ol' 55 pushed the whole thing to warp speed, taking their '50s mayhem to Australia's clubs, pubs and television screens. It was a wild ride.

Wilbur's career took another turn when, in 1977, he joined Jo Jo Zep and the Falcons. Jeff Burstin remembers when Wilde started hanging around the band, claiming 'he kind of got absorbed into the Falcons rather that actually formally joined as the sax player'. Wilbur thinks there's some truth to Jeff's assertion:

> *The Falcons were a tough band, I learnt that blowing the shit out of one note was often what was needed, not ten thousand notes delivered at the speed of light. I loved working out the horn parts with Joe, we were kind of like a team within in a team in the Falcons. He and I would always share a car on tour and we'd listen to all kinds of stuff on the stereo, reggae, Zydeco, blues, blue note jazz you name it. In the other car the cosies — as we called them — Gaz and Jeff, Tony and John, smoked dope, drank tea, got comfortable. The Falcons were one hell of a band and I still love playing with them whenever we infrequently get together.*

On his journey from Rosebud to *Countdown* and beyond, Wilbur Wilde has learnt a lifetime of lessons. He learnt stagecraft, how to play as part of a team, and how to 'honour the song'; in other words, he learnt to contribute to a performance rather than be a musical distraction. But perhaps the most important lesson he learnt was to take to opportunities that, sometimes, pushed him outside his comfort zone. *Yes* is a great liberator if you can make it work for you, says Wilbur:

> *The saxophone has taken me on an amazing journey, from rock bands to 750 performances of the Rocky Horror Show, to radio, to acting in movies and television programs like Hey Hey its Saturday and also to the cool jazz clubs of Melbourne and beyond. It's been a hell of a ride.*

I came across Wilbur's professionalism and stagecraft when he played a gig with The Hornets a few years ago. It was a typical corporate event, puddles of work mates standing around a draughty room, clutching drinks and wishing they were someplace else. We were doing our best, playing the shit out of our set, trying to get some movement in the crowd, some reaction. We were getting nothing back. Then Wilbur sidled up to the microphone and made an announcement:

'Ladies and gentlemen, I must have your attention, I want all of you in front of the stage immediately. You, I'm talking to you, I want all of you to come to the front of the stage now, the band will not play until you comply.'

People nervously looked at each other, some giggled, others shuffled forward as Mr Wilde had instructed.

'Ok now that I have your attention I want to talk to you about something very important … Ladies and gentlemen … I now want to tell you about AMWAY!'

Laughter erupted. Wilbur counted in Chuck Berry's 'Teenage Wedding', the band kicked in and the crowd went crazy!

It's clear by now that side musicians come in many forms. Some are guns-for-hire: they mix and match, swapping bands and musical genres. You can see them playing behind Renee Geyer one night and Archie Roach the next, or with an international blues musician at your favorite music festival. The most successful of these guys are not only great musicians, they're easy to work with and are reliable team players, and consequently their phone rings quite frequently. Three musicians that meet these criteria perfectly I have known, liked and played with for over two decades: Jeff Burstin, Sam See and Bruce Haymes.

CHAPTER 13

THE PROFESSIONALS

Jeff Burstin — consummate guitar player

Jeff is the kind of side musician that works freelance from time to time but is largely associated with one or two particular bands. Jeff Burstin will forever be the rhythm guitarist for two stellar Australian bands, Jo Jo Zep and The Falcons and The Black Sorrows. But this is only half of his story: he has also played with countless other singers and bands, Vika and Linda Bull, Renee Geyer, Jane Clifton and The Hornets just to name a few.

He does other stuff too. He occasionally acts as musical director for showcase shows and events, on-call studio musician and/or producer, guitar teacher, and assessor of musical performances by Victorian secondary students studying for their Victorian Certificate of Education. In other words he does everything a working musician needs to do to earn a decent living in this country.

But for Jeff it's par for the course, it's all about being part of a team. For him when the band locks in and working well it can be, in his words 'transporting', an experience that makes up for all the other stuff, the prima donna singers, the egos, the nights on the road, the bad food, the poor pay, the dud gigs.

Before meeting Jeff, I had been playing like ragged claws scuttling across musical floors. Jeff wasn't like that, he was simply on top of it all, he existed on a different musical plane. He's a big, generous man. He plays mandolin, acoustic and electric guitar, and he's got the full index of musical styles: acoustic blues, poker-faced folk, down-home country, barroom blues and the thousand faces of '60s and '70s popular music. He plays whatever the song calls for and plays it as well as it could possibly be played. Other guitar players had to work on it, some, like me, would never have it, but Jeff had it in his blood.

I got familiar with Jeff Burstin's adaptive abilities as a guitarist and musician as we drove together one Saturday morning to the St Andrews Hotel northeast of Melbourne. We'd just started playing together as a duo. Jeff had tried to teach me a few things on guitar, but it had proved insurmountable. But we got on because we both loved Dylan and The Band, Donny Hathaway. He liked how I sang and the songs I wrote, so we hooked up. We played the Flowerdale Hotel on Sundays, supported Dianna Kiss at The Espy, and played other little gigs here and there. That Saturday St Andrews gig was one of those; the pub was packed with patrons enjoying lunch and a few drinks after the traditional St Andrews Saturday morning market held over the road closed.

At the last minute Jeff had been asked to fill in later that night for a guitar player who'd dropped out of an orchestra backed rock mas at St Patrick's Cathedral. He'd only just got the chord charts for the entire performance; no recorded music, just the charts. As we drove out through the Christmas Hills, Jeff had the charts open and was figuring out his parts with his guitar somehow maneuvered around his body in the front seat of my car. In the forty-five minutes it took us to drive from his home in Abbotsford to St Andrews, he had the whole thing down. How did he do it? I sat in Jeff's Abbotsford kitchen early in 2019 and asked him just that question.

Jeff was from a musical household. His father John loved jazz and was an avid collector. Duke, Count Basie, Graeme Bell — in fact, the Bell band used to occasionally rehearse in John's lounge room. But it was another Graeme, Graeme Burstin, Jeff's older brother by seven and a half years who had a profound influence on him becoming a musician. Graeme Burstin was a guitar and piano player of some distinction in Melbourne's folk scene of the '60s. Graeme's influences tendered towards blues like Robert Johnson, early Blind Lemon Jefferson, the folk of Dylan and the country of Doc Watson mixed up with some bluegrass. Graeme's music captured Jeff's attention, but he wanted a more visceral experience, so Jeff snuck into his brother's room and played his guitar. The kid had potential so Graeme showed him stuff, chords, tricks and flicks. Pretty soon young Jeffrey was hooked on the same music his big brother played.

But there was another type of music creating a disturbance in Jeff's mind, and it ripped through Festival Hall in June 1964. It was The Beatles, and they opened up other possibilities for Jeff. They had complex melodies, unusual chord patterns and a group dynamism that captured the imaginations of teenagers all over the world.

By the time Jeff reached his early teens, he was already playing mandolin with his brother in a bluegrass band at Traynor's. This led to a position in the John Graham band Blackspur, that held down a Sunday night residency at the Pancake Parlour, and played folk society nights as well as the odd university union gig. This was a unique education for any young musician, and Jeff accumulated a lifetime of knowledge first-hand on the stages of Melbourne.

All the while, Jeff's musical consciousness was stretching. The people he played with on weekends were into the music of Greenwich Village coffee houses, but there was now a part of Jeff that preferred Carnaby Street. He needed to find a new posse of musicians to help him realise what he was looking for, and he found them — at Mount Waverley High School, where he was a student.

With this bunch of mates (including Graeme Shirley Strachan, who went on to become a carpenter, a surfer and the vocalist for

Skyhooks), Jeff embraced the music of the British invasion and the electric blues:

> I've always had those two sides to my guitar playing, the acoustic tradition of folk, country and blues as well as the electric-pop sensibility of the great British era of The Beatles, Kinks and The Who. I always loved electric blues as well; the first record I ever bought was the first Paul Butterfield Blues Band LP ... so I loved equally the acoustic and electric forms of music ... It's been those dual streams that have informed my entire career.

But Burstin needed to address the formal stuff, so he studied classical guitar for his matriculation year and then got into a Monash University music course.

Around the same time Burstin was asked to play at a jug band convention held at University House in Parkville with the Gut Bucket Jug Band. The Gut Buckets had been around for a while, playing their Memphis and Dixieland Jug band music in the folk clubs and jazz centers of Melbourne since 1965. The band included the soon-to-be celebrated Rick Amor on guitar, John Childs on vocals, and an array of mandolins, harmonicas, kazoos and washboards.

Then Jeff got a taste for the power and the passion of a full-on electrified blues band. It was a taste that was satisfied when, at the age of nineteen, he met someone who nudged him further down the electric path:

> I met Wayne Burt through another guitar player, Peter Martin when Wayne was looking for a guitarist to fill out his band Rock Granite and the Profiles. Wayne had written a lot of songs, knew some great blues covers and Ross Wilson's wife Pat shared the singing duties with Wayne, plus they had a manager, Bev Patterson, so of course I joined the band.
>
> All of a sudden, we were supporting Daddy Cool at The T.F. Much in Fitzroy as well as bands like McKenzie Theory and Lipp Arthur and the Double Decker Brothers. We toured,

played universities, inner city pubs, The Kingston, The Station in Prahran and a few larger venues. Overnight I was a professional musician.

Jeff dropped out of university — he felt he'd learnt all the musical knowledge he needed. The Profiles were making headway, supporting Daddy Cool at places like Ormond Hall, and playing gigs at Sydney University, Monash, Melbourne, La Trobe. Jeff was in the eye of that early-'70s political maelstrom, playing to Trotskyite and Marxist students, dope dealers and ratbags.

I saw Rock Granite and the Profiles support Daddy Cool's Last Drive Inn Movie Show at the T.F.Much Ballroom. Pat on vocals, Wayne Burt, Jeff, maybe Wayne Duncan on bass — they stood under palm tree props and played Burt's songs, songs like 'Desert Island,' and 'Jungle Juice.' Rock Granite set the scene for Daddy Cool's last gig (for now) and helped make it one of the most celebratory nights in a Melbourne venue up to that time.

And then Rock Granite was no more. By 1975, Jeff Burstin had moved on to play with Gulliver Smith's Company Caine, with Russell Smith on guitar and John Power on bass. That's them on Co Caine's *Dr. Chop* record. The album included tracks produced by Ross Wilson, plus some live material, and the whole project was funded and released by David Pepperell and Keith Glass. Ian McFarlane felt the new line up was somewhat superior to the original, resulting in the band playing to enthusiastic audiences in Melbourne and Sydney for a year before calling it quits.

These names — Ross Wilson, Wayne Burt, John Power, Jeff Burstin, Joe Camilleri, Gary Young, Wayne Duncan — keeping popping up for a reason. They are people who sleep and eat music, and they laid the foundations in Melbourne.

Ross Wilson is a walking concept, an architect that crackles with ideas. He steered Wayne Burt towards the idea of putting a rhythm-and-blues band together, a band which played songs of Burt's like 'Beating Around the Bush', 'Dancing Shoes', 'King of Fools' songs like that. Wayne didn't want to sing lead, so Wilson got in Joe Camilleri. John Power and Jeff Burstin were recruited from Co. Caine, and then the masterstroke, Daddy Cool drummer Gary Young, joined the band. Jo Jo Zep and the Falcons they called the band, and what a killer line-up it had! Jeff was happy playing with the Falcons:

> I love playing in bands, I love the ensemble work, figuring out harmonies, who plays high on the neck who plays low, trying things out, ideas, concepts. Getting things right, experimenting. It's what is exciting about playing with other people and it was what was exciting about playing with The Falcons.

The Falcons became a phenomenon. Wayne Burt, one of the nation's great songwriters even then, had left, and was replaced by Tony Faehse (who had played in Alvin Stardust's band). The ebullient Wilbur Wilde, who had been an integral member of Ol' 55, also joined the band. They were on the road to glory.

The hit singles 'Hit & Run', 'Shape I'm In' and 'All I Wanna Do', and the albums *Screaming Targets* (1979), *Hats Off Step Lively* (1981) and the mini-album *Dexterity* (1981), all sold by the truckloads. The band toured all over the country and internationally, including spots at the Montreux Jazz and Blues festival.

In the breaks, Jeff played tough rhythm-and-blues in the Rock Doctors with his old mates Wayne Burt, John Power, Chris Stockley and Gary Young. But once the holidays were over, it was back to work; more touring with The Falcons, more gigs, more mania. It lasted 'til the early '80s.

Jeff then joined Gary Young, Wayne Duncan and Ross Hannaford in the Flying Emus, an outfit showcasing Gary Young's country-infused songs. No more the tough guitar-slinger, it was back to Jeff's roots playing country licks in a dirt band. But the Emus only recorded one album and played a couple of gigs, including the Wandong Country Music Festival, then disappeared.

As discussed, Joe Camilleri went on to put together The Black

Sorrows. Jeff was with him all the way as Camilleri moved the band seamlessly through zydeco to country/rock and power pop. Jeff Burstin was a guitarist capable of pumping out everything from French Cajun to the straight-ahead power of songs like the million-selling 'Chained to the Wheel' from The Sorrow's *Hold On To Me* album. He could handle Tex-Mex country feels as well, as heard on the hugely successful 'Harley and Rose.'

So how did Jeff Burstin manage to hold on for such a wild ride? How did he go from playing mandolin at Traynor's in the '60s to playing power-chord guitar in stadiums in the '90s? Burstin has this to say:

> *A lot of this stuff just fell into my lap, it was a right place right time kind of thing. Sure, I have the talent to produce what is required when needed, but there are a lot of talented people out there who didn't get the breaks I did. I guess my background playing bluesgrass and folk on the stages of Traynor's and the Outpost Inn at such a young age was great training, I learnt on the job. One of the most valuable lessons I learnt back then was how to get on with people, to listen to ideas and to be respectful of other musicians. That's held me in good stead for my entire career.*

Later Burstin wrote songs and played sophisticated, grownup pop with Stephen Cummings, followed by a long stint playing acoustic and electric guitar for his fellow Black Sorrows alumni Vika and Linda Bull. For a time he played guitar for the indefatigable Renee Geyer...and for the past twenty plus years he's been playing with me in The Hornets. During that time I have seen what it is to be a complete guitar player like Jeff Burstin. He is a professional, capable of handling the subtleties of an acoustic duo format, the interplay with keyboardist Bruce Haymes in a trio, or the full-tilt bluesy blitzkrieg of the full band. I grew to understand that Jeff could handle the full musical palette of The Hornets, and then, help form it. Jeff is capable of offering intimacy and companionship with his guitar playing, and he can blast you away with the weight of his musical ideas.

When I first sat in his kitchen way back in 1995/96 I got a feeling that maybe I'd just been handed a very lucky break, maybe this was the beginning of a very enjoyable journey; and it was. It's been the journey of a lifetime.

Sam See: Enjoying the Journey

I've known and played with Sam See for over thirty years, starting with a recording session for the theme music of a radio series I had written for the ABC in 1987/88 called *The Housing Game*. Since that time we've written songs together for various projects and shared many a stage during his stint with The Hornets, in the early 2000s and beyond. We met recently at his Belgrave home and discussed his life in music. I knew I was in for a treat and Sam, as usual, didn't disappoint.

Sam See is a masterful musician; he's a cellist, guitarist, keyboardist, and a songwriter, too (we all remember 'Reasons' off Farnham's *Whispering Jack* album). As a guitarist he can play with speed and intensity, but also subtlety and soul. He's played keys for Sherbet, guitar and keys for Flying Circus and Lighthouse, slide guitar and keys for Fraternity, and guitar with Farnham, Goanna, and Brian Cadd. Now he plays killer acoustic guitar with his current supergroup The Pardoners, which includes long-term associates Glyn Mason and Lindsay Field.

Over the years, Sam has toured the US, lived and played in Canada, and lived in London, where he and Bon Scott worked as apprentice wig makers: 'Bon was pretty good, I was woeful.' He's been a producer and musical director for shows like the Bicentennial concert *Under the Southern Cross* and Steve Vizard's *Tonight Live* nightly television spot. He's worked as a studio musician for John Farnham, Tina Arena, Brian Cadd, Goanna, Swanee and The Black Sorrows, and he's an arranger too, even written the odd jingle. When Sam is around, usually something good comes out of it.

See was born in Sydney just after the war, when servicemen and women everywhere were returning to civilian life as though nothing had happened. This was the era of the Red threat, when Menzies told us that communists were everywhere; in trade unions, the public service, under beds, everywhere. Menzies also urged servicewomen to retreat back to the kitchen, and servicemen to hunker down at work. This was a time, he said, to expand the suburbs, make lots of babies, and enjoy the spoils of war. Most did just that.

In 1956 Sam moved with his family to Melbourne, just in time for the Olympics. Melbourne was on the verge of a multicultural makeover, but Sam missed the after effect of this social upheaval. He returned to the Harbour City in 1966, missing his beloved St Kilda Football Club's only flag: 'great See timing as usual.'

It was during his time in Melbourne that See's love of music blossomed. He sang in a choir, learning harmony, and he took piano and cello lessons from a hard taskmaster:

> *Otti Veit was the first cellist in the MSO and also happened to be my cello teacher. She was tough, a stickler for the correct elbow position to bow the instrument, she insisted I keep my right elbow cocked. Inevitably that elbow would drop and whenever it did I was whacked with Veit's cello bow. The same thing happened playing piano. If my hands flattened out from their high stepping horses position a ruler would crack across my knuckles. I soon learnt to love corporal punishment! So now I can't play at all without being severely beaten beforehand!*

Needless to say, although Sam loved music he hated rigid learning: 'I never really learnt to effectively sight read, but I learnt enough theory to get by.'

Then, one day, Sam was sitting in his bedroom when he heard '… George Harrison's feedback introduction to The Beatles "I Feel Fine".' Sam said it changed his life: 'I immediately wanted to make sounds just like that.'

Sam was searching the radio waves and record stores around for music by The Beatles, Stones, Animals, Pretty Things. And back in Sydney he found Miles Davis, Wes Montgomery, Kenny Burrell and Jimmy Smith at a Double Bay record shop. Sam says that he 'immediately stopped doing homework, cello and piano and took up guitar, playing Easybeats, Animals and Stones songs in schoolboy bands.' Sam was living with his parents in Sydney's Paddington at this stage, playing guitar at jam nights and almost joining a band called The Lemon People…so what's wrong with that name?

Eventually, after hanging out at The Union Jack's Club in Sydney, he met Clive Shakespeare and a crazy singing Scot, Denis Loughlin, as well as bassist Doug Rae and drummer Danny Taylor. They formed a band:

> Denis wasn't perhaps a great singer, but what a showman and a very funny man as well as consummate con man. He convinced my parents, well my Mum actually, to guarantee a loan so I could buy a Hammond organ … 'This is a great opportunity for your son Mrs See', he assured her … Clive was the guitar player, although I wanted to be, so I was stuck with the keys.

So what to call the outfit? Sam remembers:

> We sat around discussing the name, I suggested The Dingoes, very prescient wasn't I? But Clive had this vision for pop super stardom and all of its associated reckless profligacy so maybe the name 'The Dingoes' didn't fit his vision, I was over-ruled. The band name we finally agreed on was… Sherbet.

Sherbet did ok for a while, especially after Sam, and new bass player Bruce Worrall, decided to add an extra singer called Daryl Braithwaite:

> We did the dual singer thing, with Daryl and Denis, I mean the Twilights and the Amen Corner had that dual front man thing. I remember we played lunchtimes at The Downunder

Bar in The Cross, it was a front for a brothel and consequently full of GI's. Denis hooked up with this gorgeous girl who was being run by a pimp with a gun. Great plan, Denis. I was very naïve and had no idea what was going on. Then one day I saw Abe Saffron and Sammy Lee playing cards with their hired guns standing behind the table making sure no-one cheated. Suddenly The Downunder Bar didn't seem such a great place to hang out.

Soon after this brush with the Sydney underworld, Denis 'got the shits' and left the band. In 1970, following a couple more line-up changes, the band began a grueling but crucial eight-month residency at Jonathan's Disco in Ultimo:

Fraternity was the senior band at Jonathans at the time and we got the junior spot. The club owner was a bloke called John Spooner and he said that you've got the spot but on a couple of conditions: we had to rehearse at the club once a week to learn new material and he would only talk to the band via the keyboard player (which happened to be me) because I was the only one in the band who knew anything about formal music. Because Daryl didn't know what to do with his hands John came up with the idea of him using only the top of his mic stand ... and he also said to Daryl, 'If you ever wear that orange cardigan again I'll kill you!

Playing seven hours a night, six nights a week quickly welded Sherbet into a formidable live act. Eventually they were spotted by twenty-year-old university student Roger Davies, who subsequently came onboard to manage the band. But Sam had moved on by this stage:

I'd heard The Band's first album and had a musical epiphany. I knew Sherbet was going to be successful but it wasn't the music I wanted to play so I left and joined Flying Circus ... My mother told me I was crazy leaving Sherbet, she could see what was coming.

Hmm, always listen to your mother may be the moral of this story. Sam explained that the Sydney scene at the time was very collegial:

> We'd play our gig then hang out at other clubs and meet different musicians on the scene, people like Bruce Howe, Fraternity's bass player and members of Flying Circus. Flying Circus had recently won the Hoadley's Battle of the Sounds, playing their country, folky original material and when they asked me to join on keys and guitar, I jumped at the chance. Their material was moving more in The Band direction, which was where I wanted to go. We used the Hoadley's prize money to travel to San Francisco in mid-1971 and basically had the time of our lives. We lived off Haight Street, smoked dope, dropped acid, saw Aretha at The Fillmore amongst many others, but played bugger-all gigs because of the immigration department.

The band then relocated to Toronto and hooked up with music agency the Music Factory for a $10,000 deal, which sponsored a two-month tour:

> We were making much more money as complete unknowns than in Oz. Back then in Ontario the drinking age was over 21, so there was a network of alcohol-free high school dances where kids paid an entrance fee and there were often a few thousand kids at these gigs. We cleaned up! While we were in Toronto, Fraternity offered me a gig replacing their keyboard player. I had no concept of 'career' at that stage and I was more interested in playing with the best players, and Mick Jurd, Fraternity's guitar player was one of my inspirations, so I accepted.

Flying Circus toured Australia in 1971, and released Sam's Crosby, Stills & Nash-influenced *The Ballad of Sacred Falls*. After the tour, Sam moved to Adelaide to join his old mate Bruce Howe in Fraternity, playing both keys and slide guitar. Fraternity featured Howe on bass, John Freeman drums, John Bissett on organ, Mick Jurd guitar, John Eyers on harp, and a singer called Bon Scott. Sam remembers:

They'd also won The Battle of the Bands *competition and were going to England. I told them they were crazy, I showed them a copy of* Melody Maker, *it was all glam and glitter bands, and I was the cutest member of Fraternity … so it was going to be a disaster, which it proved to be. We lived in cold-water flats, hardly playing. Bon Scott and I survived working as apprentice wig makers though we did manage to land a support gig for Status Quo. That was in their* Pictures of Matchstick Men *era.*

Quo pulled up to the gig in a fleet of three separate Bentleys. When they jumped out they were dressed in King's Road finery, flicking their coiffed long hair off their faces. We were going to blow these soft bastards off the fucking stage man. Rock'n'roll!

We played our set; it was great we had a terrific response. Then we stood side stage and waited to see how the Quo could follow that. The curtain pulled back and there was a wall of Marshalls, they'd changed into their denim, turned up the PA to jumbo jet level and proceeded to blow the place apart. At the end of the show we left quietly, both the theatre and London.

Luckily for Sam, Flying Circus called, so it was back to Canada for seven years, where the band was signed to Capitol Records. 'But,' says Sam, 'the scene had changed in the time I was away.' He continues:

The licensing laws had changed, the school dance thing had died, so we were constantly touring, mostly the Ontario bar circuit, which was rugged. It was chicken-wire stuff and really if they didn't have it you wished they did, especially when I was whacked full in the face by a beer bottle at a bar in Thunder Bay. Flying Circus came to an end when the Capitol record guys who had been pushing for us were fired and the new broom wanted their bands pushed.

Then there was an eighteen-month stint playing keys for a Canadian rock orchestra, Lighthouse:

We did one cross-Canada tour where we played every town that had a big enough hockey arena. I've seen more of Canada than I have of Australia. We were very popular in pockets of the States too, those places where the radio stations played our records. So, we might be playing to nobody in Mississippi one day and then playing to a packed house in Arkansas the next. For some reason, we were big in Hawaii. I remember a particularly memorable show being supported by Tower of Power … great gig … terrifying following those guys … By the end of that stint Sam had had enough touring and got a job driving a truck for a while.

In 1976, Sam was recruited by Greg Quill to join the band Southern Cross, also including Tony Bolton, Chris Stockley and Bruce Worrall. Heading back to Australia for a tour, they recorded a single, 'Been So Long'/'I Wonder Why', for Warner's Elektra label. At the end of a disastrous tour, only Greg Quill returned to Canada:

The minute I landed in Melbourne I understood that this was where I wanted to be; it was cosmopolitan, multicultural, and on a Tuesday night in winter, there were over sixty gigs listed in The Age's Green Guide, *extraordinary!*

Sam and Chris Stockley decided to hang together and hooked up with Glyn Mason to form Stockley, See and Mason:

We signed with Premier agency and Frank Stivala — suddenly we were playing four, five, six nights a week plus lunchtime shows for 3XY Pool Parties. Then we recorded a live album and a movie 'Beg Steal or Borrow' was made and described by the distributer as hilarious — I agreed when it came to our acting!

By the time Glyn quit the band a couple of years later, Sam was very much on the gun-for-hire treadmill. He was sitting in with bands like Bluestone and playing on records for Tina Arena, Goanna, The Black

Sorrows and Brian Cadd, just to name a few. Sam eventually replaced Tommy Emmanuel — no pressure there — in John Farnham's band. This led to Farnham eventually recording Sam's quintessential song 'Reasons' for the hugely successful *Whispering Jack* album.

Sam then did a multitude of recording sessions before doing what he calls the 'St Kilda Road Shuffle': selling his wares to the advertising industry:

> *It was a tough gig but thank god or Tony Lockett for Sherri McIver, who not only gave me my break in the industry but also stood with me for years on the wind and rain soaked terraces of the Moorabbin Football Ground and watched in wonderment as Nicky Winmar spun out of packs and kicked bullet-like passes to the leading Adonis that was Plugger Lockett.*

Since the early 2000s, Sam has played with his good friend Glyn Mason in the duo The Pardoners. They've released a few critically acclaimed albums and still play dozens of shows annually where they dispense (as their Middle Ages namesakes used to do) papal indulgences to the faithful, in the form of beautifully crafted, played and sung material. Sam and Glyn often add their longtime buddy Lindsay Field to the mix to form the harmony-fuelled Field, See and Mason. It's this combination that can be heard on their album *Down Under The Covers* — a collection of Sam arranged Australian pop classics — a very classy disc indeed.

I think the lyric to Sam's song 'Reasons' sums up his career: He has lived in the moment, wrung everything he could from it, learnt from the experience then moved on. As he wrote:

'... I live for now.' Sam cares a lot about music and life and does anything he can to make both work. It's what makes him such a special musician and why he has had such a long and varied career.

Bruce Haymes: 'I'm in it for the music and everything else can get stuffed'.

On the surface it seems that, like Jeff Burstin, Bruce Haymes had everything fall into his lap. But appearances can be deceptive; it's a bit more complicated than that. Bruce has a rare talent, an ability to play the right thing at the right time. Bruce is solid and reliable; he is blessed with a humble personality making him a joy to work with. I know all this because I have played and recorded with him for well over two decades. But despite our long association I've never asked him formally how he developed his prodigious keyboard chops. So we sat down in his Northcote kitchen one day, drank tea and chatted.

Bruce Haymes was a Bright boy, his father the Shire Secretary of the small Victorian town. He learnt piano from age six and, almost from the beginning, fell in love with music. 'Apparently I was fascinated with the radio, when any music was played I would crawl to the speaker and sit transfixed in front of it for hours,' Bruce says.

By his teens he had found the Beatles, the Stones, and the Hollies. But living in country Victoria, there was nowhere to go to explore further:

> I was still studying classical piano and I found I could also work out a Beatles song … wow I can actually do this! But living in Bright in the mid-'60s, there was nowhere I could take it. I didn't know anyone that played an instrument, no more played in a band.

So Bruce kept cramming his head full of music theory, figuring that he could gain access to that musical vault when and if ever he needed it. With music pushed aside for now, Bruce finished school, enrolled in a science course at Melbourne University, moved into Newman College, went to gigs, schlepped around Carlton, did that student thing. Then one day he heard someone playing piano in the college's common room:

So I went down and checked it out ... I said to the bloke playing piano that I played a bit too. So we started to play together over the next little while. Then some like-minded students gravitated to the room and, as you do, we formed a band and learnt those beloved Beatles, Kinks and Stones songs.

It was then that Bruce's life changed:

I was playing in a cover band with my Melbourne University mates one night in the '70s. It was a shit kicker gig with five people holding up the bar and four of them weren't taking any notice, but one of them was.

Unbeknown to Bruce someone in that minuscule audience was paying attention. A few weeks later a letter arrived out of the blue from the great Australian singer songwriter Richard Clapton. Bruce recalled that:

Apparently Richard's bass player, Michael Hegarty, was one of the five people in the audience at that shit-kicker bar a few weeks previously. He had been brought to the show by a mate of mine Graham Thompson. Richard was looking for a piano player for his 'Hearts on the Night Line' tour of the US. Michael recommended me. Richard asked if I could send him some stuff, so I recorded a couple of songs onto cassette and posted it off to LA. A couple of weeks later I got the nod from Richard and a plane ticket in the mail. I was off on my first ever plane trip to anywhere, it just happened to be to Los Angeles.

At the end of the tour Bruce flew home and went back to university. He was thinking, 'ah well that's the end of that; it was an incredible experience, now it was back to the real world.' But fate intervened once again in the form of Graham Thompson:

He was playing bass in the Russell Morris band at the time and he recommended me to Russell for the vacant keyboard stool. So I was back on the road, playing eight, ten, sixteen gigs a week.

Russell was with Frank Stivala's booking agency at the time and he had us working all over Victoria and up the east coast of Australia. We carried our own PA, with a full road crew, the whole eighties rock'n'roll catastrophe. But everywhere we went there were full houses because Russell played not only his latest album, but also the hits like 'The Real Thing' and 'Wings of an Eagle'. All with an eighties twist.

That's the thing about that era, the live scene was incredibly healthy especially here in Melbourne. Melbourne's scene was soulful rootsy, adventurous, you could literally learn on the job as opposed to other cities in Australia. When we went to Sydney it was a different scene, maybe it was the pokies and the League Club thing, but the music seemed to be an adjunct to the venue, so to make an impact bands had to be crowd pleasers, the Sydney scene was far more commercial. Sure there were the Bondi Life Saver and other surf club venues but the atmosphere compared to Melbourne was very different.

Squeezing into a Transit van between a speaker and a kick drum can be a little wearing after a while. Bruce got tired; 'of the long drives, the massive PAs, the sound checks, and the bad food of the road.' So Bruce jumped ship. Then, through a circuitous route, he ended up in a quirky little outfit called The Bachelors from Prague. The Bachelors were the antithesis of mainstream rock acts at the time; they were European-café quirky, '50s jazz, mixed with funk and garnished with salsa.

The band was led by the enigmatic, Black Cat café-owning Henry Maas. Maas described the early stages of the band in an article published in *Australian Musician*:

We just did our own thing,' Henry is quoted as saying, 'We didn't really mix with the others in the music community because we

used to run our own gigs. We printed the posters and did it all
ourselves. It was all in-house.[6]

The band played the inner-city Melbourne pub and club, including
Henry's Brunswick Street café. They were groovy-bebop-'50s-milk-
bar-noir, a bit laminex, a bit mum's kitchen with the Astor radio tuned
to a jazz station.

Henry and the Bachelors created an aesthetic that swept down
Brunswick Street. Brunswick Street was, in the '80s, the epicentre of
bohemian Melbourne, a mixture of edgy pubs, retro cafés, art galleries,
comedy clubs, experimental theatres and radical bookstores. Bruce
remembered those times very well:

> *It was wild, Vika Bull worked at the Black Cat and brought*
> *her sister Linda along and of course they made their way to the*
> *Bachelors' microphone. One night we played The Continental*
> *in Prahran and I noticed Joe Camilleri in the audience, couldn't*
> *figure out what he was doing there. I soon found out when Vika*
> *and Linda joined The Black Sorrows as backing singers.*

The Bachelors appeared regularly on the ABC Comedy Show *The Big*
Gig. They also toured England, where Kerri Simpson was guest vocalist
— then they called it quits. So for Bruce it was back to university at
Latrobe to study sound production.

But he wasn't done with playing in bands, not yet. Enter another
Melbourne music facilitator who would put him on another track:

> *Peter Luscombe was playing with Paul Kelly at the time, it*
> *must have been in the early '90s. Steve Hadley and Shane*
> *O'Mara were also in the band. He recommended me to Paul;*
> *he knew I was of the right mind to fit into the band. Luckily*
> *Paul agreed and I was in! It was a crazy ride, we recorded the*
> Deeper Water *album and* Live at the Continental *and* The
> Esplanade. *For the next seven years we played all over the US*
> *and Europe, all around Australia — a real adventure. Especially*

when we recorded the ARIA award-winning soundtrack to the Australian film Lantana and the electronic album Professor Ratbaggy. Peter came up with that name by the way.

The philosophy of the album was singer/songwriter meets electronic dub, breakbeat and I was given my head. I trucked the full array of effects I had stored in my front room into the studio, fuzz boxers, delays, phasers, it was a case of ... if it bent or distorted a note and it suited the song, I used it. It wasn't an intellectual process recording that album, it was intuitive, a bit rough around the edges, but it worked.

Bruce contrasted the intuitive approach of the *Professor Ratbaggy* project with bands they shared a bill with during the promotion of that album:

I remember one particular band from Sydney, they called themselves an acid jazz outfit, but they were so clinical, so intellectual, there was no freedom in the playing. That to me sums up the differences in the Sydney and Melbourne's approach to playing music live, there's a formality to Sydney bands as opposed to a willingness to experiment, to push the boundaries, to play without out a safety net like we do in Melbourne.

Peter Luscombe agrees with Bruce's assessment:

My experience playing with a lot of Sydney players is they are very schooled, whereas Melbourne players tend to smash down the barriers. We play on instinct, rather than rely on fancy technique, because technique is a bit like Latin, it's a difficult language to master but very few people understand it.

Bruce Haymes is the very definition of a much-loved and much-sought-after side musician and record producer, and he currently runs his own Park Side Recording Studio from his front room in Northcote. Bruce isn't a clinical musician, and he'll drop a brick on his keyboard if that's what the song requires, you only have to hear the wild arpeggios he sometimes throws in to appreciate his approach.

Not only is Bruce a highly skilled and consummate keyboard player, he's easy to get along with, and a true professional. That's why he spent over a decade with Renee Geyer, had a long stretch with Vika and Linda and has played many years with Archie Roach.

I too have stood on stage and watched audiences go crazy for Bruce's solos, cheering, applauding. Sometimes I wonder if Bruce knows just how good he is.

CHAPTER 14

BUMPING OUT

Melbourne ˉis unequivocally a great music city. Right from the beginning there was a tradition of playing and listening to music in a way that was unique. Melbourne's musicians played what they liked rather than what was expected. They often have elements of the dedicated amateur about them; Graeme and Roger Bell, for example, were both dedicated hot jazz enthusiasts who initially supported their passion with careers in other fields. Roger was an engineer with the Public Works Department and Graeme worked at an insurance clerk with T&G.

The Bells' financial independence freed them to relentlessly pursue their one true love: hot, or Dixieland-style, jazz. Their single-minded approach saw them develop an extensive repertoire, and eventually they were recognised as the foremost hot jazz players outside of America, if not the world.

The Bells' band was a modernist phenomenon. This was music focussed on freedom of expression through improvisation, and it garnered respect from avant-garde modernist painters like Sid Nolan, film makers, and writers like Max Harris. These artists saw a similarity to their own aesthetic in the Bells' music. They were attracted to its freedom of expression and revolt against the accepted and conventional.

The Bells refused to be sidetracked by the expectations of the professional, mainstream music market. As stated by Bisset:

'Professional musicians were bemused by the way the Bells turned their refusal to play any other music and to their credit … their determination to stick to their favorite style was not only admirable but good publicity.'[1]

The Bells gained this 'good publicity' through *Jazz Notes,* a journal devoted to the interests of traditional hot jazz in Melbourne. Like future music magazines such as *Go-Set* and *Juke* magazine, *Jazz Notes* played a crucial role in promoting the hot jazz subgenre to Melbourne audiences. The magazine was established in 1941 under the auspice of 3UZ's Jazz Lovers Society and edited by hot jazz enthusiast William H. Miller. It became compulsory reading for the '40s music enthusiast and was a key element in encouraging the booming local jazz dance scene of the '40s and '50s.

The popularity of the exhilarating hot jazz style spread like wildfire throughout Melbourne; it was up-tempo, wild and great to dance to. Almost overnight hundreds of venues sprang up around the city, beginning the 'casual jazz' scene of Melbourne. The scene was unique, and it gave work to thousands of working musicians both from Melbourne and from interstate. The casual dance scene morphed into a network of 'dry' rock'n'roll dances in the late '50s which led to the folk/jazz club and coffeehouse circuit of the next decade.

Then the Beatles hit and changed everything. Every suburban, baby boomer teenager wanted to grow their hair, rage against the machine and play guitar in a rock'n'roll band. In a sense this was the era when Melbourne came into its own; by the '60s Melbourne had established itself as Australia's popular music capital.[2]

Melbourne's dance and disco scene was enormous; literally hundreds of venues opened their doors to music lovers every week during the '60s. In addition, Australia's premier discotheques – Berties, Sebastian's, The Thumpin' Tum and Catcher were all located in Melbourne's CBD which meant virtually all the major pop acts of the day either came from Melbourne or had relocated here. In the '60s Melbourne hosted Armstrong's, the top independent recording studio in the country as well as influential music television shows like *Kommotion, The Go!! Show, Uptight*. The country's top music magazine *Go-Set* and later *Daily Planet* and *Digger* were all produced here, and we boasted import record stores like, Standish's and Archie and Jughead's. And the central importance of the Melbourne music scene continued into the '70s and beyond with Sunbury, Mushroom Records and *Countdown*.

Melbourne has remained the live music epicentre of the country, if not the world, by virtue of the sheer numbers of venues in the city — currently 553, according to the 2017 Melbourne Live Music Census. These venues give a solid stream of work to its small army of dynamic musicians and this is underpinned by an infrastructure of influential community based alternate media, including radio and magazines. As Melbourne academic Andrea Baker writes:

'In late 2018 an industry study conducted by Live Performance Australia found that the state of Victoria had the largest industry share for live music ticket sales revenue and attendance between 2016 and 2017 ... on the other side of the coin, if being a live music capital is about music innovation then Melbourne comes up trumps. As (a) 2011 Deloitte report highlights, grassroots live music venues play a crucial role in developing music careers and incubating innovative talent in Melbourne'[3]

Baker goes on to quote Save Live Australia's Music (SLAM):[4]

'Music is not just a commodity ... One thing we are seeing in Melbourne and that's quite different to Sydney, Brisbane or Adelaide, is a close-knit community. Melbourne's music community became very, very strong through the cross pollination of the arts, community radio (RRR, PBS) and [as a result], small venues are opening up everywhere because of the relaxing of bar licenses and next thing you know there's a venue on every corner.'

Melbourne's healthy live music scene can also be partially explained by its resistance to venue lockout laws which is not the case in Sydney and for a time, in parts of Brisbane. As many live music commentators and lobbyists such as SLAM have observed, lockout laws resulted in the death of many grassroots live music venues, largely killed night-time music activity and stifled music innovation and development in places like Sydney.

There are, however, some counterarguments to Melbourne's preeminent place as a live music capital. In 2015 UNESCO recognised Adelaide as Australia's only City of Music in 2015 on the basis that it hosts numerous international music festivals like WOMADelaide and OzAsia Festival.[5] Sydney too hosts a number of the major music labels and has occasionally outstripped Melbourne in terms of national live music ticket sales and attendance.

So maybe the whole Melbourne live music capital thing is an abstract notion, a numbers game, a statement of product differentiation in, to quote Beat Poet Lawrence Ferlinghetti, 'this kiss-proof world of plastic toilet seats, tampax and taxis'. Maybe it's all about trying to sell Melbourne as a national and international global music city to try and capture an increased share of the overall music tourist dollar. Maybe it's all about trying to stick it to Sydney. Sometimes all the bragging feels a little provincial, like Melbourne has an inferiority complex or something. But there is no doubt that Melbourne is a great place to see a band on a Saturday (or any) night.

The future of this depends on how we develop as a city, how our planning laws pan out, if the collegiate nature of the music scene can be maintained, if live music can continue to excite and stir the public's imagination. As Andrea Baker writes in *The Great Music City*, if all this can continue, then music will keep 'deliver[ing] significant economic, employment, cultural and social benefits' to Melburnians.[6]

At the time of writing, in any one week, Monday through Sunday Melbourne plays host to hundreds of blues and roots gigs, where outlaw women and Stagger Lee's shout out their gospel truths in places like The Lomond Hotel in Brunswick, The Drunken Poet in West Melbourne, Fitzroy's Rainbow, Catfish, Bar Open, and The Railway in Nicholson Street, or Brunswick's Spotted Mallard, The Post Office Hotel in Coburg, or Big Pig Little Pig down in Moorabbin. Venture out of town and you can hear dirt music played at the St Andrews Hotel, a low timber Victorian tucked beside a scribble gum forest down the hill from Kinglake, or you could head down the coast to Geelong and find the New Orleans-flavoured food and musical extravaganza that is Pistol Pete's. For those who like to take their music slow there's festivals like The Echuca Winter Blues in July as well as the Port Fairy and Maldon Folk Festivals, or the Port Fairy or Queenscliff Festivals.

For nearly a century, Melbourne's music venues have reflected both the changing face of music, and broader social and political shifts, it's egalitarianism, it's more politically progressive elements and its inherent creativity. It has also reflected our darker side, our underlying racism and our sexism. There is no doubt about it, Melbourne has been and continues to be one of the world's great music cities and long may she reign.

Somewhere over The Rainbow

I think there's time for one last story. It was around the mid-'90s and Melbourne was gentrifying, rapidly. Factories and warehouses were closing and turned into desirable apartments for middle class hipsters, attracted to the café society and nightlife of suburbs like Fitzroy, Collingwood, St. Kilda and Brunswick. The irony was that the occupants of those desirable warehouse apartments didn't actually like to be surrounded by nightlife and café society at all; they complained about late night revellers and the loud music from nearby venues. In other words, they whined about the very thing that attracted them to inner Melbourne in the first place.

This meant traditional music venues like The Rainbow Hotel in Fitzroy and The Tote in Collingwood came under enormous pressure to either close, or spend hundreds of thousands of dollars on noise abatement works. In the meantime, venues were also hit with thousands of dollars in fines for exceeding noise limits resulting in many traditional venues like the Tramway and The Lord Newry both in Fitzroy North cancelling the bands.

I played The Rainbow a lot at this time. Publican Chick Ratten was tearing his hair out; even though the pub had been a venue since the '30s, the residents of the newly built apartments opposite in St David Street were driving him crazy with noise complaints. These objections resulted in visits from council officers, thousands of dollars in fines and orders for him to install air-conditioning and double-glazing. As he said to me once, *it's killing me, financially and mentally.* But he was determined that his seven nights per week venue would remain open.

Then around 1996, a new block of apartments was planned adjacent to the pub in Young Street. Chick saw the plans and hit the roof. All the apartment's bedrooms were to be located on Young Street, directly facing the hotel, guaranteeing a new round of complaints, fines and expensive renovations. He put a formal objection to the development into council.

Little did Chick know, or anyone else for that matter, that the person behind the developement was none other than the notorious 'Black Prince of Lygon Street' and head of the underground crime syndicate known as the Carlton Crew, Alphonse Gangitano. Chick had grown up on the hard streets of Brunswick, was a champion boxer and knew a thing or two about taking care of himself, so when Alphonse and his crew came into his hotel a couple of weeks after he lodged his planning objection, he wasn't fazed. Alphonse ordered a beer and some drinks for his goons. Chick waited, when Alphonse finally spoke the conversation went something like this:

'So Mr Ratten you have objected to me building my apartments over the road there, is that right?"

'Yep, that's right, if you build what I see on your plans you'll kill my business, so yes I've put in a number of objections to the council planning department,' said Chick.

Alphonse smiled and nodded. 'Hmm, ok, well let my say we can do this the easy way or the hard way. The easy way is, you withdraw your objection. The hard way is you don't.'

Chick looked at him and looked at his goons, smiled and said, 'Ah well I guess it'll be the hard way. I want those plans changed!'

Chick saw anger flash into Gangitano's eyes, so he held up his hand. 'Before we go any further, Alphonse, you tell your grandfather, that Chick Ratten has asked that you accommodate my wishes in all of this and see what he says.' Apparently Chick and Gangitano Senior had grown-up together in Brunswick.

A few weeks later Chick received a call from Alphonse inviting him to lunch at the upmarket Florentino restaurant in Bourke Street. Chick knew his refusal to back down from Gangitano was a gamble. He wondered if this invitation was a ruse for something more serious. But he decided to go ahead and accept the invitation.

He went out and bought a secondhand herringbone-patterned suit and on the allotted day of the luncheon appointment, told his wife that if he wasn't back at the pub by three o'clock she should call the police.

'I walked into the upstairs dining room of the café. Alphonse and I were the only patrons. He sat at the head of a long table and you wouldn't believe it, he was wearing an exact replica of my suit! We roared laughing!'

Alphonse said that he had talked to his grandfather and that he remembered me very well. He then unfolded the plans and asked what I wanted. I said I want the bedrooms moved and the apartments set back a little from the street, and if you do that I'll withdraw my objections from council. Alphonse nodded and put his plans away.

'Ok, no problems, let's have lunch!!'

Chick couldn't believe it, he'd won, or so he thought. Suddenly the Rainbow became a kind of clubhouse for the Melbourne Mafiosa. Be-suited and be-jewelled, crims started filling the venue most nights of the week, making the ragged blues fiends of Fitzroy decidedly nervous. Then one night a group of young punks caused some bother, a brawl broke out, glass was smashed, furniture demolished. Chick jumped the bar and belted the ring-leader, then threw him out into the street. The bloodied young buck splattered:

'You're a dead man mate, my uncle is Alphonse Gangitano ...'

And so he was. The next week the young man, sporting a blackened eye returned to the hotel with his uncle in tow. Alphonse shook hands with Chick and said,

'I believe my nephew caused bit of trouble here at the pub the other night, did some damage, am I right?'

'Yep, he did, that's why I threw him out!'

'And fair enough too, how much was it to repair the damage, do you think?'

Chick mentioned a figure and Alphonse wrote out a cheque to cover it. The young man was then forced to offer Chick an apology and a promise never to darken the pub's door again.

But the battles with neighbours and the Yarra Council took their toll on Chick's health and he called last drinks at the Rainbow a couple of years later. Tragically he never had a chance to enjoy a long retirement. Soon after closing the pub's doors, he set off for Europe with two goals in mind: to meet Joe Cocker and follow the Tour de France. He achieved both, but in his rented campervan, Chick Ratten, aged 63, died of a pulmonary embolism, his wife Ursula by his side. Alphonse of course was already dead by this stage, shot in the head in January 1998 by Jason Moran at the Gangitano family home in Templestowe.

But some things never die, take the Melbourne live music scene for example, it's a resilient beast. As soon as one venue closes another opens; The Rainbow for example was resurrected just a few months after Chick's funeral and continues as a live music venue to this very day. This is due in no short measure to a Victoria planning law reform in 2014 which gives developers responsibility for noise abatement works when building close to existing music venues. Chick on hearing about this change in planning law would, I'm sure, be smiling down from somewhere over The Rainbow.

REFERENCES

INTERVIEWS CONDUCTED 2019

Andy Baylor
Jeff Burstin
Wayne Burt
Joe Cammilleri
Rick Dempster
Bruce Haymes
Judy Jacques (via email)
Peter Luscombe
Paul Neuendorf
Margret RoadKnight
Kerri Simpson
Ken White
Wilbur Wilde

NEWSPAPERS / MAGAZINES

The Sydney Morning Herald
- Jazz Singer Georgia Lee Dies, April 17, 2010
- The Grand Old Man of Jazz had a Boyish Sparkle, June 16 2012
- '60s Female Singers Deserve Recognition, July 25, 2014
- Night Train Reaches the End of the Line, January 12, 2016
- She toured the world with the likes of Duke Ellington but is unknown in Oz, May 2, 2016
- Which City is Australia's Music Capital? Andrea Baker May 17, 2017

The Age
- Len Barnard 1929-2005 — Jazz Drummer

- Feeling Blue? Come to mama, May 17, 2010

The Guardian
- Live music 'crisis': report urges NSW to lift unnecessary restrictions on venues, November 15, 2018

The Herald Sun
- Howe, Alan, The Beatles in Australia, How Four Days Changed Australia, May 24, 2014

Music Victoria Executive summary Melbourne Live Music Census

Australian Musician Magazine
- Saluting our seminal Woman Rockers, November 29,2007

Overland Magazine
- A Short History of Communist Jazz, Sparrow, Jeff June, 2012

VJAZZ, Quarterly magazine of the Victorian jazz Archive
- The Casual Dance Scene in Melbourne, Jeff Hawes, November 2013

JAZZLINE (Victorian Jazz Club)
- Judy Jacques, Jazz, and the sheer Joy of Singing: A 70th Birthday Tribute

Liner notes to Judy Jacques, the Sixties Sessions, Mastered by Gil Matthews

Various articles and clippings supplied by Paul Neuendorf, Margret RoadKnight, Ken White

ONLINE / BLOGS

- AllMusic- artist biography Herbert Henry (Smoky) Dawson
- (The Story of) Australian Country Music
- The Dancehall Racketeers — Western Swing in Australia, Donal Baylor, July 6, 2016
- Andy Baylor Biography
- eMelbourne, Jazz
- The Encyclopedia of Women & Leadership in Twentieth Century Australia (Georgia Lee)
- Turnbull J. Malcolm, Warren Fahey's Australian Folklore Unit – Early Melbourne 1-4
- Jazz in Australia, The History of Jazz in Australia, December 13, 2018
- Flaming Hoop March 14, 2016
- Milesago
  – Gerry Humphrys
  – The Spinning Wheels
- PBS — American Roots Music: Into the Classroom — Historic Background,
- Remembering Traynor's A Collaborative Folk History
- Rolling Stone, The '50s: A Decade of Music That Changed the World, Robert Palmer
- Tim Stevens From the Archive, The Red Onion Jazz Band as Practitioners of Australian Jazz

BOOKS

- Adlington, Robert (ed) *Red Strains, Music and Communism Outside the Communist Bloc*, British Academy, Oxford University Press
- Baker Andrea, *The Great Music City, Exploring Music Space and Identity,* Palgrave Macmillan, 2019
- Bell, Graeme. *Australian Jazzman*, Child and Associates, 1988
- Beilby, Peter and Roberts, Michael, *Australian Music,* Australian Music Directory, 1981
- Bisset, Andrerw *Black Roots White Flowers*, Australian Broadcasting Corporation, 1979
- Bois, John, *The Dingoes Lament,* Melbourne Books, 2012
- Dreyfus, Kay *Sweethearts of Rhythm,* Currency Press, 1999
- Dylan Bob, Chronicles, Volume One Simon& Schuster, 2004
- Horne, Craig, *Daddy Who?,* Melbourne Books, 2018
- Linehan Norm, *Australian Jazz Picture Book*, Child & Henry, 1978
- Mitchell, Jack *Blistered Heels, Jazz and Hot Dance music in Australia in the Twenties,* Jack Mitchell, 2015
- Nichols, David. *Dig: Australian Rock and Pop Music 1960-85* Verse Chorus Press, 2016
- Sedergreen, Bob *Hear Me Talking To Ya, Tales from a Fair Dinkum Jazzman,* Melbourne Books, 2007
- Simpson, Graham *The Judith Durham Story, Colours of My Life,* Random House, 1994
- Williams, Mike The Australian Jazz Explosion, Angus and Robertson, 1981

NOTES

Beside the major interviews I carried out, this book relied on a number of the following sources which, as you can see I have listed on a chapter by chapter basis. I have tried to accurately list all source material including, where possible, page numbers. If inaccuracies exist I apologies to the authors/sources involved.

Introduction: The Live Music Capital of the World

1   Alan Ginsberg quoted in Dylan, Bob Chronicles Volume One, Simon and Schuster UK ltd. 2004
2   Sydney Morning Herald, May 17, 2017
3   Marcus, Greil *The Invisible Republic Bob Dylan's Basement Tapes,* Pan MacMillan, 1998

Chapter 1: 'Change is Gonna Come'

1   Szatmary, David (2014). *Rockin' in Time.* Upper Saddle River, New Jersey: Pearson.

Chapter 2: The Roots of Jazz

1   Oakley, Giles (1997) The Devils Music, Da Capo Press, Incorporated, 1976
2   Encyclopedia Britannica, online resource
3   BBC News Magazine in December 2012

4   Bob Dylan, Chronicles Volume One, page 5. The actual quote is: "He explained that he saw me as someone in the long line of a tradition, the tradition of blues, jazz and folk and not as some newfangled wunderkind on the cutting edge."
5   Son House, Jinx Blues (lyrics)
6   Oakley p.10
7   Baker, p111,
8   Baker, p.112
9   Christian Blauvett, BBC Culture article 'The Mysterious Origins of Jazz' (2017)
10 Jazz in America, Where did Jazz come from? (online resource)
11 Swing Review.com, History of Jazz
12 Dreyfus, Kay *Sweethearts of Rhythm,* Currency Press, 1999, page 61
13 Dreyfus, page 43
14 Dreyfus p50-60
15 Dreyfus p83
16 Sparrow, Jeff *A Short History of Communist Jazz,* Overland Literary Journal, June 20 2012
17 Sparrow, Jeff ibid
18 Sparrow ibid

Chapter 3: Modernism, Communism, Hot Jazz and Graeme Bell

Quotes attributed to Graeme Bell have been drawn from his autobiography: *Graeme Bell Australian Jazzman* Child and Associates, 1988.

1   Interview with Duke Ellington just before he died in 1974
2   Vanity Fair August 2013
3   Quotes attributed to Graeme Bell
4   Harding, Lesley & Morgan Kendrah *Modern Love: The Lives of John and Sunday Reed* The Miegunyah Press 2015, p100
5   See Harding & Morgan
6   National Museum of Australia: Post war immigration drive

The Eureka Youth League, Communism and all that Jazz.

Information for this section was largely drawn from Graeme Bell's autobiography, *Australian Jazzman*, Anthony Ashbolt and Glenn Mitchells Chapter, *Music and Communism in Australia,* published in Red Stains: Music and Communism, Edited by Robert Adlington, Oxford University Press 2013 and Jeff Sparrows Overland article, A Short History of Communist Jazz.

7   Ashbolt, Anthony Mitchell, Glen: Music, the Political Score and Communism, British, Academic Scholarship, 2014)
8   Hughes, Robert: *Shock of the New,* p89 (for a more detailed discussion on the role Bolshevism played in the development of a modernists perspective in art read pages 80 through 95)
9   Bell, p56-62
10   Bell, ibid
11   Lyrics from Stealin' written by Gus Cannon
12   Bell, p59 for further details
13   Sparrow, Overland
14   Bell, p60
15   Bisset, Andrerw *Black Roots White Flowers*, Australian Broadcasting Corporation, 1979, P121
16   Harding & Morgan p.
17   Bell, ibid
18   Bell ibid
19   Bell, p83
20   Bell, p84
21   Bell, p88
22   Sydney Morning Herald, June 16, 2012
23   National Archives of Australia, Events and Issues
24   Haese, Richard Rebels and Precursors, read also *Albert Tucker,* by James Mollison and Nicholas Bonham, The Macmillan Company of Australia, 1982
25   ibid
26   ibid
27   ibid
28   Bell, p121
29   Bell first ABC contract pg.121
30   Youth Voice Sept 1948, quoted in Ashbolt and Mitchell, Music and Communism in Australia, p138)
31   Ashbolt and Mitchell p147
32   Ashbolt and Mitchell p138
33   Bell, p122
34   Bell, p124
35   Graeme Bell interviewed by Peter Thompson, Australian Broadcast Commission's Talking Heads program, 21 August 2006.
36   Bell, p187
37   Bell, p194

Chapter 4: The Jazz Explosion — Melbourne's Casual Dance Scene and Judy Jacques

1   *VJazz* Magazine, 2013
2   Simpson, Graham *The Judith Durham Story, Colours of My Life,* Random House, 1994 p22-23
3   Len Barnard quoted in Williams, Mike *The Australian Jazz Explosion,* Angus and Robertson, 1981, p.24
4   Williams, Mike, ibid

Judy Jacques
For the majority of the Judy Jacques section I have relied on interviews conducted via email with Judy conducted in the early part of 2019 as well as a treasure trove of memorabilia forwarded to me by her.

Other information came from an article written by *Robin Ryan, Jazzline Vol 47, No 2 spring/summer 2014 Judy Jacques, Jazz and the Sheer Joy of Singing)*

5   Judy Jacques quoted in Robin Ryan, Jazzline Vol 47, No 2 spring/summer 2014 Judy Jacques, Jazz and the Sheer Joy of Singing)
6   J.J. quoted in Robin Ryan, Jazzline Vol 47, No 2 spring/summer 2014 Judy Jacques, Jazz and the Sheer Joy of Singing)
7   ibid
8   See J. J. quoted in Ryan
9   ibid
10 ibid

Modern Jazz
11 Reisner, Robert *Bird The Legend of Charlie Parker,* De Cappo 1977
12 Ken White in interview with the author

Cahpter 5: Let's Rock

1   Palmer, Robert: The 50's, The Decade of Music that Changed the World: Rolling Stone, April 19, 1990
2   Milesago, *Australasian Popular Music, the first wave 1955-63*
3   Nichols, David *Dig, Australian Rock and Pop Music 1960-1980,* Verse Chorus Press, 2016
4   Dylan, Chronicals
5   Nichols ibid
6   Hedger, Claire *Saluting our Seminal Woman Rockers,* Australian Musician, November 29, 2007

Chapter 6: What the Folk?

Information for this section was drawn largely from Malcolm J Turnbull's article published in six parts in Warren Fahey's Australian Folklore Unit, Exploring the Australian identity through history, story, song and folklore, Trad & Now, 2003-2005

1   Turnbull, Malcome J. Warren Fahey's Australian Folklore Unit, Beginnings
2   Ashbolt and Mitchell, *Red Strains: Music and Communism in Australia,* p139
3   ibid, p138
4   ibid, p140
5   Turnbull, Warren Fahey's Australian Folk Law Unit
6   ibid
7   ibid
8   Dylan, Chronicles, p46-47.
9   ibid p47

The coffee house where jazz and folk meet

Information for this section was drawn largely from Malcolm J Turnbull's article published in six parts in Warren Fahey's Australian Folklore Unit, Exploring the Australian identity through history, story, song and folklore, Trad & Now, 2003-2005

10　Robert Shelton, quoted in Warren Fahey's Australian Folklore Unit, Beginnings (Turnbull)

11　*The National Times, 15 Feb 1981*

12　Turnbull, ibid

13　Turnbull, ibid

14　Turnbull, ibid

15　Horne, Daddy Who?

16　Keith Glass: A Life in Music -Milesago Web site

17　Mary Traynor, Remembering Traynor's, A Collaborative Folk History, an online resource

18　Dylan, Chronicles, p94

19　Turnbull, ibid

Frank Traynor's Folk and Jazz Club

Information for this section was drawn largely from Malcolm J Turnbull's article published in six parts in Warren Fahey's Australian Folklore Unit, Exploring the Australian identity through history, story, song and folklore, Trad & Now, 2003-2005 especially *Beginnings*

20　Turnbull, ibid

21　ibid

22　ibid

23　ibid

24　ibid. Radic quoted by Turnbull

25　Ken White interview with the author

Tony Standish — The Frank Traynor Folk Club and Heritage Record Shop

26　Tony Standish quoted in Traynor, Mary *Remembering Traynor's Collaborative Folk History* blog

27　ibid

28　ibid

29　Ken White, interview with the author

30　ibid

Chapter 7: Women Folk — Standing at the Crossroads

1　Sydney Morning Herald, July 25, 2014

2　ibid

3　Australian Folk Songs, online resource

4　Glen Tomasetti online resource, quoted from *Vietnam Protest and Tragedy* The Express Tribune, November 29, 1967

5　ibid

Margaret RoadKnight

Material for this section is from a series of interviews with the author conducted early in 2019 as well as Margaret's WEB site.

6　Margaret's WEB site

Judith Durham

Information for this section is drawn largely from: Graham Simpson's biography of Judith, *The Judith Durham Story, Colours of My Life,* Random House, 1994.

7　Interview with the author

8　David Nichols, Dig, pg. 27

9　Simpson, p151

10　Milesago WEB site, The Seekers

11　Simpson

12　ibid

Shirely Jacobs

13   *Night train reaches the end of the line*, The Sydney Morning Herald, January 15, 2016
14   ibid

Chapter 8: 'Damn Right I Got the Blues'

Georgia Lee

This section relied heavily on The ABC program AWAYE, aired on Radio National March 27, 2010, presented by Daniel Browning and produced by Browning and Phil McKellar

1   Bisset, Andrerw *Black Roots White Flowers*, Australian p21
2   Red Hot Jazz online resource
3   Bisset p31
4   Australia Women and Leadership in a Century of Australian Democracy, Georgia Lee September 28,2012, online resource
5   Browning and McKellar
6   Women's Encyclopedia, online resource
7   The Age, April 27, 2010
8   Browning and McKellar

Graham Squance and Ken White: Authentic Grit

I relied on an interview with Kenny White conducted in early 2019 for the information contained in this section, together with articles drawn from Ken White's extensive collection of memorabilia.

9   Article cut from *Go Set*, The Ken White collection.

Dutch Tilders

10   Information for this section came from conversations with Wayne Burt, an article written by a clipping of an article written by Broderick Smith and given to me by Ken White and Dutch Tildres WEB site.
11   ibid
12   ibid
13   ibid

The Four Days that Shook Melbourne

14   Alan Howe, The Beatles in Australia 50 years on, *How Four Days Changed Melbourne,* May 24, 2014

Chapter 9: The Blues Highway

1   Beilby, Peter, Roberts, Michael *Australian Music*, pg.124
2   ibid

Chapter 10: Melbourne, Americana, Mainstream and Independent — the Marvellous Melbourne Music Scene of the '80s

Joe Camilleri

This section based on interviews with Joe Camilleri, Peter Luscombe and Wayne Burt and Jeff Burstin

1   The Drum Media, July 12, 2007 p12
2   Sarah Taylor, Cordite Poetry Review, February 1, 2015
3   ibid
4   ibid
5   The Drum Media, July 12, 2007

'80s Rock'n'roll, Everyone's Rolling in Cash Right?

6   Sarah Taylor, An Introduction to Historical Maps of Live Music in Melbourne and Sydney' for the *Cordite Poetry Review*

7 ibid (Between 2004 and 2013 it
is estimated that gig listings in
Sydney had dropped 61 per cent
and recent lock out laws have seen
audiences drop by 40 percent at
live venues according to Journey
to the End of the Night, written by
Clinton Howard)
8 ibid

**Chapter 12: Housebands, Sidemen
and Sidewomen of Melbourne — The
Melbourne Sound**

1 Keith Richards, BBC's The Story of
a Sidemen, Rock'n'Roll Guns for
hire
2 Blaine, Hal and David Goggin, *Hal
Blaine and the Wrecking Crew: The
Story of the World's Most Recorded
Musician*, MixBooks, Emeryville,
California, 1990; pp. 57-60
3 Milesago WEB site, The Strangers
4 Lisa Fischer *as quoted in the
Huffington Post in June, 2013*
* Information for this section was drawn
from Our Life in Music and Together —
Vika and Linda Bull a keynote speech
they delivered on International Women's
Day, at the One of One Breakfast on
March 8th, 2019, at the Esplanade
Hotel, St Kilda. I helped Vika and Linda
prepare this speech for the event.

Chapter 14: Bumping Out

1 Bisset, Andrerw *Black Roots White
Flowers*, Australian Broadcasting
Corporation, 1979 Bisset, page 109
2 See as the Milesago: Australasian
Music and Popular Culture 1964-
75 Music Web site.

3 Baker Andrea, *The Great Music
City, Exploring Music Space and
Identity,* Palgrave Macmillan, 2019,
p306
4 Save Live Australia's Music
(SLAM) is a collective of non-
politically aligned, independent,
local music-loving citizens. The
only pre-requisite to getting
involved is a love of live music and
act as a lobby group for keeping
music live in our cities.
5 See City of Adelaide, web site
https://www.cityofadelaide.
com.au/about-adelaide/general-
information/unesco-city-of-music/
6 Baker, p307

ACKNOWLEDGEMENTS

Writing a book such as this would not have been possible with the help, cooperation and generosity of a number of people and organisations. Firstly I'd like to thank the Australian Jazz Museum in Wantirna for its generosity in opening its amazing collection of books and photographs to me. Once again I want to thank Anne O'Rourke for her encouragement and for borrowing key source material on my behalf.

Jeff Burstin, for not only giving gladly of his time to discuss his life in music but also lending me the Graeme Bell autobiography and connecting me to Joe Camilleri. Thanks Joe for breakfast and for your fantastic stories. Thanks also to Bruce Haymes, Sam See, Kerri Simpson, Andy Baylor, Wilbur Wilde, Aaron Choulai, Vika and Linda Bull, Peter Luscombe, Wayne Burt, Kerryn Tolhurst, Rick Dempster and Ken White, all of whom also gave gladly of their time and offered insight into the Melbourne music scene as well as incredibly entertaining stories and great photographs. I want to especially thank Margret RoadKnight, not only for allowing time for a series of interviews but also giving me access to her archive of memorabilia and putting me in touch with both Ken White and Judy Jacques. Judy I want to thank you for your generosity in sharing your incredible life in music with me despite difficulties of distance and ill health. You are and always will be a real trouper. And Paul Neuendorf, thank you for lunch and also for your generosity to this project. Susie Gamble has once again enhanced her legendary status by finding the rare photographs of The Strangers, The Lincolns and Thunderbirds from her unique collection.

Finally David Tenenbaum from Melbourne Books thanks for workshopping the topic with me, and thanks for all your support in bringing the book to fruition. Special thanks to my editor Amelia Cassandra Catalano, book designer Ellen Yan Cheng, and David Johnston for his keen editorial eye as well as everyone else at Melbourne Books who has helped guide me through this process.

THE AUTHOR

Craig Horne has been a public servant and speechwriter and also a musician on the Melbourne scene over the last forty-eight years. As a teenager, Daddy Cool inspired him to take up the guitar and play in a rock'n'roll band of his own, eventually performing alongside Wayne, Gary and sometimes Hanna as members of his band The Hornets. *Daddy Who? — The inside story of the rise and demise of Australia's greatest rock band* also by Craig was published by Melbourne Books in 2018.

Other Melbourne Books music titles:

Captain Matchbox & Beyond: The Music & Mayhem of Mic & Jim Conway
    Catherine Fleming, John Tait, and Mic and Jim Conway

Cold Chisel: Wild Colonial Boys
    Michael Lawrence

Daddy Who?: The Inside Story of the Rise and Demise of Australia's Greatest Rock Band
    Craig Horne

Hear Me Talking to Ya
    Bob Sedergreen

Mick Thomas: These Are The Days
    Mick Thomas

Midnight Oil: The Power and The Passion
    Michael Lawrence

Nine Parts Water, One Part Sand: Kim Salmon and the Formula for Grunge
    Douglas Galbraith

Noise in My Head: Voices from the Ugly Australian Underground
    Jimi Kritzler

Sunbury: Australia's Greatest Rock Festival
    Peter Evans

Tait's Modern Guide to Record Collecting
    John Tait

Techno Shuffle: Rave Culture and The Melbourne Underground
    Paul Fleckney

The Ballroom: The Melbourne Punk and Post-Punk Scene
    Dolores San Miguel

The Dingoes' Lament
    John Bois

The Remarkable Mr Morrison: The Virtuosity and Versatility of Australia's Master Musician
    Mervyn E. Collins

The Seekers
    Graham Simpson and Christopher Patrick

The Seekers: Behind the Curtain
    Bruce Woodley AO

This will explain everything
    Jeff Duff

Whatever Happened to Diana Trask
    Diana Trask

www.melbournebooks.com.au/categories/music